D1707791

SHARDS OF MEMORY

SHARDS OF MEMORY

NARRATIVES OF HOLOCAUST SURVIVAL

Edited and with an Introduction by Yehudi Lindeman

Assistant Editors

Lukas Rieppel,
Renata Skotnicka-Zajdman,
and
Anita Slominska

Foreword by Elie Wiesel

Westport, Connecticut
London

Library of Congress Cataloging-in-Publication Data

Shards of memory : narratives of Holocaust survival /
edited and with an introduction by Yehudi Lindeman,
et.al.; foreword by Elie Wiesel.
    p. cm.
Includes bibliographical references and index.
ISBN 0–275–99423–6 (alk. paper)
1. Holocaust, Jewish (1939–1945)—Personal narratives.
2. World War, 1939–1945—Jews—Rescue. 3. Righteous
Gentiles in the Holocaust. I. Lindeman, Yehudi.
D804.195.S48   2007
940.53'180922—dc22   2006038807

British Library Cataloguing in Publication Data is available.

Library of Congress Catalog Card Number: 2006038807
ISBN-10: 0–275–99423–6
ISBN-13: 978–0–275–99423–5

First published in 2007

Praeger Publishers, 88 Post Road West, Westport, CT 06881
An imprint of Greenwood Publishing Group, Inc.
www.praeger.com

Printed in the United States of America

The paper used in this book complies with the
Permanent Paper Standard issued by the National
Information Standards Organization (Z39.48–1984).

10 9 8 7 6 5 4 3 2 1

To the memory of Frankje Lindeman (1935–1943)

Contents

Photos

All photographs are reproduced thanks to the kind permission of those depicted or, in a few cases, the permission of their immediate family. We acknowledge the Montreal Holocaust Memorial Centre for permission to reprint the photograph of Abram F.

Foreword

Elie Wiesel

Remember: when survivors first emerged from the ghettos and the forests and the death-camps, hopelessly determined to invoke hope and tell the tale, few were willing to listen.

Yet it is my belief—rather, my fervent hope—that now, decades later, for every survivor able to bear witness, there is a reader receptive to the story. We read in *Shards of Memory* the account of Rachel G., who "during the Shoah . . . always told herself that 'we have to live so that somebody should be able to tell what happened,'" and readers everywhere ought to feel the urge to absorb her testimony, and those of the other survivors whose oral histories are anthologized here.

I have always believed in survivor testimonies: they are unique. What they say about what was done to Jews by their enemies cannot be said by anyone else. I personally have sought, and still seek, to read and learn everything I can about that dark time; and for me, survivor testimonies are an elemental part of that tuition.

Living Testimonies, the Holocaust Video Documentation Archive at McGill University has compiled the enclosed accounts from first-person video testimonies. The editors have rendered the survivors' narratives in subtle, objective language. They convey the survivor's story; his own words; his silences. " 'We were a family,' " Saul B.'s testimony begins, "but these few words are as far as he gets before his voice catches in his throat." The accounts do not force the witness's emotions onto the reader; rather, the reader cannot but respond with deep emotion and affection to the anguish and pain that is throughout.

Let us welcome *Shards of Memory* to the canon of Holocaust literature. Like all survivors' testimonies, this book is essential to our understanding of an era that defies comprehension. It belongs to a special category of books that merit our attention, and our gratitude.

Acknowledgments

This has been a truly collective experience. When *Living Testimonies* first started gathering witness accounts of the Holocaust, it was from the outset a shared process between interviewer and survivor, in a combined—and sometimes painful—effort to recapture fragments and images of the past, and connect them into a narrative. Later on, in my seminar English 505A on Holocaust fiction, memoir, and oral testimony, McGill University students collectively helped create the groundwork for the present book, *Shards of Memory*, for which my thanks.

Most of the undergraduate and graduate research assistants who worked for Living Testimonies first encountered the video testimonies in one of my courses or seminars. I gratefully acknowledge all of them, including Tamara Bekefi, Megan Bremer, Adam Budd, David Clearwater, Jessie Evans, Lisa Glover, Janice Kong, Andrea Mason, Gabrielle McIntire, Mark Narron, Amy Reiswig, Zoë Beenstock Rivlin, and Randy Schnoor.

The majority of interviews for Living Testimonies were conducted by Paula Bultz, Yehudi Lindeman and Renata Skotnicka Zajdman. We are indebted to Paula Bultz whose presence became synonymous with quiet respect for the person interviewed and quality control. I also acknowledge the work of interviewers Erika Hecht, Irena Tomaszewski and Sidney Zoltak.

At McGill University, Professors David Williams, Leanore Lieblein and Gary Wihl, as chairs of the English Department, believed in the importance of the work done by Living Testimonies and proved it by freeing me from other administrative duties. McGill University Principals Bernard Shapiro and Heather Munroe-Blum credited the academic and human merit of the work done by Living Testimonies and showed it through their vigorous support, both moral and material.

I am indebted to Barry Stahlmann who edited the Chronology and contributed in many other ways as well, and to Dr. Richard Virr of the McGill Library's Rare Books Department. Dr. Hans Möller, head librarian at McGill, gave gererously of his time and was a source of encouragement. Without the support of Elizabeth Demers, my editor at Praeger, this book could not have been done. Thanks also to Elizabeth Potenza and Michael O'Connor for their editorial assistance.

All of us are indebted to the audio-visual staff and management at McGill's ICC (now IMS). Mario Di Paolo, Stewart McCombie, Daniel Schwob and Carmelo Sgro, your concern for the survivors' comfort, the quality of sound and video and more generally the success of the archive's work has not gone unnoticed. We also express thanks to the more recent staff of IMS, and especially to Jean-Guy Tremblay and Frank Roop.

Thanks to Montreal filmmaker Bill Kerrigan, a loyal supporter of Living Testimonies and the videographer, in Europe, of the Sinti and Roma (Gypsy) project. Thanks to Marcia Goldberg and Ari Snyder of Vanier College and Robert Bernheim and Katherine Quimby Johnson of the University of Vermont. Thanks to Professsor Marianne Stenbaek of McGill for her support while she was director of Living Testimonies.

I am indebted to the late Dr. Gabrielle Tyrnauer of Montreal and Alburg, Vermont. Her pioneer work with European Sinti and Roma Holocaust survivors will not be forgotten. The account of Harry F. in this volume is just one of many interviews championed by Dr. Tyrnauer. Thanks to Rabbi Ayla (Sarah Leah) Grafstein of Phoenix, Arizona whose drive and leadership helped get Living Testimonies off the ground. I gratefully acknowledge former Dean of Arts and Professor of History Michael Maxwell who first encouraged and assisted in the establishment of the Living Testimonies Holocaust Video Archive at McGill University.

I acknowledge the trust placed in me by Israel B., David G., Paul L., Ilse Z. and the many others whose accounts are represented in this volume. This work could not have made it into print without the many words and acts of kindness and encouragement on the part of my dear siblings Leah Kaufman and Stefanie Seltzer.

I acknowledge the wisdom, affection, and support of the many Holocaust survivors who were interviewed by Living Testimonies and whose witness accounts are not represented in this volume. They include Minna Aspler, Dana Bell, Sala Bonder, Victor David, Arnold Distler, Leo Dortort, Henry Fenster, Daisy Gross, Paul Herczeg, Hella Kolatacz, David Kropveld, Sam Orshan, Frieda Shipper, Alfred Spreekmeester, Harry Taichman, Anne Voticky, and Bonno Wiener.

Thanks to the members of the Child Survivor community of Montreal.

Thanks to Joe and Manu Wiecha for giving me logistical and loving support.

It took a lot of time and effort to get this volume completed and often I was not the best of companions. I send my thanks and all my love to my spouse and partner Françoise, a woman of valor, who endured the long process with patience and quiet encouragement and support.

Finally, I gratefully acknowledge financial support from the Faculty of Arts and the Faculty of Graduate Studies and Research at McGill University, and from the Jewish Community Foundation of Montreal and its director Manny Weiner.

Introduction

Yehudi Lindeman

Between the survivor's memory and its reflection in words there
is an unbridgeable gulf.[1]

Elie Wiesel

The feeling that your experience cannot be told, that no one can
understand it, is perhaps one of the worst that was felt by the survivors
after the war.[2]

Aharon Appelfeld

The survivor had no audience and frequently felt the isolation of
someone who cannot be understood.[3]

Raul Hilberg

Even as witnesses of the Shoah despaired at finding suitable language to
express what their eyes had seen, they persisted in writing about it. Before
being deported herself, Etty Hillesum, a young Dutch woman, wrote lengthy
letters to her Amsterdam friends about life in camp Westerbork, from which
weekly or biweekly convoys left for the East. In one such account, she
details the events of one night during which she helps some of the selected
1,020 men, women, and children with their preparations just before they
are packed into the wagons that will transport them to Poland. While
admitting that "no words and images are adequate to describe nights like
these," she is haunted by a pervasive sense of being the "ears and eyes of a
piece of Jewish history." Hence her decision to speak up, for "we must keep
one another in touch with everything that happens in the various outposts
of this world, each one contributing his own little piece of stone to the great
mosaic that will take shape once the war is over."[4]

In the course of a mass deportation in the town of Riga, during the fall of 1941, the elderly Simon Dubnov, dean of Jewish historians, along with a group of Latvian Jews, was led to his execution by the Germans at the edge of town. When he lagged behind, he was shot down by a Latvian guard working under Nazi command. According to at least one eyewitness, the renowned historian's last words were an exhortation to his fellow-Jews: "*Schreibt un farschreibt!*" (Write it down and record it!).

Another oft-cited example of the Jewish zeal to write and record is the work of the Warsaw circle of amateur historians and scribes known as the *Oneg Shabbat* archive. Although starving and facing wholesale destruction, these men and women around the distinguished chronicler Emmanuel Ringelblum were nevertheless determined to leave behind a legacy of their daily strivings and despair. As a result, they succeeded in passing on much of the history of the doomed Warsaw ghetto (1940 to late 1942) to the post-war world.[5]

When we ask—as indeed we should—why so much effort was invested by so many in keeping the particular details of the onslaught against the Jews alive and preserving them for posterity, I know of no more persuasive answer than George Steiner's: "We must keep vital in ourselves a sense of scandal so overwhelming that it affects every significant aspect of our position in history and society."[6] Yet it is an answer that in its generality may or may not be a comfortable fit for most personal witness accounts, as it implies the distancing perspective of ourselves looking backward from our own time in history.

Whatever the cause or causes, sixty years after the events, the struggle of Holocaust survivors to tell their story, to reflect upon it, and record it for posterity still remains strong. The annual output of scores of scholarly books, publications, and articles attests to this enduring effort. Some of these publications deal directly with the impact of Holocaust testimonies. This book is a contribution to that literature. It offers narrative accounts of twenty-three Jewish survivors, one Sinti (Gypsy) survivor, and one rescuer.

A consuming desire to communicate their experiences, coupled paradox-ically with a reluctance to enter back into them—about which more in the Conclusion—is palpable in many of the survivors' accounts. This is true even though the testimonies presented here have been rendered in the third person singular, which lends the prose a degree of formality and detachment not present in the original interviews. Some of the implications of this decision are discussed in the Conclusion.

It is no simple task to determine the exact nature of what motivates survivors to tell their story. Is it based chiefly on the necessity to keep alive that overwhelming sense of scandal of which Steiner speaks? On the need to let others know what occurred "in the various outposts of this world" (Etty Hillesum's graphic phrase)? Is it fuelled by past injustice? Does it stem from the survivors' need to recast the war's events, and interpret and reinterpret their own relationship to those long ago events from their present day perspective? Or does it derive from an imperative to set the balance straight, to give credit where it is due: either to luck, ingenuity, or the timely appearance of another person who alerted them in the nick of time, or rescued them from certain death? Or does it perhaps spring from the need to unburden oneself?

There is little doubt that the survivors whose eyewitness testimonies are presented here seek to draw humanity's attention to the terrible fate that washed over them like a giant wave, leaving only debris behind. Yet, in some cases, the urge to speak may have a different underlying motivation as well. Abram F. was able to escape successive selections and raids in the Lodz ghetto before he was deported to Auschwitz in 1944, shortly prior to the liquidation of the ghetto. Commenting on one such earlier attempt to arrest him, he says, not without pride, that he quickly jumped off the truck that would have taken him to his death once he saw there were only Jewish ghetto police, and "Jewish policemen had no guns."

Apart from one brother who was able to join him in Montreal after the war, Abram was the only member of his family to survive. In his testimony, the trauma and suffering are matched by a certain grim satisfaction. Though he clearly mourns the loss of all his family, he feels a certain triumph at having survived Hitler and the Nazi regime while retaining his basic humanity, and living long enough to tell the world of his success in starting a new life in Canada.

Such expressions of satisfaction are rare. Yet other survivors too, even while recounting tales of torture and degradation, often speak of luck, swift adaptation, or—more likely—the unforeseen good fortune of a helping hand, a gesture of good will. Rubin B. who describes his quick adjustment to the Auschwitz universe without malice, though with a hint of pride, credits his rescue from certain death to Mr. Beisel, a German engineer and industrialist in Buno-Monowitz, the notorious slave labor camp. David G. gives credit to a rabbi who met him when he was already on the run in Poland, early in the war. The rabbi looked the young man (he was eleven at the time) in the eyes and said, "I hope that you survive." David recalled these words many times, during his more than two years' stay in hiding in a cold, dark compartment built inside farmer Stronczyk's barn.

Mila M., encouraged by her parents and aided by her cousin Olek, who would not survive, was able to force herself though a small opening in the cattle car, and jump off the train headed for the Belzec extermination camp. Mila was eventually able to pass as a Gentile. Leslie S. from Budapest lost his parents, but survived together with his younger sister. He gives credit to their rescuer, the Swedish diplomat Raoul Wallenberg. Paul L. credits himself for taking a decision, and sticking to it. After his brother died of pneumonia, he realized that he would not survive the rigors of a second winter in a forced labor camp, so he plotted his escape. When captured and arrested, he was then placed in a police cell for ordinary criminals. In spite of the arduous interrogations, the comfort of the heated cell and the relatively ample food allowed him to restock his dwindling energies. Paul is obsessed by the details of his internment, and by the strange cycle of arrests and narrow escapes. Asked for his motivation for telling his story, he replies that he does it just to get it off his chest, so "I don't choke myself with my story."

That the survivors' drive to communicate has not diminished over time demands consideration. Evidently sixty years after the events, the once flourishing survivor communities in the New World have seen their numbers reduced by natural decline. Nevertheless, time seems only to have enlarged the survivors' appetite for sharing the stories that helped determine their destiny. But this is to overlook the aura of contempt that adhered to the Holocaust survivors upon their arrival in the new land. They were "dee greener" (Yiddish for newcomers; often translated as greenhorns) or, worse yet, the DPs (displaced persons). Both terms were pejorative.

In such an atmosphere it was not possible to speak about their past even among themselves or those close to them, let alone to other Jewish or non-Jewish Canadians. "I preferred to keep my mouth shut," says one survivor. "I never told anybody where I came from," says another, commenting on his social interaction with his peers during four years of university. "The predominant memory of survivors of their first years in Canada was not of acceptance but of rejection," writes Franklin Bialystok. Only gradually, with their rise in income and social status, did they begin calling themselves "survivors," a term that "elevated their status" in the Jewish community, and which was eventually adopted by other Canadians.[7]

It was much the same in other countries. Elie Wiesel, commenting on the contempt with which survivors were viewed in Europe as well as the United States, uses even stronger language in describing the prevailing attitudes. Recalling that survivors were perceived as "recluses, outcasts, that was how people saw them (. . .) Trouble-makers, kill-joys, carriers of disease," he attempts to make a new summary:

> The time may have come to tell you outright what we have been repeating to one another in whispers: that the survivors were considered intruders and treated everywhere without affection and certainly without love.[8]

As a result, says Wiesel, since they knew that they were the bearers of very special messages, after early but feeble attempts to raise their voices, they fell silent, their mission unaccomplished, for they never found an audience willing to listen to them.

On a more personal note, I had been a child in hiding for nearly three years when troops of the Canadian First Army liberated me on a farm in the north of the Netherlands, in April 1945. But even though as a Dutchman I returned to the comfort of my own country and language, I found it hard to be a Jewish child in a postwar world that seemed harsh and anti-Semitic in a casual kind of way. Though only seven years old at the time, this is not how I had imagined the postliberation world to be. On my way to school and also while playing soccer after school, I often encountered accusing shouts of "dirty Jew." At my elementary school in Amsterdam, I quickly sensed that the word "Jew" was surrounded by an aura of fear and discomfort. Although at least eight of my young classmates were Jewish (and therefore survivors), nobody dared admit to that identity, let alone talk openly about how he or she had spent the war years. While there was no overt anti-Semitism at school, I recall being aware that certain topics were taboo, especially anything having to do with Jews and the War. Only at home did we speak freely about what had happened to us during the war. I certainly could not imagine then that any stranger might be interested in any of the stories I could tell about the years I spent hiding from the Germans.[9]

This perceived deafness on the part of society first began to change in the course of the 1960s, as part of a more general opening up in both Europe and North America. As survivors gradually began to assert their need to find a listening ear, a more general willingness to listen to them slowly emerged. A new way of seeing the war also took place in the 1960s, especially in Europe. It implied responsibility for failing at the national level, and shared guilt for what had happened to the Jews who had been left exposed and unprotected. Looking at it in retrospect, there was a discernible developing readiness to consider a different paradigm to interpret the national and collective experience of World War II. Auschwitz progressively became the central iconic event of the war, replacing more straightforward victorious imagery such as the defeat of tyranny. The change, though gradual, was drastic and implies a problematic central place for destruction at the core of our memory of World War II.

Not surprisingly, this development roughly coincided with the Eichmann trial (1961) and the Auschwitz trials (1963–1965), as well as the publication of some key books, including Elie Wiesel's *Night* (1960; originally published in French in 1958), Raul Hilberg's *The Destruction of the European Jews* (1961), and Hannah Arendt's *Eichmann in Jerusalem* (1963). A central set of images concerning the extermination of the Jews emerged and supplanted the upbeat ending that had dominated the World War II narrative until then. With a new openness to collective failure and guilt at the national level, there now was room for "thinking about those groups and those emotions that had always been excluded from the dominant images of history."[10]

Following the popular success of the TV documentary *Holocaust* in 1978, which was also the year when the Holocaust Memorial Museum in Washington, D.C. was first conceived, the resistance to listening to the survivors' stories, on the part of the outside world, melted away and has, in the past two decades, given way to an atmosphere of receptivity. Yale University's Fortunoff Archive of Holocaust Testimony was started in 1981. In the early 1980s, Canadian Jewish Congress filmed over eighty video interviews with Canadian survivors from all over the country. McGill University's video archive *Living Testimonies* was started in 1989, and

Spielberg's hugely ambitious *Survivors of the Shoah* video archive took off in 1994, following the popular success of the film *Schindler's List* (1993). The new openness of the late 1970s took the survivor communities by surprise, for it occurred at a time "when most survivors no longer expected any opportunity to speak about their experiences."[11] More recently, and much to their own surprise, survivors have over time become a welcome commodity to an often uncomprehending, but increasingly fascinated world.

"We are the last witnesses," says Renata Z., a survivor of the Warsaw ghetto, and one of the more than one hundred survivors interviewed by Living Testimonies, the Holocaust Video Documentation Archive at McGill University in Montreal, from which the accounts that constitute this volume are taken. "After us there will be nobody left to tell the story," she adds. This notion of being precariously positioned alongside the last batches of survivors makes her refer to herself and other survivors like her as an "endangered species." It also persuaded her to share the experience of living, working, and hiding inside the Warsaw ghetto, as well escaping from the city prior to the April 1943 uprising through the network of sewers that ran below it. Ultimately, it even led her to become an interviewer for Living Testimonies herself.

Clearly, then, we cannot rely much longer on the immediacy of eyewitness accounts by living survivors like Renata. That personal gift for storytelling is now slowly being replaced by other indirect forms of discourse. These include books, visual media, and museums. In the words of Yale literary scholar Geoffrey Hartman, "the era of direct knowledge of the Holocaust as of the Second World War is rapidly coming to an end." We now live in a time of what he terms "transition," a period during which education will gradually replace direct experience of those events.[12] At the opening of the U.S. Holocaust Memorial Museum in 1993, President Bill Clinton used similar language, noting that "history" will soon replace "living reality and shared experience." To help fill the void left by the disappearance of this living, shared experience, video testimony—with its direct appeal (it is alive, unceremonial, and unavoidable), its emphasis on process rather than finished text, and the ease of its dissemination—must play a major role.

Though quite obviously a work such as ours serves an historical and educational function, it is not addressed just to historians and the classroom. As we conceived it, the book is also meant to be read by a much wider, lay audience. It is also intended as a tribute. By making the idiosyncratic voices of survivors public, this book serves to honor the individuality of those who lived through the war. Finally, it is a response to the voices of the victims that were silenced and can no longer be heard. In no small measure, this book is created in answer to the plea of those who, to adopt the language of the philosopher Alain Finkielkraut, "call us from the other shore."[13]

The people whose stories are collected in this book are diverse, though they all share an essentially similar experience. They speak different languages and come from different countries, as well as from varying socioeconomic backgrounds.

Paradoxically, they all appear very North American in the way they hold themselves and dress (something hidden from readers, but obvious to those watching the videos), and express themselves. Even as their command of the English language ranges from awkward to excellent, they seem to feel safe and, with few exceptions, comfortable and at home on the continent. The survivors represented here are men and women, young and old, though all were at least in their fifties at the time of being interviewed. They come from Poland, Romania, Hungary, Czechoslovakia, Germany, France, and Holland.

In this book we have created chapters that group survivors' narratives together according to three distinctions: gender, age, and whether one survived inside the camps or outside the camps in hiding or on the run.

The decision to separate women's accounts of the camps (Chapter 2) from the men's accounts (Chapter 3) was part of our attempt to capture the particular experience of women and men in the Shoah. Although Nazi destruction clearly did not distinguish between women and men, there are differences between men and women in terms of "what was done to them (their vulnerabilities) and what they did (their resources)."[14] Dalia Ofer and Lenore Weitzman offer strong arguments for the study of gender-based behavior in the ghettos and camps, and even living among the partisans. In some of these cases, women were asked to sacrifice themselves because of their children. Often, in rescue and resistance work, women were expected to take on special roles.[15] By grouping stories together according to gender, we intend to draw attention to recurring forms of trauma, humiliation, and resistance that are specific to women's stories as well as to men's. For example, women often emphasize the humiliation of entrance to the camps, of being stripped and shaved. Men, by contrast, frequently recount an instance of humiliation inflicted by an individual, who is often mentioned by name. Men and women are also distinct in the way they tell their stories—what kind of details they include, and what they omit or can not remember. Bringing the reader's attention to gender with these chapter divisions is part of an attempt to restore to the survivor the individuality of which they were deprived in the camps.

In spite of the prominent position and length of Chapters 2 ("Women Surviving the Camps") and 3 ("Men Surviving the Camps"), our chapter divisions make clear that not all of the witnesses in our text passed through camps. Chapter 1, "Hiding in the Open: Passing as a Gentile," has the accounts of three young women (two of them Polish and one Hungarian) who survived the war by pretending to be gentile girls. Chapter 5, "Evading the Nazis," features the narrative of Margot S. whose father left Germany and, by moving ever further east, ended up on a *kolkhoz* (communal farm) near Kirov in the USSR. It also has the rather brazen account of Irene B. who evaded the Nazis in her native Warsaw by moving across occupied

Europe to Turkey and Palestine, and then traveled to Rhodesia and South Africa, before crossing to South America and eventually reaching Canada, in March 1943. Chapter 5 also features the story of Harry F., a young Sinti (German Gypsy) puppeteer and entertainer whose family miraculously survived by eluding the Nazis and their murderous Croatian, Slovenian, and Romanian collaborators, across much of Southeastern Europe.

Besides Harry, the only other narrative that concerns a non-Jewish person is that of Hans M. With Chapter 6, we created a separate and final chapter dedicated to the story of someone who participated, as a young student at the University of Copenhagen, in the Danish resistance. The story of Hans especially highlights his contribution to the removal and rescue of the Danish Jewish population by the Danish underground.

The narratives of child survivors are grouped together in Chapter 4, "Hiding on the Run." Children, that is, child survivors of the Shoah, occupy a special category in this volume because, unlike adults, they had never known any other life than that under occupation, or if they did, they soon forgot about it. By contrast, adult survivors were often uplifted or tormented, as the case may be, by the memory of family and communal situations in pre-occupation life. Besides lacking an adult perspective and a sense of chronology, children are also different because they are arguably able to blank out some of the horror, and only absorb that portion of it that they can bear. That defense mechanism may have made them more matter-of-fact, and enabled them to ward off some of the terror of the camps and the very worst hide-and-run situations. Yet it also makes their stories more heart-rending for, as Aharon Appelfeld has pointed out, this was the only existence they knew, they "knew no other childhood."[16]

Leah K. narrates how she as the only person in her family of nine survived the months long death march from Romania to Transnistria (Ukraine). She locates the key to her survival in a chance remark made by two German officers passing the refugees in a car. They proposed to take her away from her parents because, with her long blond hair, she could not possibly be Jewish. Leah explains that this remark planted the seed of her survival. Since she realized that she did not look Jewish, she would later be able to pass as a non-Jewish girl without much difficulty. Other child survivors in Chapter 4 are David G. and Stefanie S. both of whom survived with one parent, and Leslie who, as we saw before, was orphaned but survived in Budapest thanks to the help of Raoul Wallenberg.

The texts give some indication of what it took to survive, besides plain luck, which was the most necessary ingredient. Clearly, there was no single blueprint for survival. Being young, strong, and healthy helped, as did having special skills (being a physician or a carpenter). Having experience with hard physical work helped too. But this was something most Jews lacked: they generally had urban or small-town backgrounds, and few grew up on a farm. Having family connections also made a difference, especially an older, protective brother or sister. Rena S. owed her life to her strong, protective mother who always hovered about her, and at one point made the twelve year old girl, who was still in pig-tails and short dresses, wear "adult fashion" clothes and high heels so that she would make it through the selection allowing her to move from the Krakow ghetto (which was liquidated by then) to camp Plaszow. Knowing someone in the Jewish hierarchy could make the difference between life and death too. The family of sisters Ilse Z. and Marti D. were solidly middle class and belonged, through their mother Lotte, to the small German-Jewish immigrant community in Amsterdam. After being deported from their home, they quickly obtained connections at the top of the camp Westerbork hierarchy (which was predominantly German Jewish). This protection arguably saved their lives, allowing them to be shielded from deportation for half a year, and then be deported to Bergen-Belsen, rather than Auschwitz.

Yet according to Raul Hilberg, in his essay on "Survivors," the physical condition and social characteristics of the survivor were less important than his or her "psychological profile." Hilberg distinguishes three important traits that could make the difference between life and death: realism, rapid decision making, and tenacious holding on to life.[17] Of these, realism may well be the most significant one. Rubin, shortly after arriving in Auschwitz-Birkenau, quickly realized that "vigilance, obedience and keeping a low profile" would be his only means of survival there, and that obeying orders was "one of the basic vocabularies of survival." Even so, Rubin is aware that his "days are numbered." Another example is the down-to-earth reaction of Abram after being told, shortly after arriving in Auschwitz, that his family is already dead and that it is "Jewish smoke" that he sees coming from the chimney: "We took it half as a joke to hurt you and half as maybe it is true. Maybe it is a Jewish smoke."

Rapid decision making guides many of the actions of the survivors. We already saw how the split second decision of Abram to jump off the truck saved his life. He acted as soon as he realized the Germans were gone and only Jewish soldiers were left to guard him. One other example is the escape of Leah from the terrible camp at Pechora where her chances for survival were nil. By staying and sleeping close to the gate, she was able to seize her opportunity when it presented itself, at a point when the only guard on duty was distracted by a beautiful woman just as he was opening the gate for an entering vehicle. At that precise moment, the nine year old Leah resolutely walked out and quickly blended in with the crowds. Patterns of tenacity abound throughout the text. We already looked at Paul's resolve to make his escape from the labor camp before the onset of the next winter. The accounts of Irene C., Jacob G., and Saul B. provide different but powerful examples of strength of purpose.

The testimonies we have selected for publication in this volume each show glimpses of the big movements of World War II, such as the fast German sweep into Poland or France, the bureaucratic German machine that marks and identifies Jews in much the same manner across German occupied Europe, the efficiently organized round-ups of Europe's Jews, or the slow retreat of the German Wehrmacht from east to west. In our texts, these movements come across in fragments, through the perspective of the ordinary individuals who tried to stay ahead of them, or escape them once they became trapped inside the lines of fire. The fate of the European Jews may be a collective one, but the attempt to survive the attacks on life and liberty is often best understood as an individual struggle. The same goes for the post-war movements of large groups of people on their way to being resettled, mostly in other continents, and their drive to begin all over again and start a new family. These are events best portrayed by focusing on individual lives that capture this historical flow in all its particular subjective human detail.

Finally, a note about accuracy and transcription. We have done extensive research in order to verify even the smallest and remotest place names mentioned by the survivors. Yet there are bound to be errors, for which we apologize. Also, in an attempt to make the text more reader-friendly, we decided to present some of the names of places and streets (especially those in Czech, Hungarian, and Polish) in their Westernized or more accurately, Anglicized version, without any of the special marks or accents. Thus we have Miskolc, Cinadovo, Lodz, Krakow, and Plac Zgody. We hope this will be accepted for what it is, a somewhat uncomfortable compromise, and we trust it will not give offense to anyone from those particular areas.

Notes

1. Elie Wiesel, A Jew Today (New York: Random House, 1978), 198.

2. Aharon Appelfeld, *Beyond Despair* (New York: Fromm International Publishing Corporation, 1994), 31–32.

3. Raul Hilberg, *Perpetrators, Victims, Bystanders* (New York: Harper, 1992), 190.

4. Etty Hillesum was killed in Auschwitz in November 1943. She wrote a substantial number of letters from Camp Westerbork. She is best known for her diaries, to which some of the letters are appended. See *An Interrupted Life: The Diaries of Etty Hillesum* (New York: Pantheon, 1983), 207–208, and also Etty Hillesum, *Letters from Westerbork* (New York: Pantheon, 1986).

5. Cited in Martin Gilbert, *The Holocaust: A History of the Jews of Europe during the Second World War* (New York: Holt, Rinehart and Winston, 1986), 230. See also Jacob Sloan, ed., *Notes from the Warsaw Ghetto: The Journal of Emmanuel Ringelblum* (New York, 1958), which is a selection in English from an early publication in Yiddish.

6. George Steiner, *In Bluebeard's Castle: Some Notes Towards the Re-definition of Culture* (London: Faber and Faber, 1971), 43.

7. Franklin Bialystok, *Delayed Impact: The Holocaust and the Canadian Jewish Community* (Montreal: McGill-Queens UP, 2000), 80–81.

8. Wiesel, *A Jew Today*, 196.

9. Cf. Yehudi Lindeman, "In Hiding in Holland," in *The Holocaust: Personal Accounts*, David Scrase and Wolfgang Mieder, eds. (Burlington: The Center for Holocaust Studies at the University of Vermont, 2001), 204–206.

10. Frank van Vree, "Een verleden dat niet verdwijnen wil" [A Past that Won't Go Away], *Icodo-Info*, vol. 20, no. 1 (June 2003): 28–29. (In Dutch.)

11. Sylvia Rothchild, ed., *Voices from the Holocaust* (New York: NAL, 1981), 10.

12. Geoffrey Hartman, *The Longest Shadow: In the Aftermath of the Holocaust* (Bloomington: Indiana UP, 1996), 10.

13. Alain Finkielkraut, *Une voix vient de l'autre rive* (Paris: Gallimard, 2000), 23.

14. Joan Ringelheim, "Women and the Holocaust: A Reconsideration of Research," *Signs*, vol. 10, no. 4 (1985), 743.

15. Dalia Ofer and Lenore J. Weitzman, *Women in the Holocaust* (New Haven: Yale University Press, 1998), 1–18.

16. Appelfeld, *Beyond Despair*, 36–37.

17. Hilberg, *Perpetrators, Victims, Bystanders*, 188–189.

CHAPTER 1

Hiding in the Open: Passing as a Gentile

Rose B.
August 17, 1994

From the time Rose's daughter Clare, born after the Holocaust, was a little girl, Rose used to tell her everything that happened to her during the war. Then, Rose says, the "wound was still fresh." Because of Rose's stories, her daughter would wake up crying and screaming in the middle of the night, fearing that Hitler was coming back. When her son was born six years later, she avoided a repeat of her daughter's traumatic experience by not telling him anything until he was grown. Rose, in turn, tried to push her memories away. Now after so many years have passed, Rose has some trouble remembering her experience of the war. In her testimony, Rose's omission of detail and memory gaps are evident of the years of effort to forget her pain.

Before the war, Stryj, Poland (now part of the modern Ukraine), was a city with 35,000 inhabitants, including Ukrainians, Poles, *Volksdeutsche* (ethnic Germans), and Jews. Rose recounts that for a family of observant Jews who attended synagogue regularly and kept a kosher home, life in Stryj was "pleasant and normal." In her case, it also included economic hardships. Her family was "not rich" and it was very expensive for her parents, Solomon and Klara, to raise their two daughters, Mathilda who was born in 1913, and Rose, born in 1921.

Rose was very close to her extended family, most of which lived in Stryj. Rose had "twelve uncles and aunties, twenty-four cousins in Stryj, and seven cousins out of Stryj." She continues, "That's what I lost. Everybody gone. Lost in the Holocaust. I was only one [who] survived, with my father."

Rose's father was a tinsmith and a roofer and her mother had a small china shop. Rose and her sister attended a Polish *gymnasium*. The family spoke Polish at home, although Rose recalls Solomon and Klara speaking Yiddish with each other.

In Stryj, good relations between Jews and non-Jews always depended on the character of the individual, remembers Rose. Only after the German invasion, she says, "everybody turned their backs to the Jews," but she adds that Gentiles in Stryj also helped her to survive.

The Germans began bombing Poland in September 1939. Rose remembers fleeing into the countryside with her family. When they returned to their home, the Germans had already occupied Stryj. Rose does not recall the details of this initial occupation, but she says that nothing happened to the Jews. The Germans, however, were only in Stryj until it fell to the Russians two weeks later. As Rose recalls, the city changed hands peacefully. The period of Russian occupation was "quiet" for her family. Her father was not a "capitalist" and he continued working as a tinsmith and a roofer. During this time, Rose was engaged in secretarial studies. It was not until the Russians left in June 1941 that she knew things were changing drastically.

Rose cannot describe the day the Germans marched into Stryj: "I remember everybody was scared . . . Even the Polish [people] were afraid." Soon after the Germans' arrival, her family was forced out of their home and into the ghetto that had been established near the city's synagogue. They had to leave their possessions behind as they moved into a ghetto apartment with her cousin Gerta, and Gerta's husband and children. The four of them lived in "one little kitchen."

Although the ghetto was closed and guarded, Rose's father, who was self-employed, had permission from the Germans to continue working in Stryj. She, her sister, and her mother worked at the *Arbeitslager* (labor camp) near the German military barracks. Rose's job was "segregating potatoes." For the most part, Rose is unable to give a detailed description of the ghetto. As part of the working battalion, she remembers getting up at 6:00 a.m. every morning and walking two hours to the *Arbeitslager*. Otherwise she says, "This is like a dream I don't remember."

When the Stryj ghetto was liquidated, the *Arbeitslager* was converted into a *Zwangsarbeitlager* (forced labor camp). Jews who could work were taken to the camp. All the other people from the ghetto were killed. Everyone of Rose's immediate family ended up at the *Zwangsarbeitlager*. Her mother worked in the kitchen; but Rose and Mathilda worked in the construction of German military barracks, carrying heavy loads of lumber on their backs. To this day, Rose has pain in her shoulder from this hard labor. Rose worked at the *Zwangsarbeitlager* for nearly two years. The whole time she feared that the Germans planned to liquidate the camp.

In 1943, Rose escaped with her sister. They knew of people who had previously escaped from the ghetto and the forced labor camp in Stryj aided by a gentile couple who, in exchange for money, escorted Jews to Warsaw. Rose and Mathilda paid this couple to take them on an overnight train to Warsaw. For Rose this was a "terrible trip." She and her sister traveled in separate compartments, Rose with the woman, and her sister with the man. While they were on the train, German soldiers approached her and interrogated her about what she was smuggling. Other passengers smuggled food items like butter and eggs, but knowing she would be shot if her true identity were revealed, she explains, "I didn't say that I was smuggling my life." "You see?" she repeats, "I didn't smuggle nothing but I smuggled my life."

Rose and Mathilda arrived in Warsaw on August 2, 1943. They spent the night with the couple, but then they were left to their own devices. Rose and Mathilda did not have anything; they only wanted to "get lost" in the city. They contacted friends from Stryj, a Jewish girl and her brother, who lived in hiding. The four of them met in a park. Rose went with the girl to locate an address that had been recommended as a potential hiding place, while Mathilda and the girl's brother stayed behind. Rose and the girl returned to the park after finding no one at that address, but Mathilda and the brother were no longer there. Rose never saw her sister again. "To this day," Rose says, "I don't know what happened to them." She thinks that German soldiers might have rounded them up for forced labor, which was common in Warsaw at the time; "I don't know if they went as a Polish, [or] as a Jewish, you see?" Even today, the girl, who survived the war, is angry with Rose: "She didn't want to talk to me. She said because of me, because of my sister, her brother got lost, got killed."

The girl was afraid to be seen with Rose and wanted her to go to the house of a *volksdeutsch* couple that housed people for money. The *volksdeutsch* couple took Rose in but she was there only for a few days before they asked her to leave. They told Rose that it was not a safe location for her because they had a son who had run away from the army. Two days before, German soldiers had searched their house, discovered a Jewish couple, and shot them on the spot.

Because Mathilda was older, she had been carrying all the funds that the two sisters possessed. When she found herself alone in Warsaw, Rose thought to contact one of her sister's gentile friends in Stryj. This friend was able to send her money that Rose used to buy false documents. Her papers gave her the name Irene Kotowska, but bore Rose's picture, her fingerprints, and her signature. Rose emphasizes that it was absolutely necessary for her to have the false documents because the German soldiers frequently stopped her on the street and asked to see them. Even with the documents that said she was a gentile girl, Rose was always afraid that they would think she was Jewish.

Having false documents enabled Rose to look in the newspaper for a job. First, she applied to be a domestic helper for a pregnant woman. When the woman met with her, she began stroking Rose's hair and said, "*Mein Kind*, go with God. I recognize that you are Jewish." Rose remembers that she cried and begged the woman to let her stay.

She then applied for a job with the Kaczmarski family, with whom she would stay for a year. The Kaczmarskis were a middle-class gentile family who lived in downtown Warsaw. Rose did domestic work for them, cared for a two-year old girl, and smuggled a headache-relief powder that Mr. Kaczmarski, a pharmacist, made in his home and sold on the black market, an especially dangerous task for Rose.

The Kaczmarskis did not know that Rose was Jewish and because they never went to church, Rose avoided the suspicion that she was not the Catholic girl she said she was. She was also convincing in her ability to appear uninterested when they informed her of what had happened to the Jews in Warsaw. In general, there was no disturbance, but Rose always feared the possibility of the house being searched.

While she was hiding in Warsaw, Rose recognized a man on the street as her father's former employer. Rose tried to avoid him but he stopped her and told her that Stryj had been made *judenfrei*. All Jews, including her mother and her cousins, were taken into the synagogue. Rose's father, on the other hand, was one of the few men chosen to be transferred to a work camp in Drohobycz. This gave Rose the hope that she might see her father again. She knew that everybody else had been killed.

Rose was liberated in the summer of 1944, six months before the liberation of Warsaw, while she was on holiday with the Kaczmarskis in Józefów, a small summer resort town on the eastern side of the Wisla (Vistula) River. A few weeks later, Rose revealed to the Kaczmarskis that she was Jewish and told them that she wanted to go to Otwock, a nearby town, to see what had happened and hopefully encounter fellow Jews. In Otwock Rose found a group of Jewish girls and boys to live with, so she returned to Józefów and said good-bye to the family. The Kaczmarskis, who Rose calls her "angels," were happy that Rose had survived the war and that they had contributed to saving a Jewish woman. Rose kept in touch with Mrs. Kaczmarski until 1993, when she learned that Mrs. Kaczmarski was suffering from Alzheimer's disease.

After a stay in Otwock, Rose wanted to return to Stryj to see what had happened. She says that she spent one or two days there with a family friend but found "nobody alive."

She then went to Lublin to work as a secretary, until Praga, a district of Warsaw, was liberated in 1945. She moved to Praga and found another secretarial job. In both Lublin and Praga, Rose worked as "Irena Kotowska."

Rose B. after the war

While in Praga, Rose received word that her father was alive and recovering in a hospital in Linz, Austria. He had been liberated from the Mauthausen concentration camp. She reunited with her father in 1945: "Unexpectedly I came. You can imagine this meeting. I came alone without my sister, you see?"

She and her father lived together in a DP camp in Austria until an uncle located them while trying to discover whether anyone in the family was still alive. This uncle, her father's brother who had moved to Buenos Aires before the war, arranged visas for Rose and her father and brought them to Buenos Aires in 1948. They had been living in a DP camp since 1945.

Rose was not in Argentina very long before she began to correspond with a man she had met at the DP camp in Linz. Because he was unable to accompany her to Buenos Aires, the two of them had said goodbye in Austria. However, around the same time, he was able to go to Canada and he wanted Rose to join him there as his wife. As soon as she could, Rose left for Montreal and was married three weeks after she arrived. A year later, Rose's father also immigrated to Canada. He never remarried, but lived with Rose, her husband, and her children, Clare and Fred. He died on December 22, 1970. Rose remarks that he lived long enough to see his grandson's bar mitzvah.

Rose now has two grandchildren of her own, Steven and Tyler. She concludes, "You see, today you don't remember all those moments and the scare you went through the whole time during the German occupation. After so many years you try to push away this thing, this memory."

❈ ❈ ❈

Mila (Amalia) M.
February 23, 1994

After Mila's family was rounded up from the Kolomyja ghetto, Mila, her sisters, and a cousin escaped a death transport to Belzec by jumping off a moving train. They obtained false documents and lived in hiding as Christians in Chodorov, Poland, for the duration of the war. Mila's testimony attests to her personal courage and to the humanity of those who helped her survive.

Mila grew up in a happy home in Zaleszczyki, Poland, a beautiful and prosperous summer resort town of five thousand near the Romanian border. Mila, born November 22, 1923, had two older sisters, Lola and Ziuta. Their orphaned cousin, Jasia, who was two years younger than Mila, also lived with them. The family was well-to-do and traditionally Jewish. Her father, Zigmund, was an industrialist who owned several flourmills and some property, while Mila's mother, Fanny, chaired a Jewish organization that helped the poor and the sick. The family spoke Polish at home, but Fanny and Zigmund sometimes spoke Yiddish between themselves. They had a kosher cook who prepared their shabbat dinners and a large seder meal at Passover. Mila remembers that Zigmund went to synagogue every week.

Zaleszczyki's population was evenly divided between Jews, Poles, and Ukrainians. Mila, who considered herself assimilated, attended the Polish *gymnasium* where she had both Jewish and non-Jewish friends. Her childhood and adolescence were marked by good relations with non-Jews, something Mila points out as unique to her own experience of growing up in Poland. Not only did the family have a number of non-Jewish friends and neighbors, they also participated in Christian Polish culture, attending Christmas dinners at the homes of Christian family friends who, in turn, were invited to her family's *Purim* celebrations. One year, on All Saint's Day, Mila's family had gone to the Christian cemetery to see the graves lit up by candles, honoring the dead. Mila came across the grave of an elderly neighbor who had no children. No one had put a candle on his grave, which made Mila feel so sad for him that she started to cry. Touched by her daughter's compassion, Mila's mother took her to put a candle on his grave each year.

At the outbreak of World War II, Mila's whole life changed abruptly. The bombing began immediately after September 1, 1939. Waves of refugees followed by retreating Polish soldiers passed through the town on their way across the Romanian border. Mila's father refused to cross into Romania because he did not want to abandon their property; he also was not fully aware of the danger. In retrospect, Mila is struck by how accessible safety was to them at that time; from their house, the Romanian border was only one hundred meters away.

Mila's family expected the German army to arrive in their town. When they heard rumors that the Russians were coming instead, they were relieved. Even though her father was a "capitalist," Zigmund considered the Russians "the lesser of two evils." However, soon after the Russian army occupied the town on September 17, 1939, Zigmund's business and property were confiscated. For several months after this forced take-over, the Russians employed him as the supervisor of his own business. Because of the family's fear that Mila's father would be arrested and deported to Siberia, Mila's brother-in-law, whose parents were Romanian, took the family to Kolomyja.

The family members and friends who stayed behind in Zaleszczyki were arrested and eventually disappeared.

In Kolomyja, Mila continued to go to school. On June 22, 1941, two days before Mila's graduation, the German army began its invasion of the Soviet Union. For her, this was the beginning of a period of indescribable brutality. Her first encounter with inhumanity involved a group of expelled Hungarian Jews of Polish origin who arrived in her town. A Hungarian couple and their six year-old daughter Eva used to drop by Mila's house because her family provided them with food. One day, the Hungarian family stopped coming. Later, in the ghetto, Mila saw Eva all alone in the square. She was sobbing the word "Anyuka," which Mila later found out was Hungarian for "Mama." Until that moment, Mila had distinct memories of Eva as a happy child who was full of life. The stark contrast between the image of the happy Eva and the sad and forlorn child in the ghetto still makes Mila cry.

Everyone in Mila's family, except for her eldest sister Ziuta, was confined to the ghetto in February 1942. A local woman was hiding Ziuta, her husband Dr. Wasserman, and their daughter. Before the war, Mila's brother-in-law had repeatedly treated this woman, who was a prostitute, for recurring venereal disease, and had never charged her for medical care. To repay this kindness, at the outbreak of the war, she swore she "would not let Dr. Wasserman die." She remained true to her promise, hiding him, his wife, and their little girl in a hole she dug in her kitchen floor.

The Kolomyja ghetto was surrounded on all sides by wooden fences that were not difficult to cross. Mila's family was fortunate to live near the border of the ghetto, which made it easier for a friend, Arbentild, to sneak in food and wood for them. Arbentild was a *Volksdeutscher* who went around on his bicycle peddling shawls in order to earn money to feed Mila and her family. Because of Arbentild, Mila felt she was luckier than others were.

The population of the ghetto shrank, due to the raids every few weeks, until more people were brought in from surrounding areas. Mila remembers horrible hunger and illness. People died in the streets, which created the ever-present stench of death.

The *Judenrat*, the Jewish Council of the ghetto, assigned Mila to a job outside the ghetto. She was a gardener for a German woman who worked for the mayor. The German woman's nine-year-old daughter hid bread and butter in her apron and brought it to Mila while she worked. The wife of a German officer's chauffeur, who lived nearby, also brought Mila some food. Mila was aware of the harsh laws forbidding non-Jews from helping Jews. Even though few were willing to endanger their own lives and the lives of their families by sheltering or aiding Jews, Mila indicates that there were some people who "retained their humanity."

Mila and her family planned to escape to Hungary, but on October 11, 1942, German soldiers raided their apartment. Mila and her family attempted to hide beneath the staircase but they were discovered and herded into a square with approximately five thousand other Jews who had also been caught. Late in the afternoon, they were loaded onto cattle cars. They were under no illusions about what would happen to them, for they had heard about the death camp Belzec: "We knew we were going to die."

Once the train was en route, Mila remembers feeling tired. She kept on dozing off and dreaming that she was somewhere else, then waking up and realizing that she was on the train to Belzec. Meanwhile, her cousin Jasia and her friend Olek intended to escape. By dismantling the boards near the small window, they created a hole in the train's siding that was large enough to squeeze through. The decision was made that Mila, Lola, Olek, and Jasia, together with Olek's parents, would take their chances by jumping off. Mila's parents stayed on the train, fearing that their distinctly Semitic features would hurt everyone's chance for survival if they succeeded in getting away.

One after another they jumped off and fell onto the gravel. Mila somehow managed to land unharmed, as did her sister and her cousin. They found Olek with both his legs broken. Because he could not move, he begged them all to run away without him. He said that he would kill himself by ingesting poison he carried with him. They left him by the train tracks. When they returned to check on him in the morning they found his bullet-ridden body. Olek's grief-stricken parents survived the war, although shortly after, his father committed suicide.

Mila, Lola, and Jasia made their way to Chodorov, where they sent a telegram to Arbentild, explaining what had happened. They all cried over the loss of Mila's parents, who had died at Belzec, sacrificing their lives so the children could survive. Arbentild did not hesitate to shelter, feed, and clothe the three young women. Mila reports that Arbentild told them, "I am going to save you. If I have to perish I'll perish with you." He sought the help of a priest named Petchuk, who worked in the city hall and was able to procure birth certificates and working papers that identified them as Gentiles. This priest provided false papers for many other Jews as well. "He was not part of any organization," explains Mila, "he was a simple man who decided to help." Petchuk did not survive the war.

Mila worked in the land and estate office in the German administration of Bobrka, under the command of a "cruel beast" named Orgen Scheffer. Scheffer and his "henchman" Ivan Gronnick were known for hunting down Jews in the forest and killing them. "If Scheffer had known I was Jewish," says Mila, "he would have killed me in a most merciless way." Passing as gentile girls, she, Lola, and Jasia worked in his office for two years.

In autumn 1943, all the Jews from the Bobrka ghetto were rounded up and taken to Wlodawa, a nearby Polish settlement. There, a mass grave was dug and every Jew was shot. Mila says that hearing about this event was an experience she cannot explain. She was haunted by the thought of all those people being killed. Alone at night she would hear waves of wailing and crying, as well as the "eerie barking" of dogs. It was her imagination, she explains, or else it really was the souls of the murdered Jews passing through the town. At work, it was rumored that the blood of the murdered Jews was streaming out of the mass grave. It was horrifying and unthinkable. A Pole who worked in Mila's office, Pavel Chiuczala, bragged that he participated in the killing.

Some Jews had escaped the massacre in the forest. Mila found out that the mayor of Bobrka gave them food because he saw them as protection against the *Banderovtsi*—Ukrainian partisans who were killing both Jews and Poles. Because the *Banderovtsi* represented a significant threat to the Poles in the area, two of Mila's Polish friends, Janina and Henryk Medinski, who also worked in the land office, suggested that she, her sister, and her cousin move into their family's home in Lvov. In Lvov, Mila, who did not reveal that she was Jewish, came into contact with the Medinskis' cousin Jan Kinski, who made a powerful impression on her. During the war, Jan Kinski sold all his possessions in order to save as many Jews as he could. Through his connections, he took Jews to Warsaw, where he found hiding places for them. He was blackmailed because of his illegal activities and committed suicide just three weeks before the liberation. Mila attended his funeral. To this day, she wonders how many Jews Jan saved.

When the Russians liberated Lvov in July 1944, Mila, Lola, and Jasia decided to return to their home in Zaleszczyki. Passing through decimated villages on the way, they arrived in Zaleszczyki where they reunited with Ziuta and her family. Mila stayed in Zaleszczyki for a few months, and recalls that she was received warmly and treated well by her neighbors. Some of them gave her food and furniture. Mila recognizes that she was lucky to have encountered so much kindness when so many others received none. Many other Jews from Zaleszczyki had also survived under the protection of a German man who had established a colony for the production of rubber in nearby Kolendzyany. Though the Jews who were employed by this German man were not well fed, Mila observes, they were not killed. When the *Banderovtsi* came with the intention of killing the hidden Jews, the man emerged with two pistols and drove the *Banderovtsi* away.

Eventually, Mila's brother-in-law managed to obtain papers enabling the family to immigrate to Romania. They were at the railway station in Bucharest when they heard that the war was finally over. Mila sobbed at the news. She, her sisters, brother-in-law, and cousin stayed in Bucharest for a year and a half. Lola was married in Romania and lived there with her husband for ten years before immigrating to Canada. Jasia moved to Israel. The others traveled to Prague, where they hoped to obtain visas to go abroad. This was more difficult than they expected. The message they received was that "no country wanted Jews." However, for fifty U.S. dollars, they were each able to buy visas to Paraguay. At the time, Mila's boyfriend had already immigrated to Brazil. They planned to meet up in Rio de Janeiro and get married. By the time Mila arrived in South America, her boyfriend was engaged to someone else. So, Mila, Ziuta, her husband, and their daughter settled in Asunción, Paraguay, where there was so much political unrest that Mila recalls there were five different presidents in one year.

In Paraguay, Mila, who spoke Russian, Ukrainian, Romanian, German, Polish, and a little Spanish, worked as an interpreter and social worker for

Mila M. in Paraguay, 1948

new immigrants. The entire family lived on what she earned, for her brother-in-law's medical license was not recognized there. They had no intention of staying in Paraguay on a long-term basis. Mila says she would have traveled through the jungle to Argentina, as many other Jewish refugees did, if Mila's brother-in-law had not discovered that an uncle was living in Montreal. This uncle arranged to have Canadian immigration papers sent to Mila and her family. He instructed the family to go to Montevideo, where tickets and money would be waiting for them. When Mila and her family arrived in Montevideo, there were no tickets for them because their uncle had died before he could make the proper arrangements. They contacted any relative they could for help. After a three-month delay in Uruguay, Mila and her family collected enough money from other relatives to leave for Canada.

Mila, her sister, and her family traveled by ship to New York in 1949, and from there took a train to Montreal. After arriving in Montreal, Mila worked in a coat factory for two years. At her job, she was merely part of a machine yet she was happy and very appreciative of her freedom. Not knowing the language, on the other hand, was very lonely. She felt that she could not participate in life so she also went to school in the evening to learn English. Eventually, she earned a degree in accounting at Sir George Williams University. She became the chief accountant for the Montreal Museum of Fine Arts, later working there in the administration of collections.

Mila was married in 1953. She and her husband chose not to have any children because, she says, she was afraid of bringing children into the world. She did not want her own children to be endangered and have to live with the fear of persecution that she had experienced in her life. Despite this, Mila says she feels "sane" because she is not filled with hatred. However, to this day, Mila suffers from nightmares and bad headaches triggered by her painful memories of the war. She says, "I know after today's interview I will have a terrible headache tomorrow."

She has chronicled her story for *Living Testimonies* because she realizes that it must be recorded and documented. Most importantly, she feels that she must act as a living witness to both the terrible cruelty of the war and to the people who retained their humanity. The latter group is immensely important to Mila. She believes she was able to save herself because she knew she could count on the help of others. Otherwise, she says, she does not know if she would have even jumped off the train to Belzec.

※ ※ ※

Edith Z.
February 8, 1993

After Germany invaded Hungary, Edith fled from her hometown of Miskolc to Budapest, where she spent the rest of the war passing as a Catholic. After liberation, the surviving members of her immediate family joined her oldest brother and paternal uncles in El Paso, Texas. Edith remained in Hungary and was caught behind the Iron Curtain. She and her husband, along with their newborn child, moved to Israel in 1949 and then to Montreal, Canada, in 1952.

Edith clearly remembers the day that Germany invaded Hungary in March 1944. She was attending a dance in the gymnasium of her school when news of the invasion came. As soon as the students got word of what was happening, everyone at the dance ran to their homes because they knew "this was like a death sentence." The next day, German soldiers reached her hometown.

Edith was born in 1926 in Miskolc, Hungary, one hundred kilometers northeast of Budapest. Hers was a city of about 75,000 people, approximately ten thousand of whom were Jewish. Edith's father Solomon was born in Czechoslovakia but had left that country for Hungary to avoid World War I. Her mother Sarah, who hailed from a wealthy family in the nearby town of Sender, helped out in her husband's business. Solomon was a successful citrus importer who was respected by the community. For a time, he served as the president of the *chevra kadisha*, the mutual benefit society that provided burials for the dead. The family was well-to-do. They had domestic help and spent their summer vacations in a nearby resort town, Tapolca.

Edith speaks fondly of her five siblings, Laszlo, Irving, Imra, Sandor, and Eva. They all attended Jewish school in Miskolc, and Edith went on to study at the only Jewish Teacher's College in Hungary. Her family was traditional and religious, observing *kashrut* and shabbat. On High Holidays, the men in the family went to synagogue and then came home for a feast often accompanied by a poor neighbor. Her early childhood was pleasant, she says, but quickly adds, "I don't believe that those last few years [just before the war] were happy any more, because the rest of the family was in Czechoslovakia and no good news came from there."

In 1939, Edith's American uncles came to Miskolc for a visit and suggested that some of the family leave Hungary and join them in El Paso, Texas. Solomon, however, refused to leave because Edith's paternal grandmother was ailing and too weak to make the journey. Edith's oldest brother Laszlo was the only one who managed to escape Europe before the German invasion. He was able to secure a visa for Mexico and lived in Ciudad Juarez, attending school just across the border in El Paso.

Other than the news she received from her family in Czechoslovakia, Edith does not remember hearing much about the war before the German invasion. "Everything was hushed, quiet." Some restrictions were imposed on Hungarian Jews, such as forbidding them to hire non-Jews, but on the whole, "nobody either knew or talked." Anti-Semitism was an issue, but it did not affect her much because she had no contacts outside the Jewish community. After the invasion, however, things rapidly changed for the worse. "Unfortunately I didn't see one Hungarian non-Jew who tried to express their sympathy or to help," she says.

Not long after the invasion, Jews were forbidden to attend Hungarian schools, and many of Edith's friends left Miskolc and, when they returned to their hometowns, found themselves forced into a ghetto. One Jewish friend wrote her a postcard, asking Edith to send clothes. "In a bracket she said, 'you won't need them much longer,' " meaning that soon Edith, too, would be placed in a ghetto. Edith believed her, saying "it hit you, that was the truth." The invasion came very quickly, and once it started, it was almost impossible to flee or resist. Within weeks, Jews were made to wear yellow badges and were no longer allowed outside in the evening.

Back in the winter of 1943, her father had begun hiding two Jewish boys who had recently fled Czechoslovakia using false papers. They told her family, "you Hungarian Jews, you really are very stupid. You don't see ahead." This persuaded Solomon to begin securing false papers for his family.

Before the papers came through, Edith's whole family was sent to work on a farm fifty kilometers away. They were watched by Hungarians, and lived in a stable for several weeks before being sent back to Miskolc. When they returned, the family had to move into a ghetto. Since there was hardly any room left in the ghetto at this point, the family was split up. Edith remembers hearing a group of young Zionist men trying to convince the Judenrat to procure guns and overpower the Germans. But the leaders were frightened of the Germans and told the young men that they would turn them over to the Nazis if they made preparations to resist.

When the false papers came through a few days after her return to Miskolc, Edith and one of the Czechoslovakian boys decided to take their chances and make an attempt to escape. The next Saturday, Edith put a crucifix around her neck and went to say goodbye to her father. At the sight of his daughter wearing a crucifix, Solomon broke down and Edith saw her father cry for the first time in her life. Then she and the Czechoslovakian boy tore the yellow Star of David off of their coats and, with their false papers in hand, marched out of the ghetto toward the train station. "Nobody stopped us walking out of the ghetto. That part was very easy."

Just as they arrived at the station, a bomb threat caused a siren to sound. The two escapees had to walk around Miskolc for half of an hour. They were terrified that someone would recognize them and denounce them to the authorities. When they finally made it to the train, a policeman approached them and demanded to see their papers. Edith handed him her false documents, he examined them, and then returned them to her without suspecting a thing. The rest of the train ride to Budapest passed without incident.

Two days after Edith arrived in Budapest, she was reunited with two of her brothers who had also managed to escape. The next day, her parents tried to escape from the ghetto with Eva and Sandor. At the train station, a female Hungarian janitor recognized them and called the police, shouting, "I know them, they are Jews, they are running away." A policeman came, and took her parents and youngest siblings to the station. The police told Edith's father that they would spare his family if he enlisted in a labor battalion. He agreed, and the police began to interrogate him, trying to find out what he had done with his money and property. Eventually, he was sent to a forced labor camp in the Carpathian Mountains and his wife and two youngest children, along with everyone else in the Miskolc ghetto, were sent to work in a brick factory.

While she was in Budapest, Edith sometimes received postcards from her father, but she never learned what had happened to her mother and youngest siblings. After the war, two cousins told Edith that her mother had been deported to Auschwitz along with almost everyone else in the Miskolc ghetto. Since Sarah was accompanied by the thirteen-year-old Sandor and the nine-year-old Eva, she and the children were chosen for the "the wrong side" during selection and perished in the gas chambers.

In Budapest, Edith could not live together with her brothers because, according to their assumed identities, they were not related. In the beginning, she and her brothers worked in a bottling plant. However, it was not long before their coworkers began to suspect that something was wrong. Sensing suspicion in the many questions that they asked, Edith and her brothers chose not to return to work. They agreed to meet once every day, usually for breakfast or lunch. Often, she recalls, "we didn't even sit together at one table because it wasn't safe."

Under the name Anta Irene Katerin, Edith lived as a boarder in about ten different apartments during as many months. She was in constant fear of being found out, and moved on each time she believed to have aroused suspicion. She remembers, "those were very difficult times, there was nothing to do." Every morning, she had to leave her room so that her landlord would not question her about the fact that she was not working. "We were walking the streets, many times we got into the movies, because it was dark, and we were watching the same movie again and again," she says. Fortunately, one of her father's business contacts, Vinza Schiotto, a Gentile, was able to help them by securing jobs for her brothers and lending them money. Edith remembers him as "an exceptionally nice person," and they still keep in touch.

One day, as she was getting off a streetcar, a Hungarian policeman approached Edith. He ordered her to come to the station with him so he could check her papers, because he suspected she was Jewish. She protested, telling the policeman to examine her papers right there. The policeman said it was too dark to see, and the Czech boy accompanying her suggested they move under a street lamp. Edith passed the officer's scrutiny, but just barely. She knew that it would be a mistake to go back to the people with whom she stayed, since the police would probably go there to track her down. Even though it was past the 10 p.m. curfew, Edith fled into the night.

Because she was blond and possessed false papers, Edith was reasonably safe in Budapest. She was even able to visit an uncle in the Budapest ghetto and sometimes to attend religious services held in a private apartment there. Edith states that she never witnessed any deportations from the ghetto in either Miskolc or Budapest. The only Jews she remembers being captured were those rounded up "for different reasons," and "a lot of them, they took care of it right then and there in Budapest: they shot them."

Edith concealed her true identity until the last house she stayed in. The owner of her last residence was in love with a Jewish communist, and chose to help hide Edith along with some other Jews, keeping their presence a secret. Edith also went to a Wallenberg house a few times to get food, and her brothers obtained *Schutzpässe* there for other Jews to get into protected "Swiss houses." Edith explains that many Jews received help in this way, especially those fleeing from labor camps.

In January of 1945, the Russian army liberated Budapest. Edith remembers that she was hiding in an air raid shelter with her brothers when the first Russian soldier appeared: "it was great happiness. He was a young man, and he opened his arms with everybody hugging and kissing: 'the Russians are here, the Russians are here, this is the end!' " The soldier motioned to Edith that she should give him her valuable watch. She "gave it to him happily." It was not long before Edith realized that she was not yet out of danger; the Russian soldiers began stealing valuables and harassing Jewish women. In broken Yiddish, she asked a Jewish captain in the Russian army to protect them. He ordered his men to leave her and her brothers alone, but his request went unheeded. A few days later, she left the air raid shelter, having bandaged her head with gauze to discourage the Russians from raping her.

She and her brothers gathered with a group of about ten other Jews and boarded a crowded train headed for Miskolc. In Debrecen, on their way from Budapest to Miskolc, the Russian army stopped the train and everyone inside was forced to perform manual labor in a lumberyard for the rest of the day. The next day, they were herded onto an open wagon train and they resumed their journey home. Altogether, it took them two weeks to cover the ground that normally took two hours by train.

Back in Miskolc, Edith and her brothers were reunited with their father, who had been liberated a few weeks earlier. The reunion was only the second time that Edith ever saw her father cry. The family waited for over a month before they met another relative. One day, her twin teenage cousins knocked on their window. At first she did not recognize them, and they told her that they had been taken to Auschwitz where Dr. Josef Mengele performed experiments on them. Edith knew about the work camps, but had not yet heard of the death camps. She says, "I got goose pimples, and I couldn't believe it: 'what are you telling me, these stories.' " One of the twins had contracted tuberculosis, but the American relatives were able to save his life by sending penicillin. Eventually, he was sent to recover in Davos, Switzerland, while his twin went to live in Texas.

Solomon, Edith's father, tried to start a business again, but decided to leave for the United States in 1947, as did her brothers. Not long after, Edith married. She and her husband wanted to immigrate to Israel, but since her husband had no papers and Edith was pregnant, they were forced to wait. After the Iron Curtain fell, they were trapped in Europe again. On March 16, 1949, Edith paid a guide to help them escape Hungary. They had to walk many miles, sometimes all night, take a bus, and cross a river in order to get to Bratislava, Czechoslovakia.

Here she joined up with the Zionist *Bricha*. They gave her the necessary papers and accompanied her, along with her husband and newly born child, to Vienna. Edith and her baby girl both contracted influenza in Austria, and they stayed in separate hospitals. Within four weeks, however, they had made it to Israel, arriving in April of 1949. After visiting her family in Texas, Edith decided to move to America. Denied a visa by the U.S. government, they immigrated to Montreal in 1952.

Edith felt she finally began to live again in Montreal, raising two daughters and one son. In 1989, Edith returned to Hungary to visit Miskolc and see her grandparents' graves in Sender. Edith reports that there were now only one thousand Jews in Miskolc, and that most of these had recently come from other parts of Hungary and Europe. She says, "the city of Miskolc was like a ghost town to me, I saw familiar names only in the cemeteries."

CHAPTER 2

Women Surviving the Camps

Rachel G.
September 29, 1993

During the Shoah, Rachel always told herself that "we have to live so that somebody should be able to tell what happened. That's why I'm saying my story now." For many years, she was incapable of recounting her experiences because thinking about them made her physically ill. In the 1990s, she found the strength to tell her children and grandchildren what happened to her, and even went so far as to write detailed memoirs. Much of her testimony came in the form of readings from those memoirs.

Rachel was born on March 15, 1917, in Beregszasz, a Czechoslovakian town next to the Hungarian border. She had one elder brother, Miklos, a younger sister, Elisa, and a younger brother, Louis. Her father, Bernard Kalus was a butcher and ran a small grocery store on the side. Rachel's mother, who had been very active in her own father's liquor business, helped in Bernard's shop. When she was fifteen, Rachel's family moved to her mother's hometown of Cinadovo, just ten kilometers from Munkacs where most of her extended family lived. Cinadovo was a large village with a high school and some factories. It had a large Jewish population and a synagogue. However, it was not long before Rachel, who had always dreamed of becoming a teacher, moved to Munkacs, where she studied education at a Russian-language college.

Rachel describes her large extended family as "very close" and "definitely orthodox." Her father, who was also very progressive, "never complained" about her ambition to go to college in a different city—a very unusual thing for a young woman to do at that time. She was very grateful for her father and says, "I could do anything I wanted to do."

In 1937 she graduated from college and took a job as a teacher in a town near the Hungarian border. When the war broke out in 1939, that part of Czechoslovakia was returned to Hungary. Rachel was not very frightened at the sight of the Hungarian army marching into town because, having grown up in Bergszasz, she was "close to Hungarians." On the other hand, she was dismayed to hear the Hungarians claim that the Jews were responsible for the fact that certain parts of Czechoslovakia, which had belonged to Hungary before the First World War, were not returned. A few months later she had to move to another village because the Hungarians did not trust Jews living so close to the border. Not long after that she received "a nice letter that [read] 'you are freed from your job, you can't teach anymore.'"

Since her husband, whom she had only married to stay in Hungary, had been sent away to a forced labor camp in 1940, she returned to Cinadovo. When she arrived at her family's home, she found that her brother had been sent away to a forced labor camp as well. Her father was allowed to remain, and even kept his butcher shop, because he had been wounded in the

Great War. This was a special privilege as other Jews were no longer allowed to keep any shops, personal possessions, or official jobs. These measures did not surprise Rachel because, although Czechoslovakia had been a democratic country where Jews had some rights, she remembers that the Czech "people were always anti-Semitic."

Rachel was not aware of the conditions outside of Cinadovo because hers was such a small village; everyone in the village was unorganized and completely cut off from the rest of the world. What little information she did receive came from Polish Jews who had escaped and were in hiding throughout the county. These refugees told Rachel what was going on elsewhere, but although she did not think they were lying, "it was hard to believe that things like that could happen."

The war began to threaten her life in an immediate way just after "a very sad Passover" in 1944. By then, most of the men in the family had been away for two or three years. They "survived only in our memories and in the hope that we will see them again someday." The morning after Passover, officials from the German army told all the Jews to pack their things and meet in a local schoolyard. "'Don't bother to lock your doors,'" they said. All of their valuables were confiscated. As the whole group walked to the train station, Rachel thought to herself: "What did we do to deserve this? Nothing. Nothing at all, but we are Jews."

They traveled by train for four days "to a place that looked like nowhere." It was Auschwitz. Upon their arrival, they were made to line up. That is when Rachel witnessed Dr. Mengele "playing God"; she vividly remembered how he stood on the platform and separated the prisoners, as if to say "You live, you don't. To right, to left." At this point, her forty-nine-year-old mother, fifty-eight-year-old father, and eighteen-year-old brother, who walked with a cane, were taken to the gas chambers.

Her sister Elisa and she were spared and had to walk to a shower room. Making her way through Auschwitz, Rachel smelled "a terrible smell" and saw the SS burning a pile of corpses out in the open. After they showered, the new inmates had their heads shaved, and their bodies tattooed. Then they were made to wait outside all night, "naked, ashamed and afraid," until they were issued clothing. Rachel remembers that "it was always raining in Auschwitz."

Not long after they arrived in Auschwitz, Rachel and her sister were transferred to the Birkenau section of the camp, where they lived right next to a crematorium. Their barracks housed some two hundred women who slept on straw mattresses. They all worked just next door, opening the suitcases that were taken from the new arrivals, sorting out the medication, toiletries, and clothes, and removing the yellow star from each shirt and blouse. They also prepared shipments of gold teeth and silverware. Everything was loaded up in suitcases and shipped to Germany. Sometimes she could see the newcomers arriving and she remembers how frightened they looked: "Where did all these people go? The answer came from the chimneys.

The sky was red; it hurt to look. We walked with closed eyes to work. This was hell right here on earth."

At one point, one of Rachel's friends saw her mother and young son in the line of newcomers. The mother, who had not seen her daughter in two years, was ecstatic. Rachel's friend became very excited and shouted out her mother's name. Rachel and the other inmates grabbed the girl and threw her into the barracks before she could make a scene. They suspected that if the SS guards noticed what was happening, the girl risked being ordered to join her mother and her child in the crematorium.

Sometimes Rachel saw Red Cross cars driving through Birkenau. At first she thought that help might be coming, but then realized that these cars were only delivering the Zyklon B gas. "We asked ourselves, 'where is God?' Why doesn't he put out the fires never to burn again?"

One morning, the crematorium next to her barracks suddenly exploded. Rachel saw the flames and heard SS guards marching toward it with their dogs. She also heard the *Sonderkommando*—the Jewish inmates who had to work in the crematorium—singing the *Hatikvah*. The SS men made the men line up in front of the crematorium and then she heard the sound of machine guns. The members of the *Sonderkommando* were shot for trying to sabotage the Final Solution, but kept "singing the *Hatikvah*." The plan had been to blow up all the crematoria simultaneously, but they only managed to destroy the one. After the men were shot, the girls were ordered to line up. Rachel was certain that she would be finished off as well. After searching their barracks for anyone who might have escaped, the SS ordered the girls to return "like nothing happened."

In January 1945, Auschwitz was evacuated because the Russian army was closing in. The prisoners marched without any food or rest for days, not knowing where they would be taken: "The long line of hungry people looked like a giant caterpillar, pulling its body up on the snow-covered hilly road of Poland." Many people died on the march. If they fell out of line or sat down to rest, they were shot and their bodies were left to decompose where they fell. The male prisoners had left Auschwitz some time before the women, and Rachel remembers passing by decaying male bodies. A friend of Rachel's had to march in her high-heeled shoes, and when one of them broke, she decided to take the left shoe from one of the male corpses. The girl wore a man's shoe and a lady's heel until the war was over.

After a number of days, the group arrived at a train station were they were given a loaf of bread for every five prisoners. Then they were "herded into" the open wagons of the train, and made their way to Ravensbrück. The group spent the first two days at the new camp crowded into one room. It was such close quarters that the prisoners could barely sit down. Two days later, they were given barracks where they had to sleep five people to every bed. Rachel was then taken to Malchow where she worked in a munitions factory.

Recently, Rachel has had recurring nightmares of Ravensbrück. In her dream, she leaves her barracks to look for some friends. She gets lost outside and cannot find her way back. Then she sees a group of SS guards and runs in the other direction. For an eternity she wanders around the maze of barracks in Ravensbrück aimlessly, and encounters one dying person after the other. "All I wished was to find my barracks," she explains. In her dream, she never does.

While imprisoned in Malchow, Rachel caught typhus, which was brought on by lice. "But we were very lucky," she says, "because there was no crematorium and they didn't burn the sick." Instead, she was put in a special barracks to quarantine the infected. She shared a bed with a girl who had a twin sister. One evening, the sister came to their window, crying and begging her to get well because she could not go on alone. Later that night, Rachel "felt that [the sick girl] was cold." "In the morning," Rachel explains, "they just threw her with the rest of the dead in the corridor."

In April, the *Lager* was evacuated because the Russians had kept advancing. Rachel was extremely sick and could hardly walk. Luckily, they went to their next destination, Leipzig, by train. On the way, Rachel saw that every city they passed through was completely bombed out: "The bombs lit up the sky, and were falling all around us, but we always thought they are coming right at us. Of course we were petrified, but we didn't care—it would have ended our suffering." They were given a meal of soup with some tiny strips of meat and potatoes when they arrived in Leipzig. It was not long until they had to march still deeper into Germany.

Rachel spent the following weeks marching from one *Lager* to the next, always with the Allies close behind. She remembers that the prisoners even learned to sleep while marching by resting their heads on each other's shoulders. One evening, the group stopped for the night near a forest. When they got there, they were shocked to see piles of dying men who "looked like worms, picking up their heads and hands and falling back." Rachel was so hungry by then that she ate some rotten onions she found in a garbage dump, even though this gave her an inflammation of the gums.

The group spent the last night of their march near a pond. Early the next morning, Rachel and her friends undressed and quickly washed themselves. Some days earlier they had been given some rice. They made a fire to boil the rice, but almost immediately they were told to leave. As they looked around, they realized that there were no more SS men, only the *Wehrmacht*. They had been marching for a few hours when suddenly one of the *Wehrmacht* said, " 'That way are the Russians and that way are the Americans, you are free to go which way you want.'" Rachel says, "There was no joy or laugher, only tears and fear. Our ordeal wasn't over yet, because we were still on the road deep in Germany."

After walking for the rest of the day, Rachel and her group of friends found a family of German civilians. The German family gave them *Mehlsuppe*—soup made from flour and butter—as well as some men's shoes for the girl who was still wearing a heel. The civilians recommended that they walk west toward the Americans, because they were still in danger.

After walking a while longer, they found the American troops on the other side of a river; however, they could not reach them because the bridge was bombed out. It was already evening so they left to find a place where they could sleep. The next morning they returned to the river and were greeted by a high-ranking American officer. They crawled down the broken half of the bridge into the riverbed and then the Americans lowered a makeshift ladder down to them so that they could climb up on the other side. Rachel was extremely weak by this point, but "the officer was lying on his stomach, reaching out, and pulling us to safety and freedom."

They spent the next few weeks in a school with other rescued Jews. Then they were taken to Piscany on the border of Czechoslovakia. From there, they traveled to Prague, then Bratislava, and finally back to Cinadovo. Upon returning home, Rachel and her sister Elisa were overjoyed to find that their older brother Miklos had returned from Siberia.

Rachel taught school for a number of years in Czechoslovakia before immigrating to Israel with her new husband in 1948. Eighteen months after the birth of her first daughter in 1951, Rachel immigrated to Canada because working conditions for her husband were intolerable in Israel. The young family had to sell everything they owned to pay for the airfare. When they arrived in Montreal in 1952, they only had five dollars left, which they used to pay for the taxi from Dorval Airport.

❊❊❊   ❊❊❊   ❊❊❊

Toby Elisabet R.
December 20, 1993

After being offered many unrealized opportunities to escape, Toby and her family were sent to Auschwitz. She was separated from her surviving siblings at a satellite camp of Stutthof. In January 1945, as the Russian army advanced, her camp was evacuated. During a long march through the snow, she was shot and left for dead. Her unconscious body was rescued by a French political prisoner and eventually taken to a Polish hospital. When she had recovered somewhat, she went to Prague and was reunited with her one surviving sister.

The invasion of Slovakia on the eve of the Jewish Passover in 1944 completely surprised Toby's family. When a German *Wehrmacht* officer rode into their hometown on a white horse, Toby did not understand what was happening and thought, "maybe it's the Messiah." It did not take her long to realize he was "not *our* Messiah." Later that day, a young soldier entered their home, scrutinized Toby and her younger sisters and began to peruse their diaries. While reading, the soldier became "very emotional," and said, "you are educated, wonderful people, with beautiful children. What are you doing here? Run for your lives, because you are in trouble." He told them about Auschwitz, Buchenwald, and Dachau, begging them to flee: "Go. Run and hide. I know Slovak girls, they are dressed as peasants on farms and nobody will bother them. Why don't you try? It's a little bit late, but you might have a chance." Toby and her sisters never went into hiding because they could not stand the thought of splitting up the family.

Toby was born into a middle-class orthodox Jewish family on February 24, 1921, to parents Rifka and Peretz. She is the fourth of ten children, with older siblings Ernest, Esther, and Irena, and the younger Hannah, Reala, Livisch, Mordechai, Bela, and Gordy. Her family was well known in their native Slovakian village of Vel'ke Kapusany which, Toby recalls, was a fairly integrated community: she estimates that of the approximately three thousand inhabitants, one hundred and twenty families were Jewish. The town had "everything for the inhabitants," a synagogue, a Jewish school, a kosher butcher, and a Jewish doctor. Her parents owned the only bakery in town; due to its success, they shipped pastries to nearby villages. They did well enough to hire domestic help. For Toby, "it was a beautiful family; it was the most beautiful family that existed." Her parents were extremely generous. For instance, they regularly fed the Gypsies and lodged poor students without expecting them to pay for anything. Not only was her father well known for his generosity, she adds, but everyone in his town also respected him for his wisdom. The family spoke Yiddish as well as Czech, German, and Hungarian at home and in the shop.

Everything changed at the end of 1943, and life became increasingly difficult for Toby's family. Her father's business license was confiscated, the bakery was taken over by Gentiles, and Jews were forbidden to hire servants. Earlier in the year, Jewish children had also been expelled from school. While Toby had managed to finish her secondary education, most of her sisters did not. The family could not understand why so many of their friends and neighbors suddenly turned against them. A group of locals denounced Toby's father as a communist. Luckily, the judge presiding over the case was an old family friend and nothing ever came of the charges. This judge even offered to hide Rifka, Peretz, and two of their children in the town jail. He told them, "there are tragedies today," and pleaded with them to hide, for otherwise "it won't be long and I will be missing you." The two parents refused, however, not wanting to separate their family.

After two *Wehrmacht* soldiers and one officer took over Vel'ke Kapusany, a farmer in the village offered to disguise Toby and her sisters as peasants and put them to work in his fields. He came to Peretz and said, " 'Mr. Kraus, listen to me: do you know what's going to happen to . . . those beautiful daughters? I have a few [girls] already working on the farm. Just let them come to me, nobody will ask questions.'" The farmer had always been a drunk, so Peretz did not trust him and still refused to split the family up. They would not even part with their dog.

Soon afterward, all the Jews in the village were commanded to assemble at the local synagogue. From there they were deported by open train to a brick factory in Uzhgorod, a half-hour ride away. In transit, Slovaks in uniform escorted the group. An official who came to inspect the brick factory fell in love with Toby's younger sister. He repeatedly asked Peretz to let him take the young woman. "I'll save her, don't worry," he said. Toby's sister refused to go. Two weeks after their arrival in Uzhgorod, they were told that they would be taken to a better location, and everyone was deported by cattle train to Auschwitz. Toby describes the train conditions as filthy: they were denied water and could barely breathe. "A dog on the street had a better life than we had," Toby explains.

Selections took place immediately upon arrival at Auschwitz. Toby remembers the scene with remarkable clarity and horror, recalling that Chopin was played over loudspeakers during the chaos. The new inmates were told they would receive new clothing, but Toby suspected that this was a lie. Even the air, she says, was foul, but it was some time before she understood exactly why. Toby, her father, and two of her sisters passed the selection, while her mother and youngest siblings were taken away. Her older sister was crying, "Where are my children?" As Toby watched the selection and listened to the music, she realized that "everything was false, everything is a lie."

It was not long before the surviving sisters were stripped naked and shaved "like apes." An SS officer looked at her sister Reala's blond pigtails and said *Solche herrliche Haare hab ich noch nie gesehen* (Never before have I seen such beautiful hair). Then he watched as the weeping girl's head was shaved. Next, each new inmate's mouth was examined for gold teeth. At Auschwitz Toby was not tattooed. Instead, she was given a number to wear on her clothing.

On their way to the barracks, Toby and her sister Hannah saw their father Peretz. He was in a daze, sitting confused and helpless on a rock with his face in his hands. Toby looked over at Hannah and said "look at our father, he doesn't recognize us. He doesn't know who we are, but we know who he is." Then Peretz spotted his wife and youngest children as they waited to be gassed. He jumped up from where he was sitting and ran after them. Toby never saw him again.

When she arrived in her barracks, Toby met two girlfriends from high school who had been there for over a year. One of them was whistling as Toby walked in through the door. The girl worked in the clothing selection detail (*Kanada*) and had recently packed the clothes of her own mother and sister in a box destined for Germany. She immediately told Toby that in

Auschwitz, "you come in through the gates and you come out through the chimney." Another one of her high school friends also warned Toby about Dr. Mengele, advising her not to stand close to her sisters when Mengele came through the block, since he had a sadistic interest in siblings.

In the summer of 1944, Toby and her sisters were transferred to Stutthof concentration camp. From there she was separated from her sisters and taken to a satellite work camp. The SS guards told her that her sisters would soon join her, but Toby knew this was a lie. As she was taken away, Reala jumped out of her barracks' window and ran up to Toby. She said "I know why you haven't been eating the margarine," and that she too suspected that it was human body fat from the crematoria. Reala told Toby that, no matter what, she must do all that she could to stay strong so that she might survive and eventually tell the world what had happened.

At the new camp, a satellite of Stutthof that only held female inmates, Toby was immediately confronted with a question she had been dreading for a long time: *Sprechen Sie Deutsch?*" (Do you speak German?). Toby concealed her German language abilities and refused opportunities to work "on the inside . . . on *Stubendienst*," for fear of having to collaborate against the Jews. She was sent to perform heavy labor and suffered severe malnutrition. She had stopped menstruating, and began hemorrhaging while at work one day. A uniformed engineer, not an SS officer but "probably a human being," took pity on her and brought Toby to his home. The man's wife was shocked to see Toby in such a state. She did not know what went on in the camps, thinking that the inmates were all Gypsies, and broke down crying when Toby told her that her only offense was having been "born Jewish." Later, when Toby was caught smuggling food that had been left in ditches by French political prisoners, the female *SS Oberaufseher* beat Toby and withheld her scheduled ration. Other camp inmates helped by sharing their rations with her. Toby recalls that this was in January 1945, around the time she believes she saw Eichmann during a head count.

Soon after, the camp was evacuated and the inmates began their relentless death march through deep snow. On the march, for which Toby was given two left shoes and a child's coat, Ukrainian soldiers followed orders to shoot people at random—"I told myself: 'Yes, everybody has an order here. [They were] shooting [us like] ducks.'" As she marched with her old friend from high school, a soldier came over and shot the friend in the back for no reason. She continued "on with [her] sorrow" and tried not to notice that the "snow was red, not white, wherever [she] walked."

She had lost one of her shoes and her foot had become frostbitten by the time she saw five nuns standing alongside of the road. She ran over to the nuns and hid underneath one of their skirts, "just to warm up." The guards did not notice, but when the nun began to walk away Toby grabbed her leg and the woman shouted "Maria Joseph." A guard came over but did not shoot her, "he wanted me to suffer more." Sick with typhus and pneumonia, Toby alternated between praying for death and "hypnotizing" herself into staying alive, motivating herself with a drive to tell the world of what was taking place.

One night the soldiers corralled some of the prisoners, including Toby, into a stable and told them to take off their shoes and rest. Toby did not believe them and made sure to secure a place just next to the door. Within half of an hour, the stable was on fire and a girl began to scream "*Mamma, Mamma, wo bist du*?" (Mother, mother, where are you?). Toby does not know how many of the prisoners perished in the flames, but she did know that "Mamma wasn't there anymore, she was dead."

Toby managed to flee the burning stable. When she tried to escape from the march later on, she suddenly found herself alone with an SS guard. He looked her in the eyes and said "*Ich hab' ein Befehl. Ich muss schiessen*" (I have orders to shoot). She told him that the Russians were close behind, and "*du hast kein Befehl mehr*" (you have no more orders). He shot her in the thigh and left her for dead while the rest of the group marched on. She lost consciousness and woke up hours later in another stable "like Joseph," unsure how she had been saved.

Toby was taken to an unsanitary Polish hospital nearby, in order to have surgery. She was not anaesthetized, and threw herself off the operating table when she heard the surgeon say he was going to amputate her leg. Luckily, at that moment three well-dressed gentlemen from the Prague Ministry arrived at this hospital looking for Czech *Häftling*e (prisoners). These men told her she could be evacuated to a Russian hospital, but Toby refused unless the other thirty-two women in the hospital could also be saved. The men left, secured a truck, and transported all the women to a Russian military hospital. At this hospital, Toby was treated by a Jewish doctor. He sent her home to Budapest when the hospital was forced to move to Stalingrad.

The way home was not easy. On the train to Budapest, she narrowly escaped being raped by Russian soldiers. At a lodging on this trip, she remembers seeing soap marked RJF: she was extremely upset and refused to stay at this lodging, thinking RJF might stand for *Rein Juden Fett* (Pure Jewish fat).

Toby's leg injuries were so severe that she could not walk, and a friend from the Russian hospital helped her make her way to Budapest. After a few days in Budapest, she met a cousin named Goldie who told her that Toby's sister Irena was alive, married, and living in Prague. When she arrived, a Czech policeman helped Toby find her sister, who had been in Bergen-Belsen and failed to recognize her at first.

In 1947, Toby married a Czech man who had been in the Ukraine as a cook for the Nazis during the war. He managed to escape by poisoning their food and running away after his captors fell ill. Toby and her husband eventually had a daughter, although her experiences made it difficult for Toby to conceive.

On a trip to Israel in 1973, a Polish Jew who recognized her after almost thirty years stopped Toby. He told her that a non-Jewish French orthopedic doctor who was a political prisoner had saved her during the death march. The doctor had washed her wound with snow, bandaged her with his own shirt, and taken her to the stable where she later woke up. Toby regrets that she was never able to thank this doctor. In 1973, he still lived in France, but was in very poor health.

Toby told a close friend about her experiences, but she was reluctant to tell her story to others because it was too difficult emotionally for her. She did not even tell her daughter until she began to feel that she has a moral obligation to pass her story on to future generations. Still, Toby was torn; on the one hand, she wanted to protect her daughter from the burden of knowing about her experiences and, on the other, she wanted to ensure that her story would be passed on to future generations. One of the factors that drove Toby to speak out was her daughter's embarrassment in the face of Toby's orthopedic footwear—to this day Toby has difficulty walking due to her injuries.

>≫⁄≪ >≫⁄≪ >≫⁄≪

Ilse Z. and Marti D.
March 23, 1994 and September 26, 1994

Although they were not especially religious, and did not grow up in a kosher home, sisters Ilse Z. and Marti D. were very proud to be Jewish. Their family belonged to the Liberal Synagogue in Amsterdam, to which the Otto Frank family also belonged. The deportation of Dutch Jews to Poland started in the summer of 1942, but Marti and Ilse were exempted from deportation until June 1943 because both Ilse and their father worked for the Liberal Jewish community. Eventually, they were sent to Bergen-Belsen where their father died. Ilse, Marti, and their mother survived on the "Lost Train," liberated by the Russians. Marti, an avowed Zionist from a young age, immigrated to Palestine. Ilse settled with her husband Gus in Montreal. Ilse Z. and Marti D. were interviewed on different occasions for Living Testimonies in 1994. Their separate accounts of their shared wartime experiences are merged in this summary.

Henry and Lotte van Collem's two daughters, Ilse and Marti, were born in Amsterdam, in 1927 and 1929 respectively. They both attended the Montessori School. Ilse started in the Montessori system at the age of three and stayed throughout elementary school and the beginning of high school (the Montessori lyceum). Marti remembers how much she loved going to the Montessori School with its modern system of education.

Their parents were both founding members of the Progressive Synagogue (the Liberal Synagogue) of Amsterdam, which grew quite large due to the influx of German Jews. Henry also served as the administrator for the liberal Jewish community. Their mother sang in the Jewish community choir and made "teharah" for the *chevra kadisha*, that is, she participated, as a volunteer, in the ritual cleansing of the bodies of the dead. As children, both Ilse and Marti loved going to synagogue. Ilse says she especially enjoyed participating in the *kiddush* (the blessing of the wine after the shabbat service), when she and Marti were invited to stand together and hold the *kiddush* cups. "We were always known as the little van Collem girls, we always dressed alike which was customary in those days," she says.

Judaism was also very important to Marti. She says that from the time she was four or five until the outbreak of war, going to the synagogue of Friday evening and Saturday morning was the "center of [her] life." Marti remembers already having had the desire to live in Palestine before her father encouraged her to make aliyah. He told her that he himself was too old to start a new life in Eretz Yisrael, but that she should go there. Those words affected her strongly.

Ilse and Marti's family knew Anne Frank's family well, because they belonged to the same synagogue. On Wednesday afternoons, Ilse and Marti went to the same Hebrew school as Anne and Margot Frank. Ilse was in the same class as Margot, and Marti was in the same class as Anne, who was only six days her senior. They both remember going to birthday parties at the Frank house at the Merwedeplein.

Starting in 1933, when she was five or six years old, Ilse cannot remember a time when she and her sister lived alone with their parents: there were always German Jewish refugees and relatives living in the van Collem's spacious home. Her parents put them up sometimes for weeks, or even for months, until they moved on, usually to the United States, or to South Africa, Britain, or South America. At any given moment there might be eight or nine people staying in the house. The family's home, therefore, came to be known as pension van Collem, that is, "hotel van Collem." For this reason, even though Marti describes her life before the war as "normal," her life was anything but normal because her immediate family never spent a single day alone. Surrounded by relatives, friends, and strangers, Marti often overheard stories about what the Germans did to the Jews. As she herself puts it, "it was a way of life, a way of seeing things."

Their father was Dutch-Jewish, born in 1894. Their mother was born in Germany in 1900 and moved to Holland after marrying their father. The couple had first met in Frankfurt. After they moved to Amsterdam, her father started working for his uncle as the manager of the "Billiard Factory Wilhelmina" (named after an aunt), which produced high-end billiard tables, cues and balls, including ivory ones. The factory was located on the basement floor beneath their apartment. To this day Marti is "crazy" about the smell of wood, which brings back vivid memories of the work going on downstairs in the house on the Stadhouderskade. The tables, balls, and cues were scrupulously made and finished by hand before being shipped all over the world. Marti remembers that one of the tables was sold to King Farouk of Egypt.

Their father was also the half-owner of a small factory that manufactured cosmetics. His partner in this enterprise was his wife's cousin, a German Jew. This company still exists. Ilse and Marti describe their childhood life as "solidly middle class." But Ilse adds that her family, though quite well-to-do, lived in a modest fashion.

Both Ilse and Marti comment that their father was a pessimist by nature, someone who worried a lot and always expected the worst, especially where Hitler was concerned. Ilse says, "I still see my father sitting at the dining room table [on the day of Dutch capitulation] saying, 'I am not sure how long this war is going to last, but I won't see the end of it.'" Marti also had the sense that he did not see how he would make it through the war and believes that he had an inner conviction that he would not survive. Lotte, on the other hand, had always said that Hitler would not conquer Holland because the Germans had not done so in World War I. This prompts Marti to observe that their mother was an optimist by nature, even if she was wrong in this case.

Like her father, Marti remembers that she had a pretty good notion about what would happen to the Jews. She cites the case of a man who had escaped from a concentration camp, and was scarred all over; especially his head was badly marked from crawling through the coils of barbed wire. The man stayed with the van Collem family for several weeks before moving on and eventually reaching South America.

During the German invasion of Holland in early May, 1940, Ilse recalls taking shelter in the cellar. Following the occupation, the Germans gradually imposed restrictions on the Jews of Amsterdam. New measures were imposed nearly every month. When Ilse first had to wear a yellow Star of David, she felt pride more than anything else: "I didn't feel insulted. I felt proud to be who I was. I was a Jew." Although Marti remembers feeling hatred for the Germans, she took the new measures and limitations in her stride. After all, they applied to everyone who was Jewish. This fact made it easier for Marti, at age twelve or thirteen, to accept them.

At the end of the summer of 1941, Marti and Ilse were forced to quit school due to anti-Jewish restrictions. The two girls continued their education in a private Montessori study group at the house of Professor Frijda in the Guido Gezellestraat in the South of Amsterdam, for Jewish students only. To the best of Ilse's knowledge, only one other person from this group, Leo Palasch, survived the war. In addition, Ilse and Marti attended classes at the Jewish community center.

Until the early part of 1941, the girls were still able to travel around on their bicycles. When Jews were deprived of the right to own a bicycle, their freedom to visit others and stay socially active was limited substantially. Nonetheless, Ilse remembers that she and her family quietly handed over their bicycles, because "the Dutch were a very obedient people." Marti recalls that the Dutch Jews generally reacted in a relativizing, philosophical manner to the restrictions imposed upon them. Some Jews argued that matters, after all, could still be worse; others thought that the whole thing would probably blow over. Marti believes, in retrospect, that the Germans were "very clever," and the Dutch "stupid" in their willingness to register themselves and deliver their bicycles to the authorities.

Marti remembers that the Germans also barred them from public transportation. Ilse and Marti had to walk to Professor's Frijda's house, which was a long walk from where they lived. In addition, Germans forbade the Jews to go out after 8 p.m. and they were denied access to most shops, except from 3 p.m. to 5 p.m.

According to Marti, the Dutch were not terribly interested in the welfare of their Jewish neighbors. There were those, of course, who worked for the resistance and rescued Jews, but as she puts it, except for that small minority, most of the Dutch people "couldn't care less."

The deportations began in July 1942. Ilse remembers that the family did not fully realize what this entailed because they thought that deported people were sent away to work in labor camps. Their cousin from the east of Holland had been sent to Mauthausen. Ilse remembers that they received a notice that identified the cause of his death as an illness.

Even though Jews had to hand over their radios, Henry kept a radio hidden in the basement and listened to Radio Orange from London. Ilse remembers him saying that the British were just as bad as the Germans for spreading false propaganda that Jews were being gassed. None of the van Collem's could believe the news because they always thought of the Germans as a "cultured people."

Ilse and Marti's maternal (German-born) grandmother, who lived with the van Collem's in Amsterdam, died in November 1942. Around the same time, the Dutch military police had orders to pick up their grandmother in order for her to "go to work in Germany." German Jewish refugees were among the first to be deported. The Dutch policemen came for her while the family was still sitting *shive* (mandatory period of seven days of mourning). Their mother Lotte said to them, "She is already gone." They wanted to know who had picked her up. Lotte told them, "Our dear Lord in heaven." Marti also remembers this exchange between Lotte and the Dutch policemen. In her recollection, when Lotte had said "you are too late. God already took her," the Dutch policemen responded with blank, uncomprehending stares. Marti's reaction is scornful of what she saw as Dutch collaborators: "The Germans didn't do the dirty work; why should they do it if they got the Dutch to do it . . ."

With the deportations, people disappeared from Marti's life slowly and gradually. Students did not show up in school because they had been deported to a camp or because they had gone underground. As an example she mentions the Frank family. When the Franks went underground, in the

Ilse Z. (left) and Marti D. in Amsterdam around 1937

summer of 1942, they had prepared postcards to be sent from Belgium. By this subterfuge they hoped that it would appear that they might have fled to France. Only after the war did Marti's family realize that the Franks had been hiding all that time behind the Opekta office on the Prinsengracht.

When Ilse was forced out of her second year at the lyceum, she began working in the office of the Liberal Synagogue and obtained a special protective stamp (*Sperre*) on her ID card. For the time being, this exempted her from deportation. Her father who continued working as an administrator for the synagogue was afforded the same protection. Some friends of the van Collem's begged them to go into hiding but the family decided not to desert Henry's ailing mother. Marti remembers that Ilse, specifically, was offered a place to hide, but she decided to stay with the family instead.

On June 20, 1943, the entire family was arrested during a *razzia* (raid), taken to a central square, and transported, from the Muiderpoort train station, to transit camp Westerbork, in the north of the Netherlands, near the German border. By this time, nothing could have saved them from deportation because everybody in the entire neighborhood had to go. Marti remembers that they had been instructed by the Jewish Council to prepare a few basic supplies such as blankets, a flashlight or candles, shoes and sweaters, and some food. They waited until the evening with their suitcases and packs ready. Marti remembers the moment when the doorbell rang.

Ilse and Marti around 1937

She mentions that the police were rude, as though they did not have much patience following a long and tiring day of arresting Jews. As a consequence of their deportation, Marti remembers that her father's nervousness diminished: finally the fate of the family was out of his hands.

Upon arrival at Westerbork, the men and women were separated. Marti, Ilse, and their mother lived together in a barrack. Ilse claims she was not treated too badly at Westerbork. She worked in the laundry facilities with her mother (in Marti's recollection, their father worked there as well). Marti, who was considered too young to work, attended classes and took care of little children, although she worked for several weeks with her sister digging potatoes in a field.

Every Tuesday morning, trains left camp Westerbork deporting a thousand or more people to Auschwitz. Marti remembers Monday nights, when the list of deportees was read out, as the most horrible times of her stay in Westerbork. At that point however, Marti did not understand the significance of being taken to Auschwitz; she only knew it meant being sent to Poland. Ilse remembers an outbreak of polio in the camp.

At Westerbork, Ilse says she did not have any particular sense of fear. Because she had her parents with her, she somehow felt safe and protected.

As well, one of the veteran leaders of the camp was a friend of their father's. While at Westerbork, Henry secured immigration papers for a South American country, which were supposed to ensure that the family would not be deported to Auschwitz. Marti remembers that Lotte's cousin, who cofounded the cosmetics factory with Marti and Ilse's father, also protected the family by keeping them in transit camp Westerbork for more than six months. This cousin was part of the important Contact Committee of camp Westerbork that was responsible for reporting to the Germans.

In January 1944, the family was given a choice of being deported to either Bergen-Belsen or Theresienstadt. They chose Bergen-Belsen, which Ilse recalls was described as an "exchange camp," because their mother wanted to be as close as possible to the Dutch border. Theirs was only the second transport to that camp from Westerbork. They were transported on a regular train, rather than a cattle train. It stopped in Celle and the 1,500 to 2,000 prisoners, including the van Collems, had to walk the eight kilometers to the camp, carrying their small pieces of luggage.

At Bergen-Belsen, Marti recalls a wide-open space with barracks, barbed wire, and watchtowers with machine guns. Ilse remembers they were faced with Germans who had rifles and dogs. She says her father's reaction was, "I'll never get out of here alive." Bergen-Belsen was divided into several different *Lager*. In their *Lager*, inmates were allowed to wear their own clothes. At first, the men and women were crowded in segregated barracks with about 100 to 150 people each. Marti and Ilse saw their father at meals, which men and women had together around 6 p.m. As the camp filled up with prisoners coming in from other camps, men, including Ilse and Marti's father, shared the women's barracks. Ilse slept head to foot with her father in one bunk.

Because she spoke German and Dutch fluently, Lotte became a *Barackenleitster* (second in command of the barracks). She was in charge of distributing food, verifying that everybody was there, making sure the barracks were clean, and that everyone's army blankets were straight, according to strict German regulations. Ilse shares that until the end of her days, Lotte (who died in 1993), refused to discuss her wartime experience as a *Barackenleitster*.

Along with her father, Ilse was a member of the work detail that sorted and repaired the shoes coming into the camp. Ilse states that she does not know where they came from. Marti says that they were delivered to Bergen-Belsen, "possibly from Auschwitz." There was a huge pile of those shoes, says Marti, "as big as this room, but much higher." Neither Ilse nor Marti had any notion of what this pile of shoes meant. Ilse's job was to take old shoes apart with a knife, saving the pieces of good leather for further use. Henry was in charge of quality control. Ilse's duties further consisted of cutting out good pieces of material from damaged green German uniforms, which she believes were used for patching and repairs.

Ilse has vivid memories of hunger in Bergen-Belsen. She describes receiving one ration of bread in the morning, which she could eat all at once, or save to eat throughout the day. Ilse was eighteen-years old, sick with jaundice, and weighed barely more than seventy pounds. One day, an SS man took a liking to her as "a little non-Jewish looking girl" and sent her to work in the kitchen. This was a privileged job because it was warm and she was able to eat, but the SS man taunted and harassed her for his own amusement. At the same time, the job in the kitchen allowed Ilse to give rations to her family and smuggle bits of food such as sugar and potatoes in a pouch under her coveralls that her mother had sewn together out of old underwear.

Marti remembers their *Lager* having been given special privileges, such as milk for the children. Marti was assigned to looking after little children as she was in Westerbork. She was even able to find a stove and prepare porridge for them. Marti sometimes worked in the kitchen along with Ilse when they were short of people.

In March 1945, Marti had contact with Anne Frank, who was also imprisoned in Bergen-Belsen, although in a separate *Lager*. On a number of occasions, they were able to speak across a barrier that divided them. Anne told Marti that she had lost her glasses. She also reported that her sister Margot was confined to bed with *Flecktyphus*. Anne added that she did not believe she would survive if her sister could not make it. Later, Marti and their mutual friend Annelie Goslar attempted to give Anne a small package of lard from the Red Cross, a valuable item, but one which Annelie herself refused to eat because she kept kosher. They thought if they threw it across the fence at the right time, Anne would be able to catch it. Anne said, "Listen, wait a little bit, someone is coming"; and they waited for her cue, "now you can throw it." Even so, someone else grabbed the package before Anne could. "This was all I had, I have nothing more," Annelie said. That was the last time Marti had any contact with Anne Frank.

During early morning roll calls, the prisoners were sometimes kept standing out in the winter climate or snow for up to six hours. Marti recalls that her father, who was "very Dutch," meaning very prompt, often arrived ten minutes early for the *Appell*, even on cold days. One such morning in 1945, Henry began running in place to keep warm. A *Kapo* came along and beat him. Although Ilse remembers witnessing a man being whipped savagely in the face for stamping in place to keep warm, it was only after the *Appell* that she realized he was her own father. When he came back to the barracks that night Marti recalls he was unrecognizable. Ilse says that this event caused her father to "give up all pretenses of trying to live through it." Marti likewise remembers this event as a turning point. Even though their father knew that the Germans were losing the war, he gave up completely. Henry died in Bergen-Belsen on April 3, 1945, and was buried in a communal grave.

One week after their father's death in April 1945, Ilse, Marti, their mother, and other prisoners boarded a regular train with wooden seats, and were told they were going to Theresienstadt. Marti remembers that a man whose name she recalls as Dr. Kasztner addressed them in Hebrew and said,

"You are going to a good place, don't worry." The transport, which had barbed wire over the windows, contained several thousand people. Almost everyone on the transport was infested with lice, which resulted in an outbreak of *Flecktyphus*. As they left Bergen-Belsen in that passenger train, they were astonished to see two cattle trains full of new inmates arriving in the camp. Marti thought it bizarre and incomprehensible that the Germans had trains to spare for the transportation of Jews at a time when they were clearly losing the war. During the journey, the prisoners were allowed to get out when the train stopped, in order to relieve themselves, and scrounge for food at farms along the rails. Marti remembers they ate nettles to stay alive. They passed though Berlin, which was largely in ruins. Marti says they were "very happy" about the "destruction of Berlin."

The train traveled for two weeks and never made it to Theresienstadt. Late in the night of April 21, after the train had been stopped for some time near Tröbitz, Czechoslovakia, the prisoners went outside and discovered they were in the hands of Russian soldiers. This transport became known as the "Lost Train." Marti recalls that their Russian liberators were fairly kind, although they had no food to give and were unhappy to have the responsibility of caring for one to two thousand Jews thrust upon them.

The liberated prisoners were taken to a local school being used as a hospital, where Ilse and Marti received medical care. They were put under ice-cold showers and shaven all over. None of them could walk, but they were happy to be free. Their mother who had a case of phlebitis was taken to a different area of the makeshift hospital, where she was operated on by a man who was not a doctor. At this hospital, they slept on mattresses on the floor.

After they were liberated, Ilse and Marti went freely into different homes and took what they wanted, including a half-cooked chicken out of a Russian officer's pot on the stove. But Ilse says she was too numb to feel euphoria. Today, Ilse still has difficult getting very enthusiastic about things. She feels that her wartime experiences are responsible for her permanent sense of numbness. It is still deeply disturbing to her that she was unable to cry after her father's death.

Ilse and Marti stayed in Tröbitz for six weeks. Marti remembers the uncertainty of this period: "the Russians gave us no information," she says, and because of the language gap, they could not communicate anyway. At least a month went by before anybody heard about the stranded transport in Tröbitz. Finally, three American soldiers who had been alerted by some of the former camp inmates, stopped in the village, and relayed the message to Leipzig that between one and two thousand Dutch Jews were waiting to be repatriated. They were then told to go to Leipzig where the American soldiers gave them clothing. Ilse received a blouse made out of parachute material. At this time, they were separated from their mother who had been sent to a hospital in Liège.

Ilse and Marti went back to Holland with the Dutch Red Cross, arriving in late June. During the journey, Ilse felt thrilled to see Kassel in ruins, and experienced a desire for revenge. She says that if she had had a gun, she would have killed a Nazi "with pleasure."

When they finally arrived in Amsterdam on June 29, 1945, there were Dutch flags everywhere. Initially, Ilse and Marti thought the flags were meant to welcome them home. In fact, the flags were a salute to Prince Bernard of the Netherlands who celebrated his birthday on that day.

In Holland, nobody wanted to hear about what had happened to them. For a few days, Ilse and Marti stayed in an old Jewish orphanage for boys while they waited to be reunited with their mother. Ilse recalls that they were fed with bread bought on the black market, and emphasizes, "We didn't stop eating." Marti remembers they were well provided for.

Shortly after their return to Amsterdam, Marti, who looked Jewish, was harassed. People in the streets called her a "dirty Jew." Ilse believes that this taunting is one of the reasons why her sister Marti decided to go to Palestine as soon as possible. Marti, who had made some Zionist friends in the camps, felt strongly that she "didn't want to stay a day longer than I had to stay." After a period on *hachshara* (active preparation for life on the kibbutz), Marti left on the "Exodus" on June 20, 1947. The ship was intercepted and captured by the British and returned to Bergen-Belsen, of all places. Marti finally made her way to Marseilles, and from there to Palestine.

Ilse did not look Jewish but she was called a *moffenhoer* (Kraut's slut) by people who mistook her for a collaborator because her head had been shaved by the Russians, back in Tröbitz. Dutch girls who had had relations with Germans often had their heads publicly shaved in order to shame them.

Rather than go back to school, Ilse learned secretarial skills and worked for a year at the office of the Dutch Zionist Organization in Amsterdam. Their mother helped reestablish the Liberal Synagogue and assisted with the German translation of the *Diary of Anne Frank*, which, as Ilse recalls, was completed at their house and published by a friend of their mother's.

In November 1945, through friends in The Hague, Ilse became reacquainted with Gus, a man she had met in Westerbork. Gus survived the camps of Theresienstadt, Auschwitz, Gleiwitz (where he made munitions for the German army), and Blechhammer. They married in 1949 and had their first child in 1950. Her husband Gus served two years in the Dutch Air Force, and three days after he was discharged they were on a boat to Canada. They arrived in Montreal in late October, 1951. Gus worked as a welder, foreman, and later a service manager at the S. Albert Oil Company. Ilse says they were poor at first, but quite comfortable later on. She was very happy to be in Montreal. Ilse and Marti's mother eventually settled in South Africa.

Marti had not wanted to tell her story prior to giving this interview for *Living Testimonies*, because, she says "it was not finished for me." However, she does feel that giving testimony of the events of the Holocaust is very important. In her own words, "I owe it . . . if not to everybody else, then to my children."

Ilse was interviewed once before as part of a project of Canadian Jewish Congress in the early 1980s, but stopped the process because the interview had been unsatisfactory to her. Of this current interview, she says that she was afraid but realized that it is necessary. Knowing that there are gaps in her memories, she explains, "I didn't live, I was being lived." She felt like she was a child even though she was a teenager. However, she asserts that she is not bitter about what happened: "It happened. I can't change what happened." She proposes that she may even try to write about her experiences.

Both interviews end with Marti and Ilse showing some photographs of the family which, on account of her mother's foresight, had been hidden with non-Jewish friends in Amsterdam during the war.

꘎꘎꘎   ꘎꘎꘎   ꘎꘎꘎

Irene C.
January 19, 1994

Because Irene C. grew up in a part of Romania that was annexed by Hungary in 1941, it was not until 1944 that her life drastically changed. Suddenly, without prior knowledge of what was happening to the Jews in other parts of Europe, Irene's family was enclosed in a ghetto and, shortly after that, deported to Auschwitz. From Auschwitz, Irene, her mother and her sister Olga were taken to Stutthof. Through Irene's sheer will and determination to survive, she and Olga managed to escape starvation and death from the cold.

Irene was born in Satu Mare, Romania in 1925. Her father Carl was a tailor, and her mother Ida worked the night shift as a nurse at the Jewish hospital. She had one sister, Olga, who was fourteen months older than Irene, and is still alive today. They went to a Romanian school but the family spoke Hungarian at home because her father was originally from Hungary. On her mother's side they had a large extended family that they saw frequently. Her father's family still lived in Hungary, so they saw them less often; the journey, which had to be made by horse and carriage, was lengthy even though the distance was not great.

Irene's father died in 1939, from complications of asthma. When he was still alive, he always made nice dresses and suits for Olga and Irene to wear.

Later he taught the girls how to sew and make their own clothes. He also taught them how to read and write in Hebrew. The family was religious, keeping a strictly kosher home and observing all of the holidays. Olga and Irene mingled with other middle-class Jews like themselves. They went to the dance hall, the park, and the movies with their boyfriends, always accompanied by their mother. In those days, girls from traditional families did not go out without a chaperone, even though Olga and Irene always kept the company of "nice Jewish boys." On the whole, even after she lost her father, life was very comfortable in what Irene refers to as the "good old days."

The anti-Semitism in Satu Mare did not greatly affect Irene. Everyone in her building was Jewish, with the exception of the superintendent and his family. The superintendent and his wife were very nice but their son, who was in his twenties, was rumored to belong to anti-Semitic clubs. Irene's family did not worry about this son very much; in fact, they simply dismissed him as young and ignorant.

Olga, more than Irene, had gentile friends. Irene remembers the commotion in the family after Olga had gone to a gentile friend's apartment and helped her family decorate their Christmas tree. When Irene's father Carl found out that Olga had participated in this Christian ritual, he was angry and upset. Irene commented that, unlike Olga, she would have never done such a thing.

Even into the 1940s, Irene's family remained unaware of the problems the Jews faced in other parts of Europe. They did not have a radio or a telephone, and the Hungarian newspaper that they read did not report anything about the situation, even in nearby Poland. Irene recalls that a Jewish doctor living in her building committed suicide. Because this doctor was connected with more political and intellectual circles, she now presumes his suicide relates to what he had heard about the persecution of the Jews.

In 1944, the Hungarian army marched into Satu Mare. Irene was not aware that this marked the end of Hungarian Jewry. The soldiers rode in on white horses, wearing beautiful uniforms and accompanied by a band. Irene, who was eighteen at the time, greeted this fanfare with cheers. It seemed like a parade had come to town and she had no sense that persecution was imminent.

A couple of weeks later, tanks rolled through the streets and German soldiers were everywhere, strictly enforcing the restrictions imposed on Jews. Now the Jews had a curfew, could shop only at certain stores, and were required to wear the yellow star. Irene made hers from a yellow piece of fabric and sewed it onto her coat. A friend of their late father employed Olga and Irene at a factory where they worked as dressmakers. At the time she had a boyfriend, a shoemaker, but he was sent away to Bor, a Ukrainian labor camp. Irene did not hear from him until after the war.

Soon all the Jews were forced into a ghetto. Irene, Olga, and their mother moved in with an uncle who had an apartment in the designated area. No wall was built around the ghetto, but the boundaries were guarded and any Jew who dared to leave was shot. A gentile man Irene knew from the bank in Satu Mare offered to hide her at his mother's house in the countryside. Irene refused because she did not want to leave her sister and her mother. Instead, he brought them bread and any other food he could. To thank him, Irene gave him her mother's wedding ring.

Irene had been in the ghetto for a little more than a month when they had to leave. Everyone was ordered to gather in a park so that they could be transported to Debrecen, where they were told they were going to work. For the journey, Irene's mother had made a big batch of cookies for everyone to snack on along the way. They waited for a long time in the park before the Hungarian and German soldiers came and told them to march to the train station. They were quite scared, but still believed that they were going to another city to work.

By the time they reached the train station, they were very tired, especially Irene's grandparents who were already quite old. At the station, Irene saw cattle wagons; it did not occur to her that they were intended to transport the Jewish people. Irene and her family were crowded into cars that were packed to the point of suffocation. She watched as a schoolmate with tuberculosis died on the cramped voyage.

After a number of days, the train arrived at Auschwitz. When they jumped down from the wagons, Polish *Kapos* were waiting and dispersed the group in two directions. Irene's mother was ordered to return the baby she was carrying to Irene's aunt, the baby's mother. "They go in a different direction," the *Kapo* said. Irene's grandparents Fanny and Joseph, and her uncle also went in the "different direction." Irene did not suspect that she would not see them again.

Irene, her mother, and her sister went to a room where they were ordered to remove their clothes. They were given a grey potato sack to wear, and their heads were shaved. Irene felt devastated to lose her long blond hair. They were marched to barracks where her mother, Olga, and Irene were given a bed on the third level bunk. During the night there was often at least one *Appell*. Climbing up and down from the bed was tolerable for Irene and her sister, who were young, but for their mother, who was "a little bit heavy," it was very hard.

During one of the selections at Auschwitz, Irene's mother was singled out. Irene was so upset that she risked approaching the officer in charge of the selections, Dr. Josef Mengele. "He was a monster," Irene says, but "maybe he had a minute [of reprieve]" because with a wave of his hand, he called her mother back.

Irene was only in Auschwitz for six weeks. During this time, she managed to stay fairly strong because she was given soup and bread and not made to work. On the other hand, the horror and inhumanity she witnessed traumatized her. One night while standing at *Appell*, a friend of Irene's had a miscarriage. The woman had to act as though nothing had happened, and buried the fetus in the sand with her feet. Irene saw other inmates commit suicide by throwing themselves against the electrified barbed wire fence.

From Auschwitz, Irene, her sister, and her mother were transported on cattle trains to the women's camp at Stutthof. At first, they were made to dig ditches in the dirt for no apparent reason. Anybody caught resting was beaten. Her mother, who was weak and tired, leaned on her shovel for a moment. A soldier came over and whipped her in the face. Seeing her mother's face swelling and bleeding, Irene felt angry and helpless. She could do nothing: she could not wash off the blood, place a compress on her wound, or retaliate against the soldier without being killed. Irene believes that this incident depleted her mother's will to survive.

The winter of 1944–1945 was terribly cold and they were left to die in the unheated barracks in Stutthof. There was no work and the prisoners were not fed. Even so, the soldiers continued to call them to *Appell*, making them line up outdoors in the cold. None of the prisoners had any shoes, not even wooden ones. Irene asked to work in the kitchen. She smuggled potato peelings and rotten vegetables for her sister and her mother, but her mother refused to eat. Neither her mother nor her sister ever got out of bed. They both became very sick.

One dark and cold morning, Irene was the only one who prepared to leave the barracks. She got out of the bed she shared with her mother and her sister and proceeded to dress herself with all the warm clothing she had. She was looking for a particular scarf and woke Olga to ask her where it was. Olga replied that their mother was wearing it. Reaching for the scarf, it struck Irene that something was wrong with their mother—she was not moving. Olga explained to Irene that their mother had died in the middle of the night. Olga had not wanted to wake Irene to tell her, thinking that Irene needed her sleep because she had to get to the kitchen in the morning. "So we slept with her the whole night and she was dead."

Irene could not bear the thought of having her mother's body thrown off the bunk by the woman whose job it was to remove dead bodies from the barracks. She pleaded that she and Olga be allowed to take their mother's body down from the bed themselves. Irene and Olga carried their mother to a pile of corpses outside in the yard, the only place they could put her. Walking to and from the kitchen day after day, Irene saw her mother's body become covered in snow and dirt until one day the corpses were shoveled onto a "cremo" wagon and taken away.

Meanwhile, Olga was so sick that she could not walk, but Irene remained strong of will. She went to the kitchen "no matter what." Every day she brought Olga food and forced her to eat. Irene was completely determined that even if everyone else died, both she and Olga would live.

Irene and Olga were taken from Stutthof in cattle cars to Danzig (Gdansk), where they stayed for a short while in a camp near an electrical appliance assembly plant. From Danzig, Irene's memories become foggy. She has the impression that they were transported to many places within a short period of time, as though the Germans did not know where to take them. Irene does remember arriving in Bergen-Belsen. The camp horrified her because there were so many dead bodies; no one at all seemed to be alive. From there, she recalls that she was put aboard a ship.

Irene does not know where the boat left from or where it was going. They were on the ship, without food, for what felt like many days. They could have been on the Baltic Sea or the river Elbe. Irene thinks they must have been fleeing the Allies. Before they reached a destination, the ship stopped. The soldiers ordered everybody off. Panic struck as the prisoners descended a ladder down the side of the ship. In response the soldiers just pushed everyone into the water. Irene did not know how to swim. She was drowning and only semi-conscious when someone pulled her out of the water and wrapped her in a blanket. Next she was brought to a football field in Hamburg. Olga was so sick that she was taken to a hospital. Irene was taken to a school and given a bed and provisions by the British soldiers who had liberated her.

Once she was free, Irene wanted to go back to Romania so she traveled with students of a Yeshivah who were going to Prague and then she went on alone to Satu Mare. There she stayed with her uncle. Because he was a decorated soldier who had fought in World War I, he and his family had not been forced into a ghetto or shipped to Auschwitz, but survived the whole war in Satu Mare. In Satu Mare Irene reunited with her boyfriend and her aunt gave them a big engagement party. However, as the weeks passed, Irene gradually realized that her feelings had changed. She told her fiancé she could not marry him and she went back to visit her sister in Hamburg.

Once she was back in Germany, Irene wanted to go to the American occupied zone because she hoped to immigrate to the United States. She went to a DP camp in Ainring. There, at a dance, a young man from Budapest took a liking to Irene. She, however, was more taken with the young man's roommate. The roommate began courting Irene, much to the chagrin of the first young man. Their courtship ended when Olga joined Irene in Ainring after she was released from the hospital in Hamburg. Olga and Irene's new boyfriend fell in love "in a matter of minutes." As a result, Irene ended up dating the first young man from the dance. On January 30, 1947, the two couples were married in a joint religious ceremony in Weilheim. There the four of them lived on a kibbutz in preparation for going to Palestine.

Rather than going to Palestine, they all moved to Budapest in 1947. Irene remembers the following decade as very good years of her life: her husband was the manager of a textile store and she gave birth to a daughter in 1952. But October 1956 marked a significant change: Hungary began its revolt against the Russians, which brought serious trouble for the Jews. All the dormant anti-Semitism surfaced suddenly and violently. Irene remembers hearing Hungarians yelling, "This time you are not going to Auschwitz, you are going to die here."

Irene, who was seven months pregnant, escaped to Vienna with her husband and her four-year-old daughter. There they visited the Canadian consulate, where they were given permission to board an Italian ship bound for Halifax. Olga and her husband, on the other hand, decided to stay in Hungary.

Twelve days later, Irene was in Canada with only the clothes on her back. She was so sick from the journey that she nearly lost the baby she was carrying. She arrived in Montreal on January 10, 1957. Her son Ron was born on April 23. Today, Irene's two children live in Toronto, where Irene also moved in 1993. From her perspective today, Irene says that everything is okay. Despite the terrible hardships she endured during the Holocaust, she has had a good life and she is very grateful for her wonderful family.

>)<(>)<(>)<(

Rifka G.
October 20, 1993

In 1944, Rifka's family was deported from their home in Kobava, Czechoslovakia and sent to Auschwitz-Birkenau shortly thereafter, where over half of her family perished. Rifka and her sister Julie, still in their teens, endured forced labor in a series of factories and camps. Rifka says, "I was fighting for [Julie]. I was the one who saved her even though she is three years older than I."

Before their liberation, Rifka and her sister were sent on numerous marches through the countryside. Rifka remembers it was late spring and there were potatoes growing in the fields. Once, Rifka and two other girls risked their lives and dashed for a potato, even though, Rifka explains, it was hard to distinguish a potato from a stone. In doing so, the two other girls were wounded by SS fire. Rifka was not hit. She was also the only one who grabbed a potato, which she shared with her sister—the wounded girls grabbed stones.

After the liberation, Rifka was hospitalized with typhus. Through a German-speaking doctor who translated, she conveyed to American soldiers this story of "being shot at for stealing a potato." The soldiers told her they would pass it on to an American newspaper. Rifka believes it was published. However, it is not until this testimony that Rifka has ever spoken about her experience and her loss.

Rifka grew up in a large orthodox family as part of a small, close-knit Jewish community in Kobava, Czechoslovakia. Born September 16, 1929, she was the fifth of eight children. Of her seven siblings, only three survived the Holocaust: Isaac, Esther, and Julie. Rifka's other siblings Feigele, Hannah, Tobie, and Mayer Ber, along with their parents, Chava and Joseph, were "taken away and gassed."

Before the war, Rifka had a "very nice life." Her parents ran a successful importing business. At home, they spoke mostly Yiddish but Rifka learned to speak Hungarian, Czech, and Ukrainian in school.

Although Rifka and her siblings had non-Jewish friends, the mostly Ukrainian population of Kobava created a climate where anti-Semitism prevailed. Rifka says that when the Jews were forced into the ghetto, most Ukrainians were happy to take over Jewish property. Before this, even children knew that nearly everyone "hated Jews." In one instance, while she was on her way to school, two older boys pulled her to the side of the road and viciously tried to force her to eat pork. Rifka was in tears when she arrived late for the school's "priest's hour" that all students, even the Jewish children, were required to attend. Rifka recounted the incident to the priest, who punished the boys by forcing them to kneel in a corner for an hour.

The Germans never entered Kobava. Instead, her town was occupied by Hungary. The Hungarian *Csendörseg* (gendarmes) caused trouble for the Jews at the outset of the occupation. They harassed Jewish men by tugging at their long beards. This led her father to cut his off. For a reason unknown to Rifka, the Jewish men also had to report to the gendarmes every Sunday. Later, each family had to prove that they were not Polish-born because Polish Jews were being taken out of the city. Everyone thought they were taken to work, because it was impossible to believe otherwise.

Around April 1944, the gendarmes collected Rifka from her school and, along with her family, took her by wagon to a ghetto near the neighboring town of Munkacs. The ghetto was a converted brick factory. The barracks, formerly used for drying bricks, were eight feet by seven feet. After they put down their blankets, Rifka says it was "like a big huge bed" for every family. All the Jews were forced to surrender any valuables they had. Rifka remembers a soldier inspected her long beautiful hair, which was done up in braids, for hidden money or gold.

In the ghetto, her family was left with nothing but a sack of matzos and dried farfel, which her mother had prepared before they left. Rifka remembers that they had to eat the farfel uncooked, not only because they did not have a stove but also because it was forbidden to make a fire. Rifka explains that it was the appointed Jewish leaders who "had to keep order in the ghetto." Everybody followed the orders, Rifka says, because they did not want "our own boys" to be punished.

In the ghetto, the wealthy Jewish men, including Rifka's "well-to-do" uncle, were segregated in a separate barrack and isolated from their families. When Rifka found out where her uncle was, she began bringing him food that her family had obtained from her older sister, who sent it "the black way" from the nearby Munkacs ghetto. One day, Rifka tried smuggling sunflower seeds to her uncle. As she approached his barrack, a soldier came up behind her and hit her over the back. Rifka broke into a run. As she jumped into her barrack for safety, a splinter in one of the boards tore into her leg.

Terrified and in pain, she hid under the blankets. Rifka says, "I heard those German boots walking by. I didn't dare to breathe." The soldier did not catch her. The wound on her leg became infected and left a scar.

Rifka and her family had spent four to six weeks in the Munkacs ghetto when they were told that they were being sent to work in Germany. Even after they were loaded onto cattle trains, Rifka remembers they thought they were going somewhere better than the ghetto. On their journey, which lasted for days, there were rumors that they were going to Poland. Still they thought they would soon have work to do and at least be looked after with food and water. Instead, as they approached Auschwitz at dusk, Rifka witnessed a bonfire from the small window of the cattle train. She saw two people grab a corpse by the arms and the legs and, swinging it back and forth, throw it into the fire. Shocked, Rifka told the others, and they responded angrily, asking, "how dare you say something like that?"

At their final destination, Auschwitz-Birkenau, Rifka recalls noticing numerous disorienting spotlights. A soldier told them to put on the clothes they wanted "to save" because they would have to leave the rest behind. Rifka, who was fourteen years old, thought it was better to save her older sister's clothes, which were more stylish than her own. She got off the train wearing her sister's suit, "beautiful platform shoes," and a hat. "That saved me," she says, "I looked like a twenty-year-old and not a fourteen." Dr. Josef Mengele was there to make the selection. He ordered her parents to go to the right with their younger children. Rifka, her seventeen-year-old sister Julie, and her little eleven-year-old sister Feigele went to the left, the direction for the able-bodied workers. Rifka thought that Feigele was too small to work and wanted her to stay with their mother. She begged the SS guard to recognize that Feigele was too young to go with the older girls. "Don't say nonsense," he responded. Rifka speculates that because "he knew everything of what was going on," he "didn't want to have it on his conscience."

Despite the SS guard's failure to comply with Rifka's wishes, Rifka urged Feigele to run into the other line to find their mother and father. At the time she thought she was protecting Feigele. Now she is tormented by the thought that Feigele never found her parents and that "she went all by herself to the gas chamber." "I should have never sent her," she says. Rifka believes that her anguish and guilt over this incident make her afraid to talk openly about her Holocaust experiences and account, to a certain extent, for her silence over the years. "I feel like I did it," she explains, "I didn't think that she was strong."

After being processed into the camp, Rifka went to the showers. "Suddenly, here I am a fourteen year old girl" in a room full of women who were "shaved all over." It was horrible for Rifka who had never even seen her mother without her clothes. Rifka, shivering from the cold, stayed close to her sister. She feared losing her in the crowd because everyone looked the same. By chance, Rifka and Julie found three of their cousins. "Everything went by fives" in the roll calls and the distribution of food so the five girls were happy to be together. Rifka's cousins were also older, which was a comfort to her at the time. After three or four days, Rifka's cousins were taken away to work in *Kanada*, sorting the clothes that people destined for the crematoria had brought to the camp.

Rifka and her sister were left in Birkenau amongst the "tough" Polish and Slovak girls who had been there for years. Whenever anyone cried and asked when they might see their parents again, Rifka describes how the Polish and Slovak girls made a gesture toward the sky and said, "There are your parents. You have no parents. What you see you have—you have nothing else." There were many *Appells* in the cold rain, and they had nothing to cover their shaven heads. They protected themselves as best as they could by pulling the backs of their dresses like a shawl over their heads. During the selections, Rifka says they would stand there "like soldiers," hungry and dirty. They knew that "if you didn't look good enough at the *Appell*, they would select you," so they tried to appear "nice and healthy" by slapping their cheeks for color. Rifka and her sister planned to stay together and agreed, "if you are out, I'll be out."

Rifka knew from the other inmates that people were being gassed in "showers" at Auschwitz and burned in crematoria. Each time Rifka was taken for a shower she "thought it was the end." "They tried to use methods to fool you." Likewise, after nine weeks in Birkenau, when Rifka and Julie were selected for transport to a work camp, they thought, "they must be fooling us." They were given a shower, clothes that had been confiscated from other Jews, and a pot, a spoon, and a fork "which meant a lot of richness." Wearing a coat with "a big red X on it," Rifka, along with the other workers, was placed on a passenger train. Rifka thought, "They are taking us nicely to our own deaths." She and her sister cried as they left Birkenau because "[they] knew what [they] had left behind."

They arrived at a factory at Tzileta, close to Bratislava, which manufactured textiles for the German Army. Part of Rifka's job included gathering the cotton from the fields. There, Rifka, Julie, and the other prisoners joined approximately two hundred other women, all Polish Jews who had gone from their homes to the factory without passing through the camps. A few Italian men also worked at the factory. Even though they were forbidden to speak to the Jewish prisoners, one of them saved Rifka from severe injury when her arm was caught in a textile machine.

Every morning there was a roll call. Each prisoner was identified by the number sewn on her clothes. Rifka's number was 52086. "[The factory] was not so terrible," Rifka says. The Czech owner tried to make their lives better by telling the Germans that they were very good workers and deserved to be given more food. But the Germans treated them "like animals." One morning a *Kapo* came looking for her sister who was suspected of a misdeed. Because "I would do anything for my sister," Rifka hit the *Kapo* in her sister's defense. Recognizing that she had committed a grave act, Rifka ran outside into the snow. The *Kapo* chased her saying, "I'll fix you." That day, the other inmates feared Rifka would be sent back to Birkenau. Instead the *Kapo* punished Rifka and her sister by depriving them of food for one week. The other girls shared their food with them.

Eventually, the Russians were so close that Rifka could hear the bombardments. As a result, starting in January 1945, she and her sister went through a series of camp evacuations and relocations. "We went here and there . . . wherever they could place us." The prisoners were barely fed. Even though, Rifka explains, "I was the fourteen-year-old," she devised a method for stealing food from the German shepherds that accompanied the SS, and another for breaking into food storage buildings, which involved "swinging like Tarzan on a rope."

They ended up in Morchenstern, where German airplanes were being built. They stayed for a short while. Every day, the Germans called some of the girls by their numbers to report to the kitchen to peel potatoes. This was a desirable duty because it gave the opportunity to steal a potato, or even just the peelings. But Rifka's and Julie's numbers were never called for kitchen duty. One day, Rifka reported to the kitchen anyway. She was found out and punished by having all of the hair cut off her head. Rifka remembers that a woman comforted her, promising her that one day she would have beautiful hair, a husband, and a family. "I said, 'you are dreaming,'" but she has never forgotten this woman's kindness.

Under American bombing and strafing, Rifka and her sister were evacuated from the airplane factory in trains full of munitions, and taken through the Austrian and Czechoslovakian countryside to Mauthausen. Polish men were also transported in the train. They were from the concentration camps and had left to voluntarily fight with the Germans. Hearing the cries of the Jewish prisoners, Rifka recalls that the Polish men tried to set them free. They opened the wagon doors and everyone ran "like crazy dogs" to the mountains, thinking "we are free we are free." After a few minutes, the SS caught them and ordered them back on the train. As a group, the prisoners refused. They would rather be killed on the grassy hill than go back to the transport. The SS promised that they could ride in unlocked wagons with the Polish volunteers. This lasted for a few days. When the train passed through villages, the Poles ran off to get everyone food. After the Polish men were gone, Rifka and the other Jewish prisoners were again locked in the wagons without food or water.

"I guess they just didn't know what to do with us any more because it was toward the end of the war." Many camps were already liberated. They arrived in Mauthausen, where they were placed in a "big barrack of Gypsies," at the bottom of a hill, away from the main camp. Julie became very sick and delirious with fever. She was taken to the "sick room" where she was given a bed and a little food. Rifka worried that Julie, like the other sick prisoners, would be taken out at night and killed, so Rifka spent the nights hiding under Julie's bed. If she heard anyone approaching, the two of them could try to run back to the Gypies' barrack.

From Mauthausen they were destined for Gunskirchen, another Austrian camp. The sick were told that they would be taken to the Red Cross in trucks, while the healthy ones would walk. Rifka did not believe them, thinking that anyone put on the truck would be killed. Julie, who could not walk, thought Rifka should leave her behind in order to save herself but Rifka and another woman carried Julie all the way.

They were on a death march through the forest. There was no food or water. They also passed through a number of villages. In one of them, the SS disappeared. She and others thought they might be liberated and entered a farm where they ate the food that was left for the animals and milked the cows directly into their mouths. Soon, however, they discovered they were not free. A loudspeaker was set up and a voice ordered everyone out. The SS roamed the farms and caught those who attempted to hide in piles of straw by poking around with pitchforks.

At one point Rifka was in the midst of the *Wehrmacht* (army), whose soldiers, she remembers, were much more compassionate than the SS. They even tried to feed them, which was not an easy thing for them to do because "we were like animals," she says. Rifka survived on grass. They occasionally had contact with villagers who told them that "soon it will be over."

When they arrived at Gunskirchen, deep in a dark, muddy forest, there were thousands of prisoners there. The majority of them were "whole families" from Hungary who had been deported but not taken to be gassed. At this camp, everybody was dying but she felt numb to the suffering and the inhumanity: "The dead were there piled up, whole piles near the latrines . . . but somehow you become like stone. You become immune, it doesn't bother you anymore at all." She explains, "You're just looking how to save yourself. It becomes a job to see if you can get a little bit more of that ersatz coffee that is left in the kettles that they serve it from. It becomes a full time job."

On May 5, 1945, she woke up and saw a little Jewish boy wearing a German helmet. The Germans were gone. Rifka vividly remembers the arrival of her American liberators, who came on horseback because the tanks could not negotiate the forest. She also remembers the shock of the Americans when they saw the condition of the prisoners. "They looked at us like they discover something new"; and from the prisoners' perspective, the "soldiers seemed like kings."

Many prisoners ran away and perished, but Rifka and others stayed behind in the camp. They eventually moved out of the forest but they were still afraid, even of the American-run Red Cross, and hid in nearby German villages. After convincing themselves that it was safe, they entered the Red Cross camp. Rifka, sick with typhus, was admitted to a crowded German hospital only after an American soldier threatened to cut the doctors' heads off if they did not take her in. Julie was later brought to the same hospital, but neither of them knew the other was there. In the hospital, Rifka had nightmares about her sister Feigele. Both Rifka and Julie eventually recovered, and the two of them discussed going home.

The Red Cross helped facilitate the train tickets to Kobava. Due to the damage to the surrounding countryside from the bombardments, the trip was very slow. Rifka hoped to encounter Russian soldiers because she viewed them as their true liberators. At the time she thought that if the Americans had wanted to, they could have saved the Jews. However, Rifka's meeting with Russians was disappointing because unlike the American soldiers, who were gentlemanly, they tried to take advantage of the young girls. Furthermore, they "only wanted to drink." Rifka had a little bottle of perfume that was a gift from a German villager, and a Russian soldier took it from her and drank it.

When they reached Hungary, Rifka and Julie were reunited with their sister Esther who had obtained Christian papers and survived the war working in a restaurant in Budapest. She also found the three cousins she had been with in Birkenau and her brother Isaac who had lived through the war in Russian labor camps. She and her family returned to Kobava. There, they were chased away by the new occupant of their former home. Rifka never returned. Even though she says, "sometimes I feel that I would like

Rifka G. in Holland after the war

to just walk where my mother walked," she worries that it would be too painful.

Rifka and her sisters went to Germany where Rifka pursued her education and met her future husband in a DP camp in Bamberg. Unable to meet the immigration requirements for the United States, they all went to Holland, where Rifka married and gave birth to her son Leo. Fearing the thought of another European war, Rifka and her family moved to Canada. Rifka's sister Esther also immigrated to Montreal, while Julie went from Holland to Melbourne to be close to some of her husband's surviving relatives. Her brother Isaac moved first to Israel, and then to Florida. Rifka's second son Harry was born in Montreal.

Rifka does not think that her children should be ignorant of her family's story. Initially, she did not tell her children because she "wanted them to go on with their lives." Now, she believes her story can teach her children never to "go like sheep to the gas chamber." Throughout her life it has been hard for Rifka to share her stories because she "wanted to forget," and she did not want her children to be burdened with sorrow, or made "bitter." She fears that already she "passed down [her] struggling" and her hardship through the great sadness that has been ingrained in her life. For this reason, she fears, "I could not hand down to my children [the] happiness that I maybe should have." Yet, out of love for her children and grandchildren, Rifka tries very hard to "look just ahead" because she knows she cannot bring her family back.

⊁⊰ ⊁⊰ ⊁⊰

Rena S.
April 27, 1994

Although Rena was still in her early teens during the war, she escaped the fate of the majority of girls her age by "passing" as an adult and working, first at a knitting factory in the Krakow ghetto and later in Plaszow. When Plaszow was liquidated, Rena and her mother were sent to Auschwitz-Birkenau. After a selection there, they stood in line for the gas chamber until a Kapo who mistook Rena's mother for her neighbor rescued them. They passed through Bergen-Belsen before arriving at a munitions factory in Salzwedel, where the Americans liberated them. Throughout the war, Rena had the protection of her mother who looked out for their survival. Rena also survived using her own wits.

Born in 1929, Rena was almost ten years old when Germany invaded Poland. Her family was middle-class and lived in a modern and rather upscale part of Krakow. Rena grew up speaking Polish, but not Hebrew or Yiddish. Later, her grandmother taught her to speak German fluently. Rena's close-knit family attended synagogue on holidays. They always had large gatherings on shabbat with her many aunts, uncles, and cousins who "unfortunately disappeared very quickly."

Rena describes her father, Isaac, as a "very special and soft person," and her mother, Ruth, as an outgoing and socially active woman with a sense of humor. Rena was especially close to her grandmother, Eva. She lived with them and had a "tremendous influence" on Rena. After school, Rena always ran home to be with her grandmother. "She would always listen to my stories. She always had time for me." Eva, who was from Silesia, spoke German and did not speak Polish very well. When the children "wanted to have fun [they] invited her to speak Polish." They "had a ball" making fun of her grammar.

Rena's grandmother was very well educated, having been taught philosophy and literature by nuns. She wrote poetry and plays that Rena and the other children performed at family gatherings. Her grandmother was also very "handy" and taught Rena skills such as knitting and embroidery, which later helped Rena in the factories.

Rena and her only sister Tola, who was four years older, went to a regular Polish school with a student body evenly divided between Jewish and Gentile girls. Most Jewish girls, including Rena and Tola, received additional Jewish education on the side. Rena describes herself as a fairly good student, "rotten in drawing and singing," and "comfortable with herself and accepted by her peers." On the whole, she was "happy-go-lucky" with a "little streak of rebellion," which she thinks was normal for a girl her age.

Because Krakow was considered to be a historic town and neither the Poles nor the Germans wanted to destroy it, the city "fell without a shot." One of the first measures against the Jews was the confiscation of their radios. This stuck in Rena's mind because the exchange between her grandmother and the young Nazi soldier who came for their radio gave her an inkling that something was gravely wrong. Her grandmother, who could not believe what was happening, confronted the soldier, telling him that she considered herself to be a German. She was, after all, educated as a German. The soldier responded, "If a donkey is born in a stable with pure bred horses, it remains a donkey." Having been raised to respect her elders, Rena was shocked by the soldier's disrespect.

Before the German invasion of Poland, the family knew about *Kristallnacht*. Initially, Rena did not identify with the Jews who were persecuted. She could not believe that they were "normal Jews" and thought there must have been another reason for the attack. She realized this was not the case when an Italian man appropriated her father's business and a German officer took over the family's apartment. They had to move into "cramped quarters" in an older section of Krakow near the Jewish cemetery "where the Jews were allowed to live."

Rena continued to go to school until one day her teacher, Miss Wicowska, informed the class that each *Zydoweczka*, or "little Jewish girl," should collect her books and leave, saying they would "not need to be educated anymore." Some of the Polish girls were laughing but others seemed afraid and did not know how to react. The silent ones "looked to the teacher for guidance. They didn't get very good guidance."

According to Rena, among the adults there was a "conspiracy of silence." They tried to shield the children from painful knowledge, and discussion ceased as soon as children entered the room. The cumulative loss of her friends, her school, and her home left Rena confused and bewildered. She could not comprehend the reason for these drastic upheavals.

In 1941, Rena and her family moved into the large Krakow ghetto. When the deportations started, Rena lost part of her extended family, including a cousin, Marysia, who was like a sister to her. The loss of Marysia was "very dramatic" for Rena. When Marysia's family was summoned for deportation, Rena's mother tried to save the girl by hiding her in their apartment and claiming that she was her own daughter. However, when Marysia saw her parents leaving the ghetto, she ran to join them and her two older sisters, Tinka and Nina. Rena remembers that everybody hoped they were going to a village to work but they later found out that the transports were destined for Treblinka. This was confirmed when her mother's second cousin sent her parents a postcard, which they believed came from Treblinka. It warned, "Don't go. This is a sure death."

In the ghetto, Rena says she felt like a "semi-child." She did not have to fend for herself. Her mother still washed and braided her hair. She continued to receive some education from private teachers. She participated in the ballet classes that some adults had organized in the ghetto, in an effort to maintain a sense of normalcy. On the other hand, she was aware of what was happening as more and more people disappeared from the ghetto.

In the summer of 1942, the large Krakow ghetto was closed. Rena and her family moved into the small ghetto in Krakow, sharing a two-room apartment with two other families. They lived on *Plac Zgody* (Harmony Square). Many people in the ghetto worked in a factory called Optima. The factory was operated by the Germans but "subdivided with Jewish management." Rena worked in the knitting department, mending German military sweaters and socks that were bloody, dirty, and filled with vermin, sent from the Russian front. She was only twelve years old, still wearing short dresses and pigtails, but she had papers that designated her as a fully capable working adult.

One day, everyone in the ghetto had to report for selection. Rena's grandmother was sick with pneumonia and confined to bed with a high fever. Not knowing what was going to happen to her, the family left her behind in their locked apartment, along with the elderly and senile mother of Henryk Heilmann, a family friend. Henryk and his wife Lushka went on to survive the war by working in Oskar Schindler's enamel factory.

The Jewish police started dividing people, lining them up on either the left or the right sidewalk. Rena and her mother were directed to the left sidewalk but her mother noticed that the police were pushing their own families to the right. Giving Rena a shove, her mother said, "Run! Don't look," ordering her to the other side. Rena obeyed and then watched her mother, who had "good presentation" and spoke perfect German, approach one of the guards. Rena does not know what her mother said, but she was allowed to walk over and join the group on the right, which was then marched to the factory. In the evening, they came back to the ghetto to find that by some "miracle" their apartment was one of the only ones that had not been searched. Rena's grandmother was still there.

Even though her family was still together, this *Aktion* was devastating for Rena. She explains, "It is very very difficult to talk about something where you lost the rest of your friends." That day, Rena was the only one her age who came back to the ghetto. Rena also witnessed the children from the orphanage on *Plac Zgody* being shot and thrown in trucks. From their zombie-like demeanors, Rena suspects that the nurses drugged the children with morphine in advance.

Rena continued to work in the knitting factory, along with her grandmother who recovered from pneumonia. This period was very hard for Rena because she says she "didn't really know how to cope," but "knew she wasn't supposed to ask. Adults who have a lot on their minds, don't have time for children." Rena overheard an argument between her mother and father concerning her father's invitation to join the Jewish police. Her mother wanted him to join because she saw it as a way for him to save the family. Rena's father refused, saying, "They will lead me to death but I won't lead anyone to death." At the time, Rena did not really understand what this meant.

The Krakow ghetto was soon liquidated. Some Jews were deported and others were transferred to Plaszow, well known as the camp near Oskar Schindler's enamel factory. For the selection, Rena's mother gave Rena a "fashionably short haircut" and dressed her in "adult fashion" in her own clothes and high heels. Because Rena was tall for her age, her mother told her to line up in a row of shorter women in order to draw attention to her height. This way, Rena managed to avoid deportation.

In Plaszow, Rena was assigned to a barracks with her mother, her sister, and her grandmother. She continued to work at Optima, traveling to the factory under the supervision of guards with dogs. For no practical reason, the workers had to carry heavy pieces of wood on their shoulders for both legs of the journey.

One day on the *Appellplatz*, all the inmates were forced to watch the hanging of three young men. She does not know what offense they committed. Along with the other prisoners, Rena was then forced to march past the dead bodies, and she recalls that at this time her mind had simply shut off. Watching the young men alive at one moment and then "seeing the three people hang there like rag dolls was one of the most horrible sights I've seen."

On another occasion, while standing at the door of the barrack, Rena saw the *Lagerkommandant*, the infamous Amon Goeth, approaching with his entourage and his two Great Danes. The *Stubenälteste* (the person in charge) of her barrack was nowhere in sight. Rena was "scared out of her wits" but she knew she should try to warn the other inmates. She yelled, "*Achtung!*" (Watch out!) so that the women would line up against the bunks. Then, in imitation of the *Stubenälteste*, she called out the expected formalities of camp protocol. Goeth was greatly amused, patted Rena on the head, and walked away. Once he left, Rena says "all the starch went out of me" and she started shaking and crying. From this incident, Rena concludes, "children know how to act when they have to." In the presence of German soldiers, Rena generally felt "vulnerable" and "unprotected." She explains that she was careful never to look them in the eyes.

During a selection from the factory, Rena's grandmother, Eva, was taken away for deportation. Knowing that people who went away never came back, Rena was compelled to intervene. Rena ran to the "commission" at the front of the factory and whispered to one of the Jewish leaders, Dr. Gross, who was an acquaintance of the family, that her grandmother had been selected. She attributes her courage to a childlike feeling of being "indestructible." Rena then heard that the entire paper factory, *Papiernica*, where her sister Tola worked, had also been selected for this deportation. She went back to the doctor to inform him that her sister was about to be deported as well. She realizes now that in doing so, she risked her own safety, but "children don't think," she explains. Dr. Gross managed to remove Tola from the list of deportees but Tola insisted on accompanying their grandmother. Fortunately, they were both deported to Skarzysko, where they worked in a HASAG munitions factory.

Following Tola's deportation, Rena says that her father deteriorated physically and emotionally. He felt powerless to protect his own family. In May 1944, he was selected for deportation with the children's transport (the transport dramatized in Steven Spielberg's film *Schindler's List*). The passengers went directly to the crematoria at Auschwitz.

The camp grew increasingly smaller. Meanwhile, for Rena there was a routine of working in the factory, *Appell*, beatings, and shootings. However, by the summer of 1944, Russian guns could be heard in the distance. One hot day, Plaszow was slated for liquidation. The inmates were assembled at the train station for deportation. Rena's mother Ruth realized that the camp's "big shots" were keeping to the back of the line. She and Rena joined them. The train cars filled to capacity and Rena and her mother were left in the camp. They remained in Plaszow as part of the group which "cleaned up." Rena was assigned to digging up the bodies of prisoners who had been shot. She feared "encountering a total body." "I could deal with bones. You stacked them in a pile and they were burned. Bodies of people was something else. . . . " The bodies were exhumed with a spade, taken by their arms and legs, stacked in a pile, doused with gasoline, and burned. Rena tried to shut it out but she had nightmares. She never talked about it with anyone.

In the fall of 1944, Rena and her mother Ruth were deported by train to Auschwitz-Birkenau. When they arrived, the women were given a shower and left outside naked for the duration of the cold autumn night. They hugged each other for warmth. When they were taken to a large barracks and shaved, Rena became "hysterical." For a young girl of thirteen, Rena says, "somehow having my hair shaven meant more to me than getting killed. It doesn't make sense. It's not logical: hair grows back." In the end, the barber did not shave her entire head. Instead, he left a circle of hair on top. "Believe me," Rena says, "I would've looked better with all my hair shaven but somehow that little bit of hair gave me dignity."

The inmates were given clothes that "were meant to make us look stupid and ridiculous." Ruth, for example, wore a short pleated skirt with wooden shoes. Rena wore a huge men's pajama blouse. Rena and her mother did not work. There were roll calls at all hours. She says they might have been in Birkenau for weeks but she does not really know. Rena remembers some people throwing themselves against the electrified barbed wire. Whenever this happened, her mother told her that this was not the way to act: "You must survive. That's your duty. If you allow yourself to die, you'll be handing them a victory." Ruth also told her that there would be life after the war but Rena did not see how it could possibly be true.

During a selection, headed by an SS officer whom she believes was Dr. Mengele, Rena was sent to the left. She knew she had been selected for the gas chamber. She did not harbor any illusions as to the source of the smoke rising over Birkenau: "you don't forget the stench of human bodies burning," she says. Even though Rena's mother had told her over and over that she must survive, Rena says that she remembers feeling indifferent. "Maybe it really didn't matter anymore." Not wanting Rena to go alone to the gas chamber, Rena's mother joined her. While they were standing in line to be gassed, a Polish woman *Kapo* suddenly approached Ruth and insisted that she was her neighbor from Warsaw. "This is for life," the woman said, and pushed them into the line waiting to board a train going to Bergen-Belsen.

At Bergen-Belsen, where they arrived around November 1944, the new inmates were put in large tents because there was no more room in the barracks. As it was very cold and the prisoners were not properly dressed, everyone was trying to avoid having to sleep at the coldest spot, along the edge of the tent. Rena says that she and her mother were not pushy enough to claim a spot in the middle. One night, however, there was a terrible storm and the tent collapsed. The people sleeping in the middle of the tent suffocated but those on the edges, including Rena and Ruth, were able to get out. They were brought to an overcrowded barracks that had no bunks.

Soon, Rena and her mother were selected for a transport that mostly included Greek-speaking women. They were very apprehensive, especially because they were under the impression that they were relatively safe in Bergen-Belsen. They arrived in Salzwedel, a small town in Germany, where they were made to work in a munitions factory. Because both Rena and

Ruth spoke German, their job was to verify that bullets had been calibrated correctly. Rena says that her mother somehow sabotaged her work by altering the scale of her calibration measurements. Every day they marched through the town down a main road. They worked alongside German employees from the same town who, Rena explains, were perfectly aware of the condition of the Jewish prisoners.

Salzwedel was not the "the worst place" even though the inmates worked long hours. The *Kommandant* was an old man who was "not kind but not cruel." They feared getting sick and returning to Bergen-Belsen. During the Allied air attacks, the Americans bombed the factory. The prisoners, meanwhile, were locked up inside the munitions shed. Rena recalls how the women laughed and sang songs during the raid even though they knew that the building could easily blow up at any moment. "Nobody cared," Rena states, "it would be an easy way out . . . . Besides, we had lasted that long. We felt indestructible."

Rena was liberated by the Americans. She saw the tanks enter the camp but she has no memory of the following forty-eight hours. As the Germans surrendered, the prisoners moved into their vacated barracks. Ruth suffered

Rena S., age sixteen, in Krakow, 1945

from lack of vitamins and was hospitalized. Wanting to be close to her mother, Rena reported to the hospital as a nurse.

They eventually went back to Poland and stayed there until the beginning of 1946. Trying to locate other members of their family, they contacted the Red Cross and many rabbis. They found out that Tola, who had survived the war, had been in Krakow, but left the evening before Rena and her mother arrived there. Tola ended up in a DP camp in Linz.

An uncle, who survived the war and lived in Berlin posing as a *Volksdeutscher*, spent a "kilo in gold" in order to bring Rena and her mother to live with him. The two of them traveled separately, which was a harrowing experience. Rena was apprehended at the border and spent the night in prison. Once they made it to Berlin, Rena's mother did not want Rena to stay there so she arranged for Rena to study in London. Rena, who knew very little English, traveled to London on a transport of German war brides.

Crossing the Russian zone of Germany was another harrowing experience for Rena. Being stateless and born in Poland, she "belonged to the Russians" and feared repatriation. While being questioned by Russian soldiers, she grabbed her passport and ran away, "screaming like a banshee" through the train. She burst into a car of British officers. "What little English I knew completely escaped me at that point," says Rena, but a Jewish officer finally understood what was happening and she was allowed to remain on the train.

In 1948, Rena joined her mother in Canada, where she still lives with her husband, a survivor from Slovakia. They have two children and nine grandchildren.

CHAPTER 3

Men Surviving the Camps

David A.
February 23, 1994

David miraculously survived a mass execution near Balf, on the Austro-Hungarian border. In 1956, he moved to Montreal to live closer to two surviving sisters and one brother. To this day, David sees the last of his surviving siblings, his sister Yolanda, several times a week. If not, she calls and asks him, "What's the matter. You moved out of town?" This kind of dry humor and irony emerges throughout David's narrative, making him seem somewhat detached from the experiences through which he lived.

David's family history goes back 100 years in the small village of Tinnye in Hungary, some thirty kilometers northwest of Budapest. The village had a large community of Hungarian Jews who had been prohibited from living in the capital several centuries earlier. The community was predominantly orthodox, with an eminent *yeshiva* that drew students from across Hungary.

David's uncles and his father Ignace ran a successful agriculture and livestock export business, and were friends with the local Hungarian intellectuals. David's father and uncles paid the highest taxes in the town; they owned land and employed hundreds of people, many of them peasants from the town. Although many of the townspeople were dependent on the family business for their livelihood, David was aware of strong anti-Semitic undercurrents.

David was born on October 21, 1922. As the youngest of eight children from a close-knit and comfortably off family, David led a sheltered life before the war. His oldest sister Rosa, twenty years his senior, often took him from Tinnye to Budapest, where people would assume that David was her son. Among his other siblings were Bella, Miklos, Emmanuel, Sarah, Yola, and Matilda. David had a large extended family of approximately one hundred. Of them, only ten to fifteen survived the Holocaust. They now live dispersed across several continents.

David went to *cheder* from the age of four and to the local school from the age of ten; he was then sent to an orthodox Jewish high school in Budapest, where his days were divided between secular studies in the mornings and Jewish studies in the afternoons.

Certain anti-Semitic laws began earlier in Hungary than in Germany and were strictly enforced. The *numerus clausus* excluded Jews through a simple mechanism: the percentage of Jewish businesses, students, and professionals was not allowed to exceed the percentage of Jews in the total population. David was prohibited from attending university and returned to Tinnye at the age of eighteen to work in the family business. Similar legal restrictions also revoked the family business license, forcing David's father to hire a *Verwalter* (straw man) and put the business under his name. The Jews cooperated with these laws and learned new trades, even as the legal constraints grew progressively more stringent. Soon Jews were excluded from the media and the army. Having an affair with a Christian could lead to a five-year prison sentence.

Suspecting that worse was to come, David urged his father to sell the business and leave Hungary. "I was the wise man telling them, let's go, let's move. My father looked at me like I was a lunatic." Ignace trusted Miklós Horthy, the Hungarian leader whose ties to the Jews were so close that his son married a Jewish woman. Everyone had heard that in Warsaw the Jews were being persecuted; in Hungary most considered themselves safe.

Around 1938, David's three brothers were called into the Hungarian Army. Later, one was sent to the Russian front, and two went to Transylvania. Two of his brothers went missing "somewhere in the Russian steppes" and never returned. In 1941, Hungarian Jews had to prove their citizenship; those of questionable citizenship were executed or expelled. Some managed to escape Hungary, telling unbelievable stories when they returned.

In October 1943, David was recruited for service in a labor battalion and was sent to Esztergombator, a Hungarian army labor camp where he had to wear a yellow armband. Shortly afterward, while David was still in the camp, Horthy declared that the war was lost, and that he was seeking peace. The next day, the leader of the Arrow Cross, Ferenc Szálasi, took power and the Hungarians joined forces with the Germans.

At Esztergombator, the guards erected barbed wire around David's barracks. He overheard one saying, "OK Jews, it won't be long. You'll die like the rest of them." David joined a group of twenty prisoners who cut the barbed wire and escaped. They stole a truck and uniforms from the army, and the group drove to Budapest, where they dispersed. David went to the ghetto in search of his family and found three of his sisters. He then traveled from place to place in search of the underground, using false documents that identified him as a Hungarian soldier on a six-month leave. "I didn't look like too much of a Jew just to look at me, so I passed. I was already an escape artist, experienced."

In November 1944, David located another sister and her husband, daughter, and a sixteen-year-old son. Protected by the Vatican, they were hiding in a monastery. After celebrating their reunion, David thought it best to leave. He gave in after being urged not to leave at night. In the morning, he awoke to find the monastery surrounded by two hundred Hungarian *Csendörseg* (gendarmes), SS, and soldiers. Everyone was ordered into the yard, but David hid in the attic. When he came down he found his sister crying and discovered that all the men, including his brother-in-law and nephew, had been taken away. He promised his sister that he would bring her husband and son back, and went after the other men, despite pleas that he escape. David was captured and, with the others, loaded into cattle cars and taken first to Sopron, and then to Fertorákos, and on to Balf, a village on the Austro-Hungarian border. At Balf, David unexpectedly encountered another brother-in-law.

David describes the period in Balf from November 1944 to March 1945 as unreal. Sixty percent of the prisoners perished. They slept on hay in the villagers' barns, brushing the snow off their bodies in the mornings. Their rations were a daily portion of soup and half a kilo of bread every three days. "Food was absolutely nonexistent. Eight-hundred to a thousand people standing in line and getting a bowl of so-called soup." Hygiene was also nonexistent; the prisoners had no means of washing and no change of clothes. The number of prisoners was marked outside the barns; they were summoned for roll call at 6 a.m. every morning. The soldiers threatened to shoot every tenth Jew if anyone went missing. The peasants were too afraid to risk helping them.

The prisoners dug eight-by-ten meter antitank ditches in the frozen ground, to ward off the advancing Russian army. Ironically, when the Russian liberators finally came, they arrived on horseback, undeterred by the ditches. Instead, the ditches were used as mass graves for the prisoners who had dug them.

When no German soldiers were around, the guards who belonged to the *Organisation Todt* labor battalions sometimes allowed the prisoners to rest and warm themselves over the fires. Eventually, David had some luck; he was recognized by one of his father's former employees, "you're an A., come here, I need a butcher." He started working in the camp kitchen, where he had access to extra food and hot water. In December 1944, a typhus epidemic broke out. "People were dying by the dozen. There was no food and no heat. It did not take long for people to die." David explains that the "hospital" was located in a village about six kilometers away. He says,

> All the sick were loaded up on open carts pulled by a tractor and taken
> to this village for treatment. By the time they got there, they were all dead.
> So they were burned. That was the hospital treatment: short and sweet.

The farmers in the area were also getting sick: "this disease typhoid is not anti-Semitic," jokes David.

David was able to take his sixteen-year-old nephew into the kitchen as an assistant. However, his brothers-in-law remained in the barns and fell ill. David and the nephew brought them food from the kitchen. Just when they regained their strength, David contracted typhus. For twenty days, David was feverish; those days, "disappeared from [his] life completely." David recovered a few days before March 31.

By the end of March 1945, the Russians were advancing toward Balf. The Nazis marched the healthy prisoners west to Mauthausen on March 27, leaving the sick and the "in between," including David, in Balf. The 190 prisoners who remained, thought that they only had to endure until the Russians came; they thought they had survived. The sixteen-year-old nephew ran away with a friend.

On March 31, an SS Commando arrived and ordered the remaining prisoners to leave the barns. A healthy prisoner had taken David's shoes several days earlier: "I was half dead, who needs shoes?" The prisoners were weak and slow. If someone was too sick to walk, he was shot with a "neat little machine gun." He testifies,

> They ordered everyone into the ditches. There were thousands of soldiers. They were absolutely cool, slow. Never mind the approaching front. They aimed at the head and shot one. Then, if there is a reflex they put more bullets. No rush. Aim and shoot, like in a game. When my time came, a young guy came with a moustache. He looked at me; he murmured something. I covered my eyes. He shoot me here [in the wrist]. I didn't lose consciousness. I just fell down. I get bullet here [in the brow] and there and another one [in the arm and leg]. Then I guess he thought I had enough and moved on to the next one. The two brother-in-laws, one beside me, one next to me. I saw them. Died both of them. This was going on for maybe an hour, not more, until everything was quiet and we were lying there dead.

After the shootings, the soldiers threw clumps of dirt on the bodies in order to see if any would flinch. Eventually, all that remained was a dead silence. David refers to this event as "the killing of me and my comrades."

A few hours later, David heard voices. A Jewish boy had brought the Russian liberators. He was yelling in Hungarian: "If anyone is alive, don't be afraid!" David and two other prisoners answered the call. Using a stick, the Russians pulled the sole survivors out of the ditch. Walking the several kilometers to the nearby inn in Balf, David left a trail of blood.

The Russians put David on a table and then left until the next morning. They ordered a *Volksdeutscher* to drive the three survivors in a horse-drawn buggy to a Russian military hospital in a village twenty kilometers away. As soon as they left the village, the driver, who "was shaking from what the Russians had told him," jumped out and ran off, leaving David to drive the buggy. Further along, they met a Russian soldier with a three-legged horse. The Russian "traded" horses with David, causing their short journey to the hospital to take several days. Near the hospital, David exchanged the horse and buggy for a drink of milk. By the time he finally arrived, one of the survivors had died of blood poisoning.

David's clothes were "glued" to his body from all the blood and the dirt. "The only way to undress me was with scissors." Nuns bandaged David's wounds. A Russian medic came and dislodged the bullet from his leg with a piece of metal wrapped in gauze: "He pulled and pushed and pulled. Eventually the bullet fell out. Then the doctor looked at me and said, 'now you're okay.'" David could not see with his left eye and has since only regained partial vision. After two to three weeks he was able to walk with a crutch, and left the hospital for the village of Siojut. From Siojut he went to Budapest on a train carrying French prisoners of war.

David arrived in Budapest in terrible health, "I don't think Picasso could make a picture like I was looking." A makeshift Jewish hospital had been established in a school building. David convalesced there for eleven months. Word got around that he was looking for his family and he was reunited with his mother and sisters. His father had perished in Auschwitz; his mother died in 1946, a year after her liberation, as a result of the hardships she had suffered in the ghetto.

After recovering, David was declared "60 percent invalid" and discharged from the Hungarian army. He joined a Zionist organization. He went to Vienna and Italy before arriving in Israel in 1949. He spent six months on a kibbutz and then started a transport company in Jerusalem in partnership with the nephew who had escaped from Balf. In Jerusalem, David married an Auschwitz survivor. However, in 1956, together with his wife and son, David left the successful company he had founded in Jerusalem and started life again in Montreal, in order to be near his two surviving sisters and brother. They had wanted to move far from Hungary and Canada had been the first country to accept their immigration applications. David's first wife died in 1975 and David remarried in 1988.

Recently, David returned to Balf in order to help exhume the bodies of his comrades from the massacre, who had been buried in the ditch that they dug. The bodies were reburied in the main Jewish cemetery of Budapest. In 1992, a monument and plaque were erected on the site of the execution in memory of the victims. David emphasizes the importance of remembering this event. He feels no anger toward the soldier who shot him: "It wasn't his fault. He was just the tool to pull the trigger . . . It took a while, almost fifty years, till I can talk about it. I didn't talk for too many years." For him, talking serves as a warning that "it shouldn't happen again. Enough is enough."

❊❊❊ ❊❊❊ ❊❊❊

Jacob G.
November 24, 1993

Jacob G. worked as a carpenter in a forced labor camp in Radom, Poland, during most of the war. Eventually, he was transferred to various camps in Germany and was finally liberated by American forces while in transit near Staltach (just south of Munich). Before immigrating to Montreal in 1948, Jacob worked in Germany for several years as a manager in a children's nutritional centre. Jacob read much of his testimony from short articles that he wrote for his children and grandchildren.

Jacob was apprehensive about the prospect of giving a testimony on his wartime experiences. Despite his reluctance to relive past trauma, he agreed to the videotaped interview because he felt a responsibility both to the past and to posterity: "if we that are still alive will not bring [our experiences] out into the open when there are now so many so-called professional historians denying what took place, . . . what will happen when nothing is left behind?"

In the summer of 1969, Jacob had been asked to make a statement against Weinrich, the head of the Gestapo in Jacob's hometown of Radom, Poland. After testifying to the German consul in Montreal, the stenographer read his testimony back to him to verify that it was accurate. As he listened to his own story, Jacob felt so overpowered by the force of his memories that he became physically ill and passed out before she could finish. Consequently, Jacob never signed his own testimony to verify its authenticity. Then, in 1972, he was asked to appear at Weinrich's trial in Bonn, Germany. Though he was extremely reluctant to relive his trauma yet again, Jacob decided to go because he felt it was his moral duty to those who had perished. At the trial, the presiding judge had Jacob's testimony from Montreal in front of him. The judge moved to strike Jacob's recollections from the evidence because the date Jacob had given orally for when Weinrich ordered the "resettlement" of fifteen hundred Jews in January of 1943 contradicted what his document from Montreal indicated. It seems that the secretary of the German consul in Montreal had made a typing error, indicating the date as January 12 rather than January 15. Jacob told the judge that if he could prove that Jacob had signed the Montreal testimony to verify its authenticity, Jacob would strike his own recollections from the evidence. When the Judge noticed that Jacob's Montreal testimony did not bear Jacob's signature, he simply said, "court adjourned." This experience taught Jacob that survivor testimonies are often the only evidence of what actually happened during the Holocaust, and that, since there are many who would discredit the memories of survivors, it is crucial for witnesses like him to document their wartime experiences as clearly and accurately as they can.

At the trial in Bonn, the prosecutor asked Jacob if he remembered any of the SS officer's names. He said, "I remember not only their names, but also their ranks." He then listed some of the SS officer's names, one after another. A woman sitting on the jury asked Jacob to repeat one of the names, and as he did so he noticed her face turn white as a sheet of paper. That was when he remembered that most of the SS officers he knew had come from Hamburg, which was also where the jurors came from. This woman was likely a relative or a friend of the SS man. When the prosecutor asked Jacob to stay in Hamburg and make additional statements after the trial had ended, Jacob declined. He was afraid for his life after having named the names of so many ex-SS officers from Hamburg.

Jacob was born on October 2, 1922, in Radom, a Polish town of about 100,000 people, approximately one third of whom were Jewish. He was the third of four children in an orthodox family. His father, Aron Baruch, was a leather worker. The rest of Jacob's family consisted of his mother Chaya Lea, his older sister Reisel, his older brother Chaim, and his younger brother Elek. The family practiced Judaism vigorously, attending synagogue regularly.

Despite his family's orthodoxy, Jacob looked for a broader approach to life, developing a strong social conscience and becoming involved in some secular movements. After graduating from elementary school in 1936, for example, he joined a Zionist group with a socialist political agenda, *Hashomer Hatza'ir*. This was not unusual for Polish Jews at the time. As Jacob explained, the trend among his peer group was "to look for a just society."

Three months after Jacob completed his apprenticeship as a cabinetmaker, the war broke out and the shop where he worked closed. Eight days after that, the German army marched into Radom. Immediately after their arrival, the Germans selected a group of leaders from the Jewish community to form the *Judenrat*. The Germans required skilled carpenters and, in October 1939, the *Judenrat* dispatched Jacob to work in the *Truppenwirtschaftslager der Waffen SS*, a forced labor camp on Kolejowa Street 18. After a ghetto was created in Radom in the spring of 1941, he and the other eighty-six laborers had to march to work from the ghetto, always accompanied by an armed SS guard.

At the mention of Kolejowa 18 "the Jews trembled with fear." Whenever the infamous SS officer, Max Klingenberg, went into the ghetto seeking additional manpower to unload 100-kg sacks of merchandise for the day, people tried desperately to evade him. If caught, they were "beaten on the spot." Since there was a constant shortage of food in the ghetto, most of these laborers had neither the strength nor the skill to carry out the arduous tasks assigned to them; as a result they suffered whippings and other indignities. It was also standard practice among the Germans to cut off the beard and *payes* (side locks) of any orthodox Jew before returning him to the ghetto.

Jacob and his brothers lived in the Radom ghetto until the summer of 1942, when a typhoid epidemic broke out. Because their work consisted of handling foodstuffs destined for the German army, they were separated from their family and relocated to a small enclave adjacent to Kolejowa 18. This enclave was enclosed with barbed wire and surrounded by a watchtower where guards were stationed around the clock. On a Sunday in August of 1942, Jacob and his coworkers were permitted to visit their families in the Radom ghetto. Since they had not seen their friends and families for several months, they were afraid of what this unusual decision by the Germans might mean and suspected that it was a sign the ghetto would soon be liquidated.

Later the same afternoon, Jacob and his coworkers returned to Kolejowa 18. When the SS officers entered the camp the following morning, Jacob saw that their "boots were caked with chunks of dry blood" and assumed the worst: "That was the last time we have seen our mother." Later, Jacob learned that most of the Radom ghetto had been "evacuated" and many of its inhabitants sent to Treblinka.

On January 13, 1943, Jacob and his brother Chaim were assigned as part of a carpentry detail to cover the windows of cattle cars with barbed wire and wood. Jacob and his coworkers had "no idea what these cars were used for." Later they discovered that they had helped build the transport trains for the second and final evacuation of the Radom ghetto. They only realized this fully when they saw the remainder of their "friends and family being herded onto them."

In the spring of 1944, six inmates managed to escape from Kolejowa 18, but another inmate informed on them and within minutes of their escape, the SS arrived with a German shepherd dog. The six men managed to elude the SS and made it all the way to the forest just outside of Radom. However, within a few days, Weitzman, one of the escapees, was back in Kolejowa 18. After interrogation and severe maltreatment, he was put back to work in the camp. He told the other inmates that as soon as he and the other escapees reached the forest, they were met by the *Armia Krajowa* (AK). The AK fired on the group of escapees the moment they realized that they were Jews. Weitzman was the sole escapee to avoid the bullets. No one else survived. Feeling that he could find no safety anywhere among the Poles, "he voluntarily had to come back to the concentration camp where he so-called found security. He did not survive." Jacob does not really know how the Polish civilian population regarded the treatment of Jews, but he will never forget that "when the *Aussiedlung* (deportation) of the ghetto took place, . . . many of the Poles were standing at the fence, waiting to get in [to the ghetto] in order to get whatever was left behind. I hear stories that some of the Poles had taken in some Jews in hiding, I personally have never encountered it while I was in Poland."

Jacob's brothers, the last members of his family, also worked at Kolejowa, and "we were each willing to risk our lives to save each other." The youngest, Elek, worked under a particularly ruthless SS corporal, Gumbinger, in the vegetable warehouse. One of his duties was to polish Gumbinger's boots before quitting work in the evening. One night, Gumbinger "being drunk as usual," had misplaced or lost his pack of cigarettes and asked Elek for his package. Elek said that he did not have any cigarettes and told Gumbinger to search him so that the latter might verify that Elek was telling the truth. However, "instead of searching, [Gumbinger] started to molest [Elek] by punching him in the face and kicking him in the shins." Elek, who knew that he might not survive this beating, opened the door and ran toward the inmates' quarters with Gumbinger chasing after him. Since Gumbinger was drunk, Elek managed to get away.

After supper, Gumbinger sounded an unscheduled *Appell*. Elek was terrified. Instead of joining the ranks, he insisted on remaining in hiding under the bunk bed. Jacob knew that if Elek did not appear at the roll call, a search would take place, and he could be shot for disobedience. He took Elek by the hand and promised that he would not allow Gumbinger to touch him. At the roll call, Gumbinger was "so drunk that he could barely open his eyes." Elek's name was the first one called, but Jacob stepped out of line in his stead and asked why Gumbinger called for his younger brother. Jacob was whipped in the face for insubordination and ordered to step back in line. Then the same scene was repeated twice. When Gumbinger raised the whip to beat Jacob the third time, Chaim (his older brother) grabbed the SS corporal's wrist, twisted the whip from out of his hand, and threw it over the barbed wire fence.

Within seconds "the chief of the guards appeared with two soldiers, guns ready to shoot." Gumbinger shouted that "they should join him in killing all the Jews." However, the chief guard realized that "he was dealing with a drunk," removed Gumbinger, and locked him out of the compound where the inmates lived.

The next day, Jacob saw Gumbinger accompany Chaim to a garage that "was known as the slaughterhouse because whoever was taken there came out as a cripple." Recognizing that his brother was in mortal danger, Jacob called out to Chaim and asked him to bring a pail of water. Chaim came into the carpentry shop to bring Jacob the water, and Gumbinger soon followed and began chasing Chaim about the shop with his whip. While his brother was running from the SS corporal, Jacob hurried to the office of *Staffscharführer* (staff sergeant) Lorenzen, who was in charge of the SS personnel and who had publicly ordered Gumbinger not to whip the Jewish laborers anymore. At first, Jacob did not manage to speak, but started to cry. Eventually, he explained all that had transpired to Lorenzen, and the two made their way back to the carpentry shop. Gumbinger was hiding around the corner of the office building and, unaware that Jacob was accompanied by the *Staffscharführer*, brought his whip down over Jacob's head. Lorenzen then took Gumbinger into his office. Soon afterward Gumbinger was transferred to the Russian front. The "punishment Gumbinger received was not for the love of the Jews by Lorenzen, but for disobeying his order—which was from a superior—not to use a whip." After this incident, another officer (Pitasch) warned Jacob that if he ever committed any infractions whatsoever, he would be decapitated.

In March of 1943, on "a very cold rainy day, with a strong easterly wind" he and a fellow inmate, Leon, left the shower room several minutes later than prescribed. Consequently, the SS guards took the two men to the front of the garage "known as the slaughterhouse" and ordered them to strip. Jacob tore off his clothes immediately. One of the guards began spraying Jacob with a powerful stream of extremely cold water from a fire hose. Jacob moved closer to the guard so that the water deflected by his body would hit the guard and make him wet. "The little Jews were expected to cringe, to cry out in pain, and to beg for the spectacle to stop." Jacob, however, made up his mind "there and then that under no circumstances would I as much as utter a sound, no matter what the consequences could be."

In the meantime, Leon pleaded with the second SS guard, asking for permission to remain in his underwear. In response, he was beaten with a metal-tipped leather whip. Soon after, Leon joined Jacob under the stream of cold water. Under the shock of the cold, Leon "lost control of himself" and started to plead and beg with the SS to stop. The SS guards then resumed whipping him, as well as Jacob. Next, Jacob and Leon were handed the sort of steel brushes used to remove caked up clay from military trucks, and ordered to rub each other with the brushes. Jacob made sure to apply the brush to Leon with little pressure and always on different parts of his body. Jacob pleaded with Leon to do the same, but Leon, who was still out of control, did not hear him even "as the water washing off my body became red." "All of this did not give the sadistic guard the desired satisfaction" and the beatings resumed once more, this time accompanied by shouts to rub harder. Jacob "surely felt each lash of the whip, but I felt no pain. My will to survive became innate, wishing to have the opportunity to repay [the SS guards] in kind one day. Several weeks later, I could still only lie on my stomach as a result of the lashes on my wet body. I swelled up like a balloon. The radial bone on my right wrist was broken while I had been trying to protect my face from the whip. The left shoulder joint was injured and I could hardly use that shoulder for several weeks."

Reading from the text he prepared before the interview, Jacob says, "examining this event in retrospect, the reason I felt no pain when I was whipped was due . . . to the fact that at times reality is not what it is but what one makes it to be. They had taken away my freedom, killed most of my family, taken away all of my possessions. I was forced to do heavy labor with a bare minimum of food. I was exposed to different abuses and indignities. However, the one thing they could not deprive me of—they could not take away my inner self, my integrity, and my inner freedom of action."

As the Russian army advanced in the middle of 1944, Jacob and the other laborers were sent from Kolejowa to Szkolna. They remained there for three weeks as the Russians continued their advance toward Germany. After the Russian army captured Lublin, everyone at Szkolna, roughly 3,000 men, women, and children, were forced to march to Tomaszow, where the Germans separated the men from the women and children. Three days later, the whole group was loaded up into cattle cars and taken to Auschwitz. This time, all those who were unable to perform manual labor—mostly children and the elderly—were taken away to the gas chambers. "The children and the older people knew where they were going," although for some reason the others did not. Jacob was stunned when he overheard a particular six-year old boy, who turned to face the other children and said " 'don't cry, our parents which are standing there don't know where we are going, let them think we will still be alive.' "

That very evening, the healthy men were loaded up into cattle cars again, headed for a work camp, called Vaihingen, near Stuttgart. At the new camp, Jacob was put to work on the night shift, building an underground ammunition factory that was to be invisible from the air. Here Jacob had contact with some non-Jewish forced laborers. He had fallen ill with diarrhea and knew that this "was one of the symptoms that within a day or two you was a goner." That night, an alarm sounded and he lined up next to a non-Jewish Belgian laborer. The Belgian man saw that Jacob was weak and prompted Jacob to tell him about the diarrhea. "He said 'why don't you take some sugar, that will stop the diarrhea.' I said 'where should I take sugar?' He said 'wait, I'll get it for you.' He brought me a half glass of sugar, which saved my life."

After his shift one morning, Jacob saw his two brothers lined up in a group destined for another nearby camp. He did not want to be separated from his brothers because "I knew that neither I nor they had an opportunity to survive if we were separated." He pleaded with one of the Jewish *Kapos* to join his brothers and the *Kapo* consented after Jacob gave him his daily portion of bread. In late October 1944, Jacob and his brothers were transferred to Hessenthal. While he was in Germany, Jacob did not have any contact with the civilian population. None of the civilians made any attempt to help the Jews or showed compassion toward them, but this might have been due to the fact that "they were not allowed to come close to us either."

In early April 1945, Jacob heard rumors that he would soon have to leave Hessenthal. The next day, he and the other Jewish laborers were loaded into cattle cars again after standing all night in the rain. While they were in transit, the train was first shot at and then bombed by unsuspecting allied fighter planes. Two bombs exploded beside Jacob's car. The car was completely torn apart, and the survivors had a chance to get out. When the fighter planes were gone, the SS got all the other prisoners off the train and captured those who had escaped. They shot and killed all the weak and the injured before forcing the rest of the group to march to Dachau, a journey that took a week.

Jacob remained in Dachau for two or three weeks before the SS loaded them onto cattle cars once more. This time, they were being taken further south, "in order to finish us off." He goes on to say, "The day before the liberation a miracle happened which was death in disguise. The Red Cross, for the first time, was permitted to hand out food parcels to Jewish inmates. Starved people opened the parcels, opened one can [of food] after another, containing pork, others condensed milk, and within hours they had diarrhea. People were dying *en masse*." Fortunately, Jacob and his brothers were careful not to eat too much, saving the contents of their packages for several days. This allowed them to avoid the others' dismal fate. Reading from his prepared text, Jacob says,

> In transit, one morning we looked out of the cattle cars and we see black people. I have never in my life seen a black person. They were hiding in

the forest. And sure enough, within an hour they took all the SS that guarded us, they took the ammunition away from them, and we were free people. My two brothers stepped down from the wagon and went to the front of the train in order to get some food. Although I have seen that I am liberated, somehow I didn't think that this applies to me. I was sitting in the car—nothing interested me until my brothers came back with a loaf of bread. This was our dream, to have a loaf of bread that you can slice and eat to your heart's content. And somehow that brought life into me.

Jacob did not accompany his brothers. Before the war he had fallen in love. He had managed to keep a picture of his girlfriend, Bela, with him, sewn into his pants. Jacob decided to remain in Germany and search for Bela. At one point, he traveled all the way to Bergen-Belsen near the northern coast of Germany on the roofs of electric trains, hoping he might find her there. Although he did manage to locate a number of women from Radom,

Jacob G. in Mittenwald, 1946

they could not even tell him if his fiancée was still alive. Disappointed, he returned to Feldafing.

There Jacob met a man who was on his way back to Radom. He showed the man the photo of his fiancée and said "if you ever see this girl—this is her name—tell her that I am alive in Germany." A few months later, Jacob found himself working as a server in the American Officer's Mess at Mittenwald. "One afternoon, a certain Captain walked in and said 'Jacob, I arrested your girlfriend.' I said 'what are you talking about, I have no girl-friend.' He said 'you don't believe me?' I said, 'No, I haven't got any.' 'Hop into the jeep.' I hopped into the jeep. We come down to the jail. There was my fiancée and her sister."

Bela had left Radom because she received the message that he was alive in Southern Germany. The day before she left, the Polish army had killed a newly wedded Jewish couple with the same surname as Jacob, an event that persuaded her to give up the idea of living in Poland. Jacob married Bela in Mittenwald in January 1946. Within less than three years, the two immigrated to Montreal, where they still live today.

>⋈< >⋈< >⋈<

Israel B.
June 18, 1992

Israel B. gives a detailed account of life in the two ghettos of the city of Radom. One of five children, he survived the Aktion *during which his parents and three siblings were seized and sent to Treblinka. Israel spent much of the war in Pionki, where munitions for the German war machine were manufactured. He was then deported to several other camps. Following his liberation by the American Army he learned he was the only one of his family to survive the war.*

Israel was born on September 7, 1921, in Radom, Poland. Israel's parents, Rafael and Simla, operated their own small tailoring business out of the two-room apartment on Slowa Street. He is the second of five children: Joseph, Israel, Abraham, Chavah, and Menachem. At age five he began attending *cheder*. At age nine he enrolled at Berek Joselewicz, an all-Jewish public school. There he learned German, a subject that would prove useful later on.

Israel remembers striking indicators of Polish anti-Semitism. Once, a Catholic priest intervened in one of the frequent attacks Israel received from

Catholic Polish boys on his way to school. The priest told Israel's attacker: "If you don't behave, we will sell you to the Jews for use as matzos." The priest was referring to the so-called "blood libel," the ancient and persistent belief that Jews use the blood of Christian children for religious purposes during the preparation of the Passover seder. The priest's words left Israel in a state of shock. He realized for the first time that, in the eyes of most Poles, Jews were worse than second-class citizens.

Israel points out that Jews in Poland were "citizens" only in so much as they paid taxes like everybody else. In every other sense they were not recognized as full or equal members of society. Jews were not allowed to occupy government positions in Poland, and only limited numbers of Jews could enroll in universities. And even then Jews had to sit to the sides of the classroom.

At the time of his graduation in 1935, Israel was about thirteen years old. He entered an apprenticeship with another tailor, and remained away from the family business for two years. During that time, Israel worked without pay from 8 a.m. to 6 p.m., six days a week. After his apprenticeship, he returned to work with his parents and older brother. He notes that there was a growing tension between Jews and Poles, and he increasingly tried to avoid his non-Jewish neighbors.

On September 1, 1939, the day of the German invasion of Poland, a bomb exploded on the train tracks near Israel's neighborhood, shaking his family home. The family decided to evacuate to his mother's hometown of Kazanow, twenty-five kilometers from Radom, where they stayed with his mother's older sister. However, when German tanks entered Kazanow and the town was occupied, they decided to return to Radom, traveling by horse and wagon.

German soldiers stopped the family and arrested Israel and one of his brothers. Along with a few hundred others, the two brothers were put on trucks headed to Kielce. There they were confined to horse stables, without food, for approximately three days. They were then given a bit of soup and a piece of bread.

Some of the inmates received packages of food from their local relatives. Israel, who did not know anyone from the large Jewish community in Kielce, once obtained a package that had gone unclaimed by its intended recipient. After two weeks, Israel and the other prisoners were released, and they were allowed to go home. He and his brother returned to Radom on foot. The journey took two days. They spent the night in an abandoned house.

Back in Radom, German soldiers came looking for Jews to take them for work. Poles often pointed out to the soldiers who was Jewish. At the work site to which Israel was taken as a day laborer, the men had to perform useless tasks such as moving stones from one place to another. Some of the men were beaten, and there was at least one death every day. During this period, Israel's brother Joseph left Radom and escaped to Russian-occupied territory, leaving Israel the eldest child in the household.

In 1940, Israel's family received an expulsion order. With all the other Jews of Radom, they were forced to move into the ghetto. Since there was not enough space in the larger or Walowa Street ghetto, they had to move into the small (Glinice) ghetto. Several families were assigned to a single house without indoor plumbing. Water had to be brought up one pail at a time, and instead of a modern toilet, they had a little hut at the back of the house. When the family moved to the small ghetto, they were able to bring the tools of their trade along with them, including the sewing machine and pressing iron.

Initially, the inhabitants were allowed to move freely between the large and small ghettos. After some months, the ghettos were closed, fenced in, and placed under constant Polish and German surveillance. All Jews were forced to wear a white armband with a blue Star of David on their right arm. The Jewish ghetto police escorted all Jews who worked outside the ghetto, including Israel, who worked for a short time in a munitions factory just outside Radom. Shortly before the ghetto was closed, Israel's brother Joseph returned from the Russian side because he had heard that there was less hunger in German occupied territory.

However, there was little to eat in the ghetto after it was closed. Israel, facing starvation, decided he would risk leaving the ghetto: "I said, 'Just go, what's the difference, if I am going to die here or die outside?' I decided to leave the ghetto and go out to work, where I didn't know." He found a job in the fields of a *Volksdeutsch* village about six kilometers outside Radom, where he communicated using the German he had learned in school. The German villagers knew he was Jewish. They paid him with potatoes, bread, and butter.

For at least two months, each Monday morning Israel removed his blue-and-white armband and left the ghetto. He returned by side-roads on Friday evenings with the food that he had earned. He replaced his armband only when he was near the ghetto. This routine was risky, because the German police summarily shot any Jew they apprehended outside the ghetto, and there was a persistent rumor that any Polish person who caught a Jew outside the ghetto, and handed him over to the Germans, would get a reward of sugar and whiskey.

In order to enter the ghetto, Israel had to pass by the Jewish police guards, who did not wear uniforms, but were recognizable by their special armbands, their hats bearing a star, and the wooden sticks they carried. Israel recounts an incident where a Jewish police officer caught him sneaking back into the ghetto. The policeman demanded food from Israel's bag of provisions. When Israel refused, a loud argument ensued which drew a number of Jewish onlookers. At the sight of the gathering crowd, the police officer "got scared and he let me go."

On another occasion, while Israel walked through the fields on the way back to the ghetto, a group of Poles spotted him. They trapped him, saying, "here's a Jew: we're going to get a kilo of sugar and a bottle of whiskey." The Poles thought that an approaching uniformed *Volksdeutscher* was a German policeman and wanted to hand Israel over to him. Fortunately the

Volksdeutscher was from the village where Israel worked and recognized him. The *Volksdeutscher* took him away from the Poles, and escorted him back into the ghetto. Commenting on this incident, Israel points out that survival was not a matter of being smart, or doing something extraordinary, but of luck. He survived because the man knew him. In any other circumstances, he would have been handed over to the Germans and killed.

In spite of the acute danger, Israel went on working outside the ghetto for several more weeks: "duty was calling, there was hunger, I had to go." However, a few weeks later he heard that a group of eleven or twelve-year-old children from the ghetto who begged for bread were caught by the German villagers and killed on the spot. He never returned to the village again.

In 1941, Israel was taken to work outside the ghetto in a German military factory that manufactured rifles. He received a special *Ausweis* (permit) to leave and come back, but still had to be escorted to and from work every day. Meanwhile the situation in the ghetto deteriorated rapidly. Large numbers of people died from starvation: "the children, all the people in the street, there wasn't enough time to bury them. . . . It was desperate. . . . I saw it, I saw it every day."

In August 1942, the Germans liquidated the smaller Glinice ghetto, and deported Israel's whole family to Treblinka. Israel was at work in the factory at the time and therefore was unaware of the deportation. Afterward he managed to escape to the larger ghetto and hide. One night two weeks later, Jewish police and Germans came knocking on the doors, ordering everyone outside. When Israel showed a German soldier his work permit for the factory, he was taken along with a group of others to one street of the ghetto. There they remained until the liquidation had passed. At this point the Germans deported nearly all of the ghetto's inhabitants to Treblinka to be killed.

The liquidation of the large (Walowa) ghetto, in August 1942, took two entire days. Israel remembers one incident especially well, because it illustrates the relationship between Poles and Jews. During the first night, while the Jews were still being rounded up, a large crowd of Polish people stood outside the ghetto's gate. Israel, who was part of a crew of Jewish cleanup workers, was working in close proximity to the crowd at this gate. He saw and heard the Poles shouting and screaming that the Jews should be removed sooner so that they could enter and loot their homes right away.

Some time after the liquidation, during the second half of August, Israel was caught by the Jewish police, taken to a location outside the ghetto, and given a shovel. Along with other surviving Jews, he was forced to dig a large hole, and told to make it as deep as they could. Soon, wagons full of bodies arrived, pulled or pushed by other Jews. Israel had to lay the bodies sideways so that they would fit in the mass grave. Israel remembers a woman and her three children who had been caught hiding outside the ghetto. When they were caught, the Germans took them to the edge of the grave and shot them in the head; "we had to bury them."

It is not true, Israel says, that Jews "went like sheep to the slaughterhouse." As witnesses to atrocities, they were systematically weakened in body and mind, over a long period. "When we went to the slaughterhouse, we had no other choice. We were so weak, we just didn't care any more. They brought us to such a stage from 1939 to 1942." He explains that everyone's spirit was broken to the point where resistance was no longer possible; hunger was an everyday reality and no one knew what would happen next.

A few weeks later, Jewish policemen inside the ghetto rounded up Israel and a group of other Jews. They were taken by military truck to a gunpowder factory in Pionki, thirty kilometers from Radom. The factory was guarded by Ukrainians in uniform, and managed by German civilians and officers. Israel worked in the furnace room, unloading coal from wagons and shoveling it into the ovens.

Sometimes the wagons contained not coal but alcohol, which was used in manufacturing gunpowder. Using homemade metal canisters, Israel started stealing the commercial alcohol, in order to trade it for bread. He hid these canisters in a heap of coal that he could access inside the furnace room; later he smuggled them past the Ukrainian guards. "I was lucky, I wasn't caught," he says. Those who were discovered smuggling the alcohol into their living quarters were hanged, while everybody else had to stand and watch. "That didn't stop me: I was still doing it," Israel says. He developed his own method, by bringing home a large container filled with soup (which passed the inspection), and hiding the smaller canisters inside. One day his method nearly failed him when he noticed the canisters floating to the surface. At the very last moment, he bent down and picked up some stones, which he placed on top of the small containers so they would sink. "This is the way I went through," he exclaims with a big smile, adding, "You see, it's a matter of survival." Then he grows more serious and says, "Believe you me, as much as we can laugh now, it wasn't a laughing matter."

At first, there were only a few hundred Jews in Pionki. Later, other prisoners were transferred there from ghettos and other camps, including Krakow and Theresienstadt, as more and more workers were needed for the manufacturing of munitions. By the end of 1944, the population numbered over three thousand.

Israel says that people assigned to the final stages of the gunpowder making process used to sabotage their work by leaving the material in for so long that it ignited. In the process, the saboteurs often seriously burned themselves. Israel explains that this sabotage was not organized, but the result of individual initiatives.

Jews who escaped the camp were killed when caught. This occurred on a number of occasions, but Israel did not witness any such executions, for they took place outside the camp. If any escapees managed to elude the Germans, they ran the risk of being killed by the partisans of the AK (*Armia Krajowa*), the Polish Home Army who, according to Israel, would "shoot Jews first and Germans second."

Toward the summer of 1944, the prisoners working in the factory began to hear shooting. Israel learned from the Polish factory workers that after the Battle of Stalingrad the Russians had begun to push the Germans back. As a result, their guards (both the Germans and the Ukrainians) became if not more friendly, at least more humane. However, the Russian advance stopped short at the Vistula River, five to six kilometers east of Pionki.

During the summer, nearly all of the 3,000 factory workers were sent on cattle cars to Auschwitz. Israel and approximately 300 young men remained behind to prepare the machinery for transport back to Germany. These men were taken to the city of Czestochowa by train, which derailed during the trip. Israel heard gunshots, and the German soldier who was guarding the prisoners told them: "Listen, . . . it's the AK. If they find out you are here, they're going to kill you all." In Czestochowa, the prisoners dug trenches to hold off the Russian advance. When the trenches were done, the men were put on a train to Sachsenhausen, a concentration camp near Oranienburg, not far from Berlin.

Upon arrival in Sachsenhausen, the men were divided into groups and taken to a room where they were stripped of their clothing. Israel was still wearing the same civilian clothes he wore in Radom. As he was forced to undress, he had to give up the family photographs he had managed to keep with him. Israel was ushered into a second room where a barber cut and shaved off all of his body hair. In a third room there were showers. He had heard about the showers of Auschwitz: " 'Now we are finished,' we said to each other. But fortunately for us, water came down." He was given a striped uniform with a Star of David made up of a red and a green triangle on the back. His number was 94690, and was shown on the front and on the back. His block consisted of the 300 Jewish men from Pionki.

In Sachsenhausen, Israel noticed that a block near his own barracks (his barracks was part of block 53) was fenced in with barbed wire. The prisoners inside received better treatment and more food. He found out that they were "artists" who were forging foreign currency—British pounds and U.S. dollars.

At the end of 1944, the prisoners were taken to clean up after the bombardments in and around the camp. The Americans bombed in the daytime, and the British bombed at night. Israel recalls standing outside, counting the number of planes in a passing squadron, while the SS took shelter inside. "We were laughing," he remembers.

After a few weeks, Israel was taken to Glewen, where he unloaded the machines he had previously prepared for transport in Pionki. To his amazement, he even found a couple of the canisters filled with alcohol, which he had put inside one of the machines in Pionki, while loading it.

He remained in Glewen until the Russians approached, at which point he was transferred back to Sachsenhausen, where he stayed until April 1945. When he returned to Sachsenhausen, Israel saw that the block that had housed the "artists" was empty. Someone from another block told him that the artists had all been taken away and killed.

At one point in April 1945, Israel looked out of a small window and saw some Red Cross trucks arriving. They brought food, but Israel did not get any. At another time he "sold" his daily piece of bread for a package of tobacco. However, his newly purchased treasure contained nothing but sawdust: "I was crying like a baby," he says.

Around April 20, 1945, Israel heard many shots fired. The prisoners were lined up in rows and marched out of Sachsenhausen that same day. Armed German guards forced the prisoners to run. "Whoever did not have enough strength to run was killed on the spot." That night they slept in the woods. The next morning they had to run again, with the German guards, some on foot and some on bicycles, chasing them west. This went on for more than a week, until around May 1. Their hunger was acute. Only once or twice did the Germans give the prisoners pieces of bread; mostly they ate whatever they could find along the road. While on the run, Israel was able to dig up some potatoes once or twice. Although he passed through villages, nobody ever offered him any food.

On the second or third morning of the march, Israel woke up to see prisoners lying dead or "half dying" with flesh removed from their upper thighs. He believes that Russian prisoners from Sachsenhausen had cut pieces of flesh from some of the sleeping people in order to feed themselves. In so doing, Israel notes, the Russians did not kill them. After Israel and the rest of ten or twelve companions became aware of this apparent cannibalism, they took turns standing guard while the others slept.

A truck with two German soldiers sitting in the front drove up beside the prisoners. Israel sensed that there was food in the truck and so ran over, removed the cover from the back, and discovered that the truck was full of bread. He took a loaf back to his companions. Soon the prisoners all rushed over and began to grab the bread. Israel overheard one of the German soldiers in the truck asking the other, "Why don't you shoot?" "I'm afraid," was the other's reply. At this point, Israel began to feel that "something had changed." His belief was confirmed when, on May 2, he heard a German soldier say, in German, "the war is over. Hitler is dead."

The news of Hitler's death emboldened Israel. The next time they passed through a village, he went into one of the houses. He took a big pot of food off the stove and went out. A German soldier was right beside him, but he did not say anything. He shared it with his companions, because everybody was hungry. They were still not liberated.

On May 3, near the German village of Schwerin, a jeep full of American soldiers passed by. One of the soldiers spoke Polish, and explained to the prisoners that they were liberated. "I sat down on a big stone on the road and I started to cry," remembers Israel. "I said to myself, 'I am liberated. For whom? Who do I have now?' I knew all my family was gone; there was nobody left."

In Schwerin, the Americans placed the prisoners in military barracks formerly occupied by the Germans. The Americans gave the prisoners only bread and soup on the first day, and would not let them leave the barracks.

Israel B., age twenty-six, in Stuttgart, 1947

Israel tried to get out, but was told to go back. Gradually, the Americans increased the prisoners' daily food ration. Israel realized later that the Americans did so to prevent the prisoners from overeating and getting sick or dying. In Bergen-Belsen, thousands had died from overeating.

Because Schwerin was supposed to be in the Eastern zone under Russian occupation, the Americans moved Israel's group to Lübeck, the closest place outside the Russian zone, which was under British administration. They were given a place to stay and were fed. But for weeks after the liberation, Israel still carried a sack of potatoes on his shoulder: "I said to myself, 'who knows what will be tomorrow?'" Some of the men left for Poland. Israel did not go back to Radom. He has never had any desire to go back there, not even when he visited other countries in Europe, long after the war had ended.

Israel stayed in a "nice, clean white house" in Schwerin. Through two girls who were also staying there, Israel met his future wife, Tziporah. She was originally from Drobin, a town near Plonsk, and had survived three years in Auschwitz. They were married in January 1946, in the old synagogue of Lübeck. For the celebration, Israel found a restaurant and planned the menu, which included meat and fish. He also hired an orchestra. A friend made the "whiskey."

One day in January 1946, a man came to Lübeck and told Israel that many Jews from Radom were living in Stuttgart. Israel and Tziporah immediately agreed to go there. Due to damaged rail lines, it was a week before they reached Stuttgart, where Israel saw many people he knew from Radom, including a cousin and his wife. Israel's cousin told him that Joseph, Israel's older brother, had died two or three weeks before the liberation in a camp not

Israel as a volunteer policeman for UNRRA, 1947

far from Stuttgart. Israel's parents, together with his two younger brothers Abraham and Menachem, and sister Chavah, were all killed in Treblinka.

Israel's daughter was born in Stuttgart on January 6, 1947. She was one of the first children born to the survivor community there. Meanwhile, Israel did not want to stay in Germany. He was a Zionist and wanted to live in Palestine, but he was told that the situation there would make it impossible for him to go with a wife and a newborn child. During the summer of 1947, a commission that included representatives from Canadian Jewish Congress, the Manufacturing Association, and the needle-trade union, arrived in Stuttgart looking for tailors. Israel passed the examination, and at the end of 1947, he and his family received Canadian visas. They departed by boat from Bremerhaven on January 6, 1948, the date of his daughter's first birthday, arriving in Halifax and continuing to Montreal by train. He worked in the needle trade and subsequently as a taxi driver. His sons, born in 1950 and 1956, both graduated from the McGill University Faculty of Medicine, and work as a rheumatologist and a hematologist, respectively. His daughter runs a business, together with her husband. At the time of the interview, Israel and his wife Tziporah had six grandchildren.

≫✺≼ ≫✺≼ ≫✺≼

Paul L.
November 12 and 19, 1991

While trying to escape from Paris to the unoccupied zone of France, Paul and his brother Jacques were captured by the Germans. Paul, who believes that it was "humanly impossible to survive," thinks it was a miracle that he lived through the almost three years between his capture and his liberation.

Paul was born in Poland on August 5, 1922, but moved with his family to Paris in 1926. Because he had moved to France when he was so young, Paul thought of himself as a Frenchman rather than an immigrant. He was the youngest of Mendel and Yenta's three sons. There were also three sisters. In the early years, Paul's family had an apartment without a drain in the kitchen, so that they used a pail to throw water from their balcony; but later they lived in an apartment in the beautiful Marais district of Paris, in the fourth arrondissement, not far from the Jewish district.

His father Mendel, who had a long, unshorn beard down to his waist, was often addressed as "Monsieur le Rabbin" even though he was not a rabbi; he was a *mo'el* and a *shochet*. The family was traditionally religious and observed all holidays. Paul explains that this religious upbringing helped to give him "courage and hope" when he later saw people killed in the camps. Despite everything, he continued to believe in God: he participated in secret prayer services in camp, and said *kaddish* for his brother when he died in 1943.

Paul was seventeen on September 3, 1939 when France declared war on Germany. Paul remembers that as the Germans approached Paris, on June 10, 1940, the French government radio told all young men to flee the city, in order to resist the Germans on the Loire River. Paul and one of his brothers left by tandem bicycle in the middle of the night, along with thousands of others who were on bicycle or on foot. They encountered bombing on the road near Nogent-le-Rotrou, about fifty kilometers southeast of Paris. Paul and his brother jumped into a ditch and survived.

The Germans occupied Paris on June 14, 1940. Shortly after June 25, when Marshal Pétain signed the armistice, Paul and his brother returned to Paris to live with their two unmarried sisters and their widowed mother, Yenta. Paul's father had died in March of that year, three months before the Germans entered Paris. Paul remembers that in June and July 1940, people said the Germans "are not that bad . . . It's not like in Poland": synagogues were still open, and Jews still had freedom of movement in the city. Furthermore, being forced to carry a *carte d'identité* was not a new policy for citizens in France. Jews even read *Aujourd'hui*, a Nazi paper distributed in France, and some recommended it as "a good paper." For Paul, this is how the Germans gradually "[got] the people caught in the system."

In the fall of 1940, Jews had to register at the police station and had *Juif* stamped on their ID cards. Once this happened, Paul explains, "you could not escape the system." A few months later, Jews had to hand over their radios to the police so that they could no longer listen to "Free France" and other Allied radio programs from London. By 1942, Jews in Paris were required to wear a yellow star on their clothing and keep an 8 p.m. curfew and they were restricted to the last car on the subway. Paul remembers that he and his friends used to carry briefcases in order to hide the yellow star so that they did not have to abide the restriction to ride in the last car. Paul also describes a sense of fear: you never knew who your enemy was.

In May 1941, the Germans sent postcards ordering the Polish Jews of Paris to present themselves to the police for verification of their identity, and to bring a blanket. "For verification of identity, I didn't see the use of a blanket," thought Paul, so he and his family did not go. Paul's worst suspicions proved true when the Nazis created the first internment camps, Pithivier and Beaune-La-Rolande. The people who did go for verification

Paul L. (right) with his brother Jacques in Nice, January 1942

were taken there, and some of them remained for up to a year. At this time, Paul hid at a friend's apartment.

In November–December 1941, the Nazis began arresting eminent French Jewish people. They sent them to a third internment camp, Compiègne. According to Paul, they wanted to prove that no Jew would be protected by the so-called French government. In the fall of 1941, when the underground resistance killed a German soldier in the streets, fifty Jews were shot in retaliation. A sign was posted as a warning, listing the names of all the people who had been killed, including Mr. Jolles, Paul's friend's father. When the first arrests of women and children took place on July 16, 1942, Paul says the people knew that the Germans intended to do in France what they had done elsewhere in Europe. Paul refers to that day in July as "the darkest day for the Jews of Paris."

Paul and his family evaded the arrests by leaving their home in Paris. They went into hiding with his brother, Jacques, who rented an apartment ten to fifteen miles away from Paris on the river Seine. During this period, Paul felt that it "could not happen to us," a feeling that allowed him to maintain some optimism. It also allowed him to feel safe and gave him a reason to live: "If you think it is going to be the end of the world, you don't survive."

On the other hand, Paul was safer than others because he had no accent, his name created no suspicion, and, as early as 1941, he had a false identity card, bought by his brother from the police, bearing the name Paul Laurent. This card was what Paul describes as a "false true" card: "false because it is not yours but true because someone has this name somewhere." Paul Laurent, for instance, was born in a little village in Northern France.

During the summer of 1942, Paul's family decided to go to Vichy, the unoccupied zone of France. The family paid for Paul's mother, Yenta, and the youngest daughter Rachel to be smuggled to Lyon in a secret compartment in a forty-foot long trailer bringing food from Vichy to Paris. Paul's older sisters Feiga and Fanny (who was married) made it to Lyon by crossing the border on foot. Fanny hid her two daughters in a convent not far from Lyon. Paul's brother Leon, along with his wife and child, survived the war in Auvergne. They stayed in Aurillac, a village in the Cantal County. Leon joined the resistance and returned to find his family in Paris in 1945.

On September 8, 1942, Paul and his brother Jacques attempted to cross the border into unoccupied France so that they could join their mother and sisters in Lyon. Near Tours, a German-French patrol checked their IDs and allowed them to pass. The guards walked away, then changed their minds and apprehended Paul and Jacques, who were then brought to the police station for further verification of their IDs. Paul and Jacques were separated and beaten. From the next room, Paul could hear his brother calling out "dis oui," (say yes), admit that you are Jewish. For twelve days, they were jailed in Vierzon and in Orléans, and subsequently deported to Pithiviers, where they remained for only two or three days. On Yom Kippur, September 20, Paul, Jacques, and about one thousand other men, women, and children were locked into cattle cars. Barbed wire blocked the train's tiny windows. At the time he did not know the transport (convoy number 35) was destined for Auschwitz.

On the way, Jacques thought they should escape, but because Germans had told the prisoners that ten people would be shot for every one that escaped, the other prisoners prevented them from doing so. After three days, the train stopped in Eichtal in Poland's Upper Silesia. About 150 men between the ages of fifteen and fifty were taken out and sent to work at a small camp. The train went on to Auschwitz without Paul and Jacques. The camp leader in Eichtal yelled at them on the day of their arrival saying that if they did not work they would be sent to a camp where, "you go in through the gate and you come out through the chimney." Paul did not understand what this meant.

At Eichtal, Paul and Jacques worked on the expressways for the Deutsche Autobahn system for two weeks, and were then transferred to Kochanowitz, a forced labor camp in Upper Silesia, which belonged to the German railroads. Paul, Jacques, and about 400 to 500 men worked building additional railroad tracks for the war effort. They carried railway rails, built bridges, and shoveled sand. Paul recalls being beaten for "sabotaging" when he could not throw shovelfuls of sand the right way. After three months of extremely difficult labor, Paul could hardly walk any more. After a full day's work on the railroad, the prisoners had to work on building the camp, where there was no electricity and everything had to be done in the dark.

"There is more than physical suffering," Paul says of camp life. He describes the pain of quarrelling with others, including his own brother, over a slice of bread, a spoonful of soup, or who would have to empty the urination pail in the middle of the night. His brother Jacques, who had said to Paul "So what, we are strong. So we work. We work until the end of the war," contracted pneumonia and died on May 14, 1943. He was buried without a coffin.

In June 1943, the camp was evacuated so it could become a rehabilitation camp for German soldiers. The inmates were transported to Borsigwerk and continued work on the railroad. The summer fortified Paul. He also received some extra food from people who pitied his loss of Jacques, Paul's brother and constant companion. As fall came, Paul feared the consequences of another winter at the camp. He remembered his brother had said, "If the war is not over before the winter, we will have to escape, we have no chance to survive." Paul began to accumulate clothing. Other inmates thought escaping was crazy and without his brother, Paul felt hesitant and alone. Despite this, he set a deadline. On Tuesday November 23, 1943 at 1 p.m., Paul walked into a cement barrack and hid in the corner. At the end of the day, the prisoners were counted in lines of five; his absence was noticed, but Paul was not found.

When it was dark, Paul smuggled himself onto a train marked "Gleiwitz" with open wagons containing sacks of coal dust. The train stopped in Gleiwitz at 3 or 4 a.m. in the morning. A German working for the

Bahnschutzpolizei (railway police) shone his lantern right in Paul's face: "this was the end of my freedom." Having previously obtained false papers from some Dutch workers which said he was Jean Charles Tosti, from the camp Konigshute, Paul spoke to the man in German, pretended to be a free French worker who wanted an evening off to see women in the city, and tried to convince the German that all he had done wrong was travel without paying. At the police station in Gleiwitz, nobody believed him. He was taken by streetcar—ironically marked *Für Juden verboten* (Jews not allowed)—to Gleiwitz's town jail. Because he fit the description of a runaway, he was interrogated and beaten. Paul "threw in the towel," admitted he was Jewish, and gave them his true name.

Instead of being returned to the camp police and hung in front of all the prisoners, Paul was detained by the railroad security police. He believes that the railroad police wanted to take the credit for arresting a Jewish escapee. Paul was put in a filthy cell with nine other people, most of who slept on the vermin infested floor. Repulsed, Paul asked to be placed elsewhere. A guard complied, taking him to a "beautiful" cell with other Frenchmen who slept on a cage bed and played cards. The next day, when Paul included "Israel" between his first and last name, which the Nazis insisted that all Jews do, the guard said, "You didn't tell me you were Jewish." Paul was sent back down to his original dirty cell. For Paul, this was still a vast improvement over working outside in a camp.

In jail, Paul's interrogators wanted to know who had helped him escape. They stripped him and found money he had hidden in his clothes, earned from selling half rations of bread. Paul remembers being told, "You aren't like the other Jews, you have guts, you deserve to go free." They wanted him to prove himself by fighting a strong German guard. When Paul refused, they mocked him saying, "You're just a coward like the rest of them." Paul explains this was a tactic "to diminish you."

Paul remained in the Gleiwitz jail until December 6. He and fifteen others were then taken on a truck to Auschwitz. An orchestra played at the gate. At Auschwitz, Paul's group was held in the shower room for twenty-four hours without food. Later, an inmate tattooed Paul's arm with the number 167307, which was inscribed crookedly because Paul, in reaction to the pain, kept pulling his arm away. Paul had to quickly learn to recognize his number when it was said in Polish. He was stripped, shaved, and put in quarantine block B. Paul recognized someone he knew, one of the barbers, who told him that if he ever wanted soup to go to him in block 4-A. Paul did so later, only to discover that he had to share the soup with the guard at the gate, which he passed on his way back to his barrack. A friend, Szlama Lefkowicz, solved this dilemma by helping Paul bring in the soup without going past the main gate.

Paul was in quarantine in Auschwitz for seven weeks, until January 20, 1944. His time in prison and in quarantine gave Paul a break from work and he became "more normal."

He was given a jacket with the letters "IL," standing for "*in Lager*," on his sleeve. Because his past escape was not yet known in Auschwitz, Paul did not yet have the red mark painted on his chest and back that signified his status as an escapee, and served as a target for the guards. That same day, on orders from Himmler, the loudspeakers proclaimed that 2,000 were to be killed. Paul was sent for the selection. The prisoners were stripped and had to carry their clothes over their right arm as they passed in front of a "so-called doctor." An SS man copied down the numbers of those selected to be gassed, and then all the prisoners were sent back to their barracks. Fortunately, Paul passed the inspection, but those whose numbers had been taken down were "dead people walking around with us." Paul reflects on the sadism of this: "I think if you want to kill someone, kill him, don't make him wait forty-eight hours or more." During the night, some of these men committed suicide by jumping from second floor windows.

Three days later, some of the inmates were told to stay out after *Appell*. They thought they were going to be taken to work in the coal mines, but instead they were lined up in front of *Stubenführer* Bernhard Krüger from the security department of the RSHA (*Reichssicherheitshauptamt*), the Reich's "spy and counter spy" service. Krüger chose fifty-five people, including Paul, who were put in a separate barrack. The next morning, Paul and the other fifty-four men left by train for Berlin, and were brought to Oranienburg-Sachsenhausen, a concentration camp of 16,000. Paul was given the new prisoner number of 75204. The fifty-five men were put in quarantine in barrack 19, "a secret barrack, and a camp within a camp." The group was told they were to join block 18, which had barbed wire around it, but nobody knew what it was all about.

The quarantine lasted until April, and being kept inside during the winter meant that Paul recovered somewhat. In April, blocks 18 and 19 merged. Both barracks were surrounded by barbed wire so that contact with the rest of the camp was impossible. One building housed 140 people, including the sixteen SS guards who belonged to the *Sicherheitsdienst* and lived together with the prisoners, while the other building was a printing shop to counterfeit foreign currency and documents. Some of the men working on the project called *Operation Bernhard* had been convicted counterfeiters before the war.

The operation had been successfully forging British pounds and was working to also perfect the forgery of American dollars. The project also falsified French *cartes d'identité* needed for German spies, baccalaureates from the Université de Lyon, receipts for payment of insurance from the Compagnie L'Urbain, declaration of change of domicile papers, papers for the evacuation of civilians from Brittany, and "little red cards" for the NKVD. Paul adds that at the end of the war they had a box of passport stamps for every South American country, and he speculates this is why many Nazis could escape there after the war. They also produced booklets for German spies on, for example, how to destroy railroad tracks and made

British stamps with propaganda messages such as "this war is a Jewish war." Because he was not "mechanical" at all, Paul says he ruined many such stamps. "This they called sabotage, but I couldn't help it."

Reading from notes he wrote immediately after the war, Paul describes the forgery procedures in detail. He was a *Hilfsarbeiter*—an assistant who sorted through the fake pounds and checked to make sure the printing was good. He slid each note, from bundles of five hundred, onto a piece of matte glass, with a light above and below. With a knife he removed any traces of wood from the notes, or pinned them to cover up a defect in the printing. The Germans had their own engravers who were constantly improving the plates. The forgery produced denominations of five, ten, twenty, and a few fifties. These were produced in various qualities, the highest of which was used to pay German spies like "Cicero."

Paul states that he and the others "knew that [their] days were numbered." Only Jewish prisoners were made to work in this operation, and they were told that there was an order to kill them once they were no longer needed. Paul felt completely unprotected, and thought that only a miracle could save them. Paul reassured himself and fellow inmates that the Allies knew about the forgery activities in the camp and that they would ensure that the prisoner-forgers would survive to bear witness to what the Germans had done. Meanwhile, the Germans were under pressure to expedite the forgery operations, but Paul explains, the inmates worked slowly in order to stay alive.

Paul managed to steal the *Blockälteste*'s original list of prisoners from blocks 18 and 19, a document he has retained. It lists the prisoners' names as well as details about what each received in the camp, like a knife, a towel, or a spoon. After the war, Paul added people's nationalities so that he would remember who everyone was. Paul explains that this group of people became like a family. They were totally isolated from others in the camp and guarded as they were taken out of the barracks for a shower once a week. They never spoke to other prisoners along the way but instead had to sing the songs the Germans taught them, Paul remembers, "because we had to act like happy people." While in Oranienburg, Paul says he still thought of himself as "little kid" and a fellow prisoner, Leo Epstein, became like his protector and mentor. They stayed in touch following the war.

When the Americans and the Russians were advancing on either side, the operation, both equipment and workers, was transported by train to Mauthausen, in Austria. On March 2, 1945, Paul and the other *Operation Bernhard* prisoners were placed in the Mauthausen jail, once again in order to separate them from the other camp inmates. Like everyone at Mauthausen, he was forced to look at a corpse hanging by its feet near the camp gates, which the Nazis had placed as a warning for "people to be scared and to behave." Paul says he remembers this image very well; it is the saddest thing he ever saw.

On April 15, Paul and the other Operation Bernhard prisoners were evacuated from Mauthausen and taken, along with their equipment, to the small camp of Schlier-Redel-Zipf. Paul says, "I saw the marvelous Danube River on my travels but I didn't have a chance to admire it." At this camp there were underground tunnels for German ammunitions; the prisoners were Spanish republicans who had taken refuge in Southern France but were "given back" to Hitler by Marshal Pétain when he came to power.

In Schlier-Redel-Zipf they unloaded the counterfeiting equipment and started digging in order to pour a two- to three-foot concrete base on which to set up the machines. Before long, the printing factory was up and running, but by May 3, they had to move again. The prisoners were moved by open truck, but had no idea where they were going. Because the equipment was left behind in Schlier-Redel-Zipf, they were convinced they were headed "for liquidation."

The three trips were planned in order to bring the 140 men by truck to the camp at Ebensee, in the Salzkammergut region of southern Austria. Paul went in the second group, convinced that the first group had already been killed. Instead, the first two groups were placed in the SS barracks, away from the rest of the camp's inmates. The third group was marched through the woods and not driven from Schlier-Redel-Zipf, as there were already white flags everywhere in the area.

By this time, the camp's loudspeakers were blaring that the prisoners should resist the Russians and let the Americans in. The SS left the watch-towers in the hands of *Wehrmacht* veterans telling them not to kill anyone, but to hand them over to the Americans. However, it was not clear what should be done with the hundred Jews from Operation Bernhard. The SS lined them up and marched them from the barracks to the gates of the Ebensee concentration camp. One of the SS thought the prisoners should be killed because they belonged to the RSHA and would be able to pass on secrets. There was an actual order to kill the Operation Bernhard prisoners for this very reason but it was with a guard in the third group, which fortunately had not yet arrived at Ebensee. Scared and undecided, the SS led the prisoners into the camp. "My liberation," Paul says, "was when I was mixed with the other people of the concentration camp of Ebensee."

On May 5, only a few hours after Paul and the others had lost themselves in the camp at Ebensee, the third group from Schlier-Redl-Zipf arrived. When the SS finally received the order to kill them, the group had already dissolved; because the secrecy of the operation had already been compromised, the third group was also permitted to join the other 8,000 people of the Ebensee camp. Paul and the others were "free."

The next day a single tank from Patton's 3rd Army rolled in. "People got crazy," Paul says, describing it as a moment filled with both joy and animosity. For Paul, the first night of liberation "was a nightmare." He remembers people stole food and weapons and set one of the barracks on fire. Some people were driven to beating and killing each other in revenge for the maltreatment from one another in the camp; others were afraid to walk around the camp. Paul and his friend Hans Blass stayed up all night, for fear of what might happen.

The Americans tried to organize the camp, bringing food into the *Appellplatz*. However, this mass distribution meant that the weaker inmates were unable to get any food. The food itself, Paul remembers, was "poison for us" and gave some inmates dysentery because they had not eaten any fat for so long.

Paul and Hans left the camp and went to a nearby village, where Hans was able to find a place to stay. The first thing Paul wanted was a pair of leather shoes to replace his wooden clogs. He even asked for shoes a few sizes too big; he had been wearing tight shoes for so long "[he] didn't want to suffer anymore." People in the stores were kind and respectful because of their striped prison uniforms. Hans, who spoke English, became friendly with the Americans, who gave him and Paul both permits to carry a revolver and the authority to protect the citizens of the town of Ebensee from looters. Everyday, the two friends returned to the camp for news. They left on a repatriation transport for France two weeks later. They traveled in freight cars that moved so slowly it took a week for them to arrive.

On May 24, in the city of Thionville on the French border, the border guards claimed not to have enough *cartes de repatrié* to let them in because they were still waiting for them to arrive from Paris. Hans insisted they be given special treatment because of the documents they had received from the American soldiers. The French border guards agreed and Paul and Hans were given the necessary cards, plus showers, haircuts, and 2,000 francs. They arrived by regular train at the Gare de l'Est in Paris. Paul remembers the sad arrival; thousands of people were at the station, yelling out "Have you seen so and so? Were you in that camp?" Meanwhile, the Red Cross told them they had to take a bus to a "centre for control" to verify their identity. Paul asked a stranger in the crowd to look for his sister at the family's old address and tell her that he was alive and in Paris.

Paul's sister Fanny met him at the repatriation center. She asked him, "where's Jacques?" Paul's response was "we were separated." Only a year later did he tell his sister the truth, which destroyed her hope that Jacques was sick somewhere in Russia. Paul also reunited with his mother, who survived the war with Paul's sisters in the unoccupied zone of France. Before they saw each other, the family was worried about the shock it would bring her, so she was given an injection by a doctor in advance. His mother told him she was always worried about her "little Paul" but thought that Jacques would be okay because he was strong. Paul, however, never told his mother about Jacques' death. In 1966 she died, still hoping that Jacques was alive.

Paul says that after the war "not everything was so sad." He feels lucky that he had a family to come back to and who took care of him. Paul could not eat properly and was sent to Vichy for liver treatment. After Vichy, the French government sent Paul to a convalescent camp in the Haute Savoie, as well as a camp at Menton, on the Riviera, where he met Simon Rosenberg, who was also a survivor and became Paul's best friend.

Paul in Paris in early 1946, age twenty-three

In Paris, Paul went to see Colonel Labadie at the counterespionage office of M.G. (Ministère de la Guerre, the War Ministry) to report on his participation in the Nazi forgery campaign. He was sent to the office of the D.G.E.R. (Direction générale des Études et Recherches) where he was told that everything about Krüger's operation was already known. Paul was politely thanked for coming forward, but no one was interested in what he had to say. As for the British pounds he had been forging, the SS had thrown them into a lake before the end of the war.

In 1947, a group of fifty-five French citizens went to Auschwitz on a collective visa. Paul was among them and he hired a translator in Czestochowa to accompany him to Kochanowitz to find his brother's grave. He found out that the camp where his brother died was converted into an SS convalescent camp and later burned. Eventually, Paul was able to find the graves of eleven people, and the police agreed to have it fenced off. In early June of 1967, Paul and his sister Rachel went back to Auschwitz to give Jacques a proper burial. In Czestochowa, a contact, Mr. Gutman, made arrangements for Paul to dig up Jacques' grave. However, Paul was told that the municipality had dug up the eleven graves and reburied the bodies elsewhere in an unmarked mass grave. Despite this, Paul dug in his brother's grave himself until he found one vertebra, which he put in a coffin and buried in the Jewish cemetery of Czestochowa.

In the postwar period, the French government was always changing, the currency was devalued, and Paul wanted to start a new life "on firm ground." He immigrated to Canada in 1951, settling in Montreal because of the French language. His sister Rachel also lives there now.

Paul has told his wife and children about his experiences as well as the nightmares he continues to have. He wants his family to know about what happened but he also thinks that it is important to exteriorize his memories: "If I get my story off my chest," Paul says, "I don't choke myself with my story."

֎֎֎֎ ֎֎֎֎ ֎֎֎֎

Saul B.
August 12, 1993

Saul's testimony is extremely emotional. He begins his interview with "We were a family," but these few words are as far he gets before his voice catches in his throat. Separated from his family, Saul spent five years in a series of Nazi labor camps. Though his testimony reveals his exceptional ability to perform hard work, there is, as he points out, no rational explanation for why he survived.

Saul was born on February 11, 1921 in Lodz, Poland. He was one of three boys and four girls in his family. His father Israel was a textile dealer, and his mother Dina took care of the family and the house. Saul, his parents, and his siblings Netel, Sora, Rochel, Bela, Jakov, and Beirish were a happy, "extremely orthodox," upper middle-class family. Saul recalls that they were "very united" within their immediate and extended families.

Saul attended both Polish and Jewish schools, where he became fluent in Polish and German. After completing his studies, he began learning how to produce textiles, a vocation he continued until the war began. In Lodz, Saul had contact with Gentiles through the "normal routine" of life. He also remembers instances of violence and aggression, such as a "mini pogrom" on the last day of Passover in 1935. On that day people vandalized his home. Saul describes how they seized their expensive down bedding only to cut it open and shake the feathers out of the third story window onto the street below.

Despite the violence and the curfew that was temporarily imposed on Jews in Lodz in the late 1930s, Saul says, "We made the best possible out of it." He and his family became aware of the growing persecution of Jews in Germany mostly through the magazines and books that were always plentiful in the household. They knew, for instance, that in 1938, Germany had expelled thousands of Jews of Polish origin for repatriation. These Jews remained in an open field in Zbaszyn (a "no man's land") until Poland finally accepted them.

Saul recounts that even though the mobilization of veterans began in March 1939, "nobody expected that [war] would happen" because of Poland's alliance with France and England. Saul himself was never drafted because he was only eighteen and the draft for the army began at twenty-one. When the war did begin, on September 1, 1939, Saul was outside the café Astoria on a crowded city street. Saul chokes on his words as he recalls people running out of the café announcing, "the war has started." He ran home where his family was listening to the radio for news about the German advance.

On Sunday September 3, 1939, two days after the war broke out, the Polish army arrived in horse and buggy, took whatever they needed from the hardware store, and left the store with only a requisition paper. The next day, a German pilot was captured in Lodz after he evacuated his burning plane. Saul remembers this pilot being chased through the streets by people shouting, "Kill him! Kill him!" Then people in Lodz began stockpiling as much food as they could buy. Soon supplies were scarce; bread was almost impossible to find, and dry goods such as rice, sugar, and barley became valuable commodities.

Shelling, bombing, and rumors that the police had left their station in Lodz had Saul's family thinking they should flee toward Warsaw. However, there were also rumors, Saul says, that the *Volksdeutsche* were blocking the roads out of Lodz, and that there were shootings. Saul's father worried that leaving would cause the family to separate from each other, and Saul's brother-in-law was concerned about Netel, his pregnant wife. They ultimately decided to leave their home but were deterred by the masses of people in the road with their horses, buggies, cows, and chickens. They returned home "to sit and wait."

The following Friday, Saul saw German soldiers, armed with machine guns, enter the city on motorcycles. The next morning, he watched from his home as the German army rolled in with their tanks and occupied the city. The existing German population of Lodz (which was considerable) began wearing swastika armbands, seized businesses, and took charge of the city administration. Soon, posters appeared in the streets announcing that it was illegal for groups of three people to meet together, and that should it

Saul B. (right) in Lodz, 1936

so happen that ten people were found in one house, everyone would be shot. These laws, Saul observes, pertained to all people, not just the Jews. Shortly, however, an ordinance was issued requiring Jews to sew a yellow Star of David (which they were required to craft themselves, ten centimeters by ten centimeters) on the left breast and right shoulder of their clothing. Any Jew without this marker would be shot.

During the occupation, Saul's family continued to observe Jewish religious holidays despite the grave consequences for those who were caught. On Rosh Hashanah, Saul's family gathered together with neighbors and held services, blowing the *shofar* in the basement of a nearby building to avoid being heard by Gestapo guards. They held Yom Kippur services with equal secrecy.

November brought the announcement that a Jewish ghetto was to be formed. Saul recalls that by mid-November there were still people unwilling to move to the assigned ghetto until one night when, after curfew, German soldiers broke down doors and shot people in their homes. This event incited a panic, and the next day Saul remembers, "the people came in droves to escape with their life." In the ghetto area of Baluty Marysin, thirty to fifty people were crammed in houses with no running water, only a pump and public toilet in the yard. They slept on tables, under tables, "wherever possible." Tearful at this point in his interview, Saul says he stayed in a three-room apartment with his parents, seven children, and the Goldman family from Kalisz, who, in a desperate state, had been taken in by Saul's brother. Food was rationed, extremely scarce, and had to be bought from the ghetto kitchens with equally scarce "ghetto money."

By May 1, 1940, the Lodz ghetto was sealed with boarded fences and six-foot high barbed wire, and guarded by *volksdeutsche* sentries who stood one hundred feet apart with machine guns. The German-formed Jewish police also monitored the ghetto. In the case of the Lodz ghetto, Saul explains, Germans had come into the Jewish *Gemeinde* (community) asking for the oldest of the Jews (rather than the most prominent of the elders). Chaim Rumkowski was thus designated to head the Jewish police. At the time, it was considered a privilege to work for this force, since the police received extra rations.

Saul recalls that there was nothing for him to do in the ghetto because he had no work, and there were no radios. He also explains that a group of "valuable Jews" who knew how to recycle textiles were given green armbands and taken outside the ghetto to train other people in this skill. Because they returned to the ghetto on weekends, they were able to smuggle in food for their families. When a rumor circulated that a group of boys would be taken to the summer resort town of Wisniowa Gora ("like Ste. Agathe here" Saul explains) to cut trees in the forest, and earn twelve marks of "ghetto money" a month, it looked like an opportunity both to earn money and to get out of the ghetto for a while and Saul was eager to volunteer for this "opportunity." At the time it seemed lucky that Saul and his brother Jakov were among the 800 chosen. Saul says,

> There are certain episodes in one's life, which remain with you forever. One such event is the day when I was about to leave the Lodz ghetto, December 10, 1940. Outside the barbed wire fence, inside the ghetto, appeared just before curfew, my late father, where I was looking out the window from the barracks, standing there motionless and looking at me, salt tears running down onto his beard. I have never seen in my entire life my father crying and this scene has always remained with me.

It was the last time that Saul saw his father. He would also never see his mother or his eldest sister and her family again.

When he left for labor assignment, Saul, along with the other young men, had to report to German doctors for examination. At nightfall, the eight hundred men were marched to the ghetto outskirts. During a two-hour wait for a passenger train (with broken windows), the SS Guards made them repeatedly roll down an embankment of deep snow. Later in the night, when they passed the Koluszki station Saul realized that "they fooled us," they were traveling west, toward Germany, not eastward to Wisniowa Gora as they had been told. As the train passed through Poznan and Zbaszyn (the "no man's land" the refugees had been in), Saul fantasized about a possible escape plan with his friend Moishel Werstowski. They imagined escaping to Paris, where Moishel's brother Srolek lived, and then across the Pyrenees, and into Spain. This was, Saul explains, the reverse of the escape route taken by refugees from the Spanish Civil War, something he had read about in a magazine when he was younger.

When the train reached its destination at Sternberg and Neumark, the prisoners were chased out, lined up, and told, "you are in Germany, and you are going to stay here." They were made to wear the Star of David, had the "laws" read out to them, and were separated into two groups. Saul, in a group of about four hundred, was marched to a labor camp called Pinnow über Reppen, five kilometers away. Here there were no barracks, only boards, and the prisoners were required to build the barracks themselves. Their guards, "torturers" as Saul remembers them, were members of the labor battalion *Organisation Todt*, who wore black uniforms with a "death's head" (or skull) on their caps. These guards often beat the prisoners with tree roots directly on their bare backs. In this labor camp, Saul recalls a particularly brutal Lithuanian foreman named Romanowski, who claimed he was "taking revenge" on the Jews. Saul also remembers that the German villagers who saw the prisoners marching to and from work each day were always willing to report Jews who were doing anything "wrong."

Saul and the other prisoners cut trees and used spades to dig out the ground for what was to become the *Reichsautobahn*, the main highway from Berlin to Moscow. Saul was very strong and was considered one of the best workers in his camp. There was no work on Sundays because the foreman had the day off; the "Sunday privilege," as Saul facetiously calls it, consisted of being subjected to cruel treatment by the guards, including orders to run, jump, and jog while being chased by dogs, or being whipped with rubber batons on their way to and from the showers. On an occasion when Saul was unable to work due to an injury, he was severely beaten by an *Organisation Todt* guard who threatened to kill him if he did not report to work the following day.

During this period, Saul was kept somewhat informed of the war through what he or the other prisoners were able to overhear on the Germans' radios or in their conversations. In particular, the prisoner who was assigned to be the Germans' barber, one Wagmann, was able to bring back important news from the German foremen's barrack, regarding, for example, developments on the eastern front. One day when Saul was assigned to help a local farmer load hay onto a truck, he overheard some guards referring to Ribbentrop's visit to Moscow. As a result, the camp anticipated the arrival of Russian prisoners, and an *Organisation Todt* guard had come to retrieve Saul before the day was over. That day, the Jewish prisoners were very hopeful about Russia's potential to weaken Germany; Saul recalls Wagmann's words as "Maybe now our salvation can come." However, Saul also remembers that this hope competed with his disappointment at not receiving the sandwich he would have earned from the farmer for a full day's work.

Saul remained in this labor camp until August 1941, when another camp needed seventy prisoners. Saul asked Romanowski to be included in this transport to Leimnitz über Mezervitch, a camp with no electricity, near Frankfurt an der Oder. Because Saul was an exceptional worker, with reluctance, he was allowed to go. The leader of the new camp was a civilian named Jabolkof, whom Saul describes as a "beast." In the middle of the night, the guards frequently ordered the prisoners out of the barracks. They stood against the doors and beat them as they tried to exit, and then forced the prisoners to line up and sing songs, or else be shot. When it got cold outside, Jabolkof ordered the prisoners to dismantle the chimney pipes from the barrack stoves and line them up outside his office. This way the prisoners could not light a fire without choking from the smoke.

In this camp, people suffered from malnutrition, and many died. Officially, the prisoners were supposed to receive thirty grams of bread a day, but instead they received thirty grams of bread every three days. Furthermore, the bread was weighted with raw potatoes rather than flour (which the baker was rumored to have been stealing). The bread gave the prisoners cramps and made them sick.

In January 1942, during a roll call in the middle of the night, two young men, Kruj and Lubochinski, were stripped and tied to a lamppost in below freezing weather. The other prisoners had to bring forth buckets of cold water, line up, and watch the guards pour the water over the heads and naked bodies of the two young men. Saul explains, his voice strained, "These are things which it always stays in your mind."

Saul continued to work on the *Autobahn* in Leimnitz, and he continued to receive regular beatings from the guards. One day, Neie, one of the German office leaders, hit Saul over the back. This time, Saul retaliated by grabbing him by his lapels, throwing him in the mud, and stepping on him. Saul was locked in a barn until guards marched him back to the camp to see a doctor. The doctor diagnosed him as having suffered a nervous breakdown. "This was a salvation," Saul says. The next day he was allowed to work again. Saul believes that this leniency was partly due to his reputation as a good and obedient worker.

However, one day in the fall, while hauling stones up a steep slope, Neie, along with two military men and two civilians, seized Saul and told him they were taking him to be hanged. Before leaving the camp, he was given papers to sign whereupon Saul discovered that all the while he had been making money: eight pfennigs an hour. After "expenses" like room and board had been deducted, Saul was given ninety-eight pfennigs. With this small amount of money in his possession, the two civilians and the two military men drove Saul to an unknown destination. Confronted with the reality of his pending execution, Saul's thoughts turned to his family. While a prisoner in Leimnitz, he had been allowed to both send and receive postcards from his family in the Lodz ghetto. The thought of his family finding out about his death anguished him. Saul, visibly distraught, explains, "what I think then is beyond thinking."

Saul ended up at a Gestapo jail in the city of Schwiebus, where he was the only Jew among the German and Polish *Berufsverbrecher* (professional criminals). Saul was fed surprisingly well, receiving potatoes with gravy, bread, and coffee, though there was no bunk in the cell and insufficient heating. On what he thought might be the last day of his life, Saul was given a shower and a blue prison uniform and assigned to help three Germans peel potatoes. No longer afraid of any consequences, Saul treated the Germans with insolence; ironically, this won their respect and friendship. Saul explains that he learned in the Gestapo jail, "If you bow your head, everybody will hit you."

While awaiting his execution, he was assigned to a room with four bunks, and rather than being jolted out of bed for midnight *Appell*, beatings, and death threats, he was forced to be in bed before dark and not up before dawn. Saul says it was like being at a "four star hotel." With nothing to do, Saul took the initiative to make the beds and clean the cell, which impressed the German warden. After two or three days, Saul was taken to the Gestapo office and interrogated about his family history. Due to the doctor's report about his nervous breakdown, as well as a report from Leimnitz that indicated Saul was a good worker (which Saul suspects was the doing of Schlamek Edelstein, a Jewish office assistant in the camp, to whom Saul continues to feel greatly indebted), he was sent back to his jail cell. The warden told him that his sentence was now a fourteen-day incarceration, after which he would be returned to Leimnitz. The other prisoners said that he was lucky to get such a short sentence; Saul felt lucky to be away from the camp. In fact, he now remembers the experience as crucial to his survival because he was able to regain his strength. However, because of his good behavior, Saul served only seven of the fourteen days.

After his return from jail, Jabolkof mysteriously changed his attitude and started to favor Saul. While the prisoners were unloading a carload of coal, Jabolkof instructed Saul to "rest a bit." At lunch, Jabolkof told Saul to go to the kitchen and ask Gotheine, the man dishing out soup, to fill up his bowl completely. Jabolkof also designated Saul to haul the water to the kitchen, for which he received an extra bowl of soup per day. One day, Jabolkof even offered Saul half a loaf of bread.

Meanwhile, Saul's brother Jakov was thirty miles away in camp Spiegelberge. The brothers were allowed to write cards back and forth, although these were censored and needed to be carefully worded. While Saul was in jail, his brother had even been to Leimnitz (sent with a cement truck) and was told the story that Saul had been taken away to be hanged. Jakov wrote a coded letter to their family in the Lodz ghetto, which said, "Saul is where cousin Yidel is," referring to a cousin who had been arrested by the Gestapo. Saul was later able to write to his family and communicate that he was still alive. As Saul remembers it, all he wrote was, "I haven't heard from you in a while."

In spring 1942, Saul was transferred to another forced labor camp called Fürstenberg an der Oder, which he describes as getting "out of a hell to a lower hell." Here he worked for a company called DEGUSSA—Deutsche Gold und Silber-Scheideanstalt, Frankfurt am Main. The company was building houses along the river, and Saul's task was to unload bricks from boats.

In the fall of 1942, Saul was again transferred, this time to a camp called Finkenheerd an der Oder, where he dug canals and carried railroad tracks at a hydroelectric construction project for Märkisches Electrizitätswerk. In this camp, Saul remembers a German foreman, Max Fuchs, who would occasionally allow the prisoners to rest from work, and would take up the work himself so his supervisors would not detect a lapse in productivity. Max Fuchs also risked his life by smuggling in food for the prisoners. Saul remained at this camp for seven to eight months, until spring 1943.

Saul was then sent, along with eighteen others, to a labor camp at Schwiebus where they worked on the construction of a factory and bridges. After six or seven weeks here, a guard informed the prisoners of Himmler's order for the Reich to be made *judenrein:* all Jews were to be put in concentration camps. In July 1943, Saul and the other inmates of labor camps in Germany were locked into cattle cars and brought to Auschwitz. Along the way, a Polish man working the railway switches told them that they were going to be gassed at Auschwitz. Saul and the others did not believe him.

When the train doors opened at their destination, Saul encountered German shepherds and the SS with rubber batons who proceeded to beat the prisoners off the train. Saul was selected to work at Buna-Monowitz, a satellite camp of Auschwitz. He recalls about twelve thousand prisoners at Buna. Upon arrival, Saul was stripped, searched, tattooed, shaved, showered (with a "balsam" purification), and issued a striped uniform. His arm now bore the number 142301.

Saul was in Buna for a year and a half, and for the first four to six weeks he stayed in one of three tents for new arrivals, each of which housed a thousand people. His first job at Buna was washing soup barrels, for which he received extra soup. Next he worked at the I.G. Farben factory, which was camouflaged by a thick man-made fog between 10 a.m. and noon every day, the approximate time the British carried out their daily bombings of Buna.

In 1944, Saul was reunited with his brother Jakov when a new transport of Polish Jews came in. The brothers discovered they were actually staying in the same tent. In March 1944, Saul sent a letter home to the Lodz ghetto. The prisoners were permitted to write letters of exactly thirty words (including the address), though they were forbidden to use the word "Auschwitz," and were instructed to use "Monowitz" instead. In retrospect, Saul views these letters, which also only permitted that they report everything was okay, as a particularly insidious mechanism of Nazi deception.

Saul remained in Buna until the camp was evacuated on January 18, 1945. Twelve thousand people were marched to Gleiwitz in a snowstorm. After two or three days of marching, they were taken to a train yard for selection. Saul recalls this incident as "shootings and shootings and shootings." Those who escaped being shot, including Saul and Jakov, were put on open cattle trains that held 150 people per wagon. They traveled from January 21 until the beginning of February. There was nothing to eat or drink. People died of cold and hunger, and corpses were piled up against the wall. Saul subsisted on the snow he could scoop up by using several belts, looped together, to lower a cup to the ground. As they passed through Czechoslovakia, local people risked their lives by standing on bridges and throwing food down into the open train cars. In a state of extreme starvation, the prisoners desperately fought over the food, often crushing it before anyone had the chance to eat it.

Saul's train arrived in Buchenwald with more passengers dead than alive. Jakov and Saul were temporarily assigned to barrack 59. Not many days later, Saul and twelve hundred others were sent on cattle trains to Zwieberge. Jakov was not among the twelve hundred and Saul never saw him again. This transport was not overcrowded; there were only fifty Jews in each train car, as well as four SS who kept a lookout for British planes flying overhead. On February 9, 1945, near Reinsdorf bei Artern, British fighter-planes opened fire on the train. Saul dove onto the floor and tried his best to take shelter. A bullet passed through Saul's leg, and killed Mushovitsky, a Belgian man lying next to him.

Saul's was the first group of Jews to be brought to Zwieberge, where they were put to work building a factory under the mountains. Saul worked drilling holes and blasting. He says that there was no air to breathe at the construction site, and that prisoners were often killed by falling rocks. "It was torture." At Zwieberge, Saul recounts, there were "killings by the dozen." After work, Saul says, he and the others had to bury the corpses from that day.

Soon Allied planes flew so low that the pilots would roll the planes and wave to the prisoners. One day the prisoners were given the choice of staying in the camp or going on a march. Saul chose the march and found himself among four thousand people walking in columns of five. The SS led the way with horses and buggies, while another group of SS walked at the rear for the purpose of shooting prisoners who could no longer walk. Despite a wounded leg, Saul marched for fourteen days. They were given no food or water, and risked being shot as they grabbed at leaves from the side of the road, or from overhanging trees, in order to have something to eat. As more and more people died, Saul thought of escape. He and another prisoner determined that with the Americans and British advancing from the west, and the Russians approaching from the east, the Germans would not have time to waste by looking for them. So when the procession came to a young forest, with leaves and foliage close to the ground, some prisoners began to yell "*dekuk*" ("take cover"). In the first moments of SS confusion, many of the prisoners ran into the woods.

Having successfully evaded the SS guards' bullets, fourteen prisoners regrouped in the forest. They constructed a shelter and stole potatoes from a nearby field. The following morning, they discovered that two people in the group had already died. Later that day, the German Army, digging ditches near the forest, caught the prisoners and brought them to a nearby village. The twelve prisoners were made to stand against a wall with their arms in the air for an hour and a half. Then the mayor of the village ordered them to be locked in a farmer's barn, where they ate the spoiled potatoes the farmer kept for his pigs.

The group departed with the German Army, recruited to pull their "field kitchen." During a lunch stop, a German soldier gave Saul a sandwich. After witnessing Saul share this sandwich with the other prisoners, the German soldier was moved to offer a second sandwich for the group. Later, a truck came by and hitched up the field kitchen. The prisoners' labor was no longer required.

On the night of April 20, 1945, the group ended up in a small city with military storehouses. At this point, Saul was no longer aware of precise locations. Once again, Saul was undressed, showered, disinfected, and dressed in new military and civilian clothing. Otherwise, everything was in disarray. The Allies were advancing and the Germans were packing up and preparing to evacuate the city. The prisoners spent the night in a basement room. No one among them felt that they could go on and they decided that if they were ordered to leave they would simply say they could no longer walk. Later when an older soldier came into their room and tried to rouse them, they said they would not go. He raised his gun to shoot them but was deterred by a German Jew who saved the group by appealing to the German's compassion as a husband and a father. Saul recalls him saying, "Sir, don't you have a wife and children? Don't you want ever in your life to meet your wife and children? So do we." The soldier became emotional and said that he would let the prisoners live, but warned that the land around the barracks was mined. Once the Germans had gone, Saul and the others discovered stores of bread, liquor, canned food, "everything." That night, nobody slept.

Out of a window in the early morning, Saul spotted a Russian soldier at a distance. A little later, at 8 or 9 a.m., a Russian soldier on a horse rode into the yard where Saul and the others were hiding. Saul remembers that all the prisoners began to cry.

After his liberation, Saul was still afraid to walk about freely, but his aim was clearly to get back to Lodz. Taking a horse and buggy from a farm, Saul and others destined for Poland went to Frankfurt an der Oder. There, Saul received permission to go to Poland from a Polish registration office. Saul, of course, had no identification papers, only the number tattooed on his arm, to which he quickly gestures and says, "this is my document." Saul made

Saul (right) age twenty-four, in Lodz in 1945

his way by train to Poznan, and from there jumped on a train to Kalisz. In Kalisz he heard that a Russian military train was going to Moscow, via Lodz. Saul was able to sneak onto this train, disembarked at Pabianice, and proceeded by streetcar to Lodz.

It was May 4, 1945. Over ten thousand Jews had already registered in the Jewish *Gemeinde*. When questioned by the people at the registration office about where he had come from and when he had left, he was told that it was impossible to have been gone five years and to have come back alive. "Don't ask me," Saul says, "ask the fellow upstairs."

In Lodz, Saul was intent on locating surviving family members. He found one of his sisters, emaciated and her head still shaved. She and two other sisters had survived in Germany. His youngest brother Beirish (later named Barry), who had been taken with his mother on the last transport from the Lodz ghetto to Auschwitz in 1944, had also survived. The five surviving siblings found out that their mother had died in the gas chamber at Auschwitz, and that his father had died of hunger in the Lodz ghetto in 1942.

Saul does not describe the five-year period of his life immediately after the war, but in 1950, he arrived in Halifax, Nova Scotia on a boat called the *Beaverbrae*. From Halifax, he took a train to Montreal's Windsor Station where he was met by one of his sisters who brought him to her house. Saul says he immigrated to Canada because he hoped it could become a permanent home. With his brother, he opened a sewing-machine business, and in 1955 he met Diana and felt he was ready to start a family. "Life has to progress," Saul says, "We cannot go around with the trauma day and night." Saul and Diana were married on June 5, 1955. Ten months later, a daughter, Lydia Beth, was born, named after an aunt whose entire immediate family perished during the Holocaust. Seventeen months after that, Diana gave birth to Irwin Sheldon. He is named after Saul's father Israel.

Saul says, "I have told this chapter of my life in memory of my dear beloved parents, Israel and Dina, and my sister and brother-in-law, Netel and Jankel, and their two year old daughter Hinde, and many members of my family and friends who were so gruesomely [killed] by Nazi Germany only because they were Jewish." He also believes that "It is [his] duty to leave testimony," and is concerned that "the time is running out." "There will be no witnesses," he says, which he thinks is especially grave in view of Holocaust deniers like Keegstra and Zundel.

Saul ends his testimony by expressing his hope that no human being will ever encounter the same kind of misery and torture he endured during the Nazi era.

Abram F.
August 2, 1989

Abram F. survived four years in the Lodz ghetto before being transported to Auschwitz in the summer of 1944. He was then transferred to a factory in Czechoslovakia, where he worked until the end of the war. Throughout this time, Abram was driven by a desire to prevail over the Nazis: "It was always a wish and a dream, when I looked at the German I said, I will outlive you. And I did. I knew Hitler's dream was to see the funeral of all the Jews, but I outlived him. I lived long enough to see Hitler's funeral, so I live a happy life since then . . . ."

Before the Nazi occupation of Poland, Abram, born on April 28, 1919, was the youngest of the five children in his family. He had three brothers, Eli, Mordechai, and Hirsch, and one older sister Mindel. They lived in Baluty, a poor and almost exclusively Jewish neighborhood of Lodz. His father Yitzhak was a cabinetmaker. All four sons worked in the business. At fourteen, Abram left public school to work as a cabinetmaker. When his eldest brother was drafted into the army and his other siblings were all married, Abram took over the shop. He was sixteen or seventeen. Abram explains that they made "the kind of furniture [their] family could not afford" for wealthy Jewish customers. They did not make a good living but in retrospect, he views his father as an artist—"He never looked at his watch."

Abram's father was an atheist and a socialist; "he was antireligious, but also a full-blooded Jew nationally." The household was Yiddish speaking. Abram was influenced by the ardently socialist environment in his home and, at age ten, joined the children's organization of the Bund, the Jewish Socialist Party. He also remembers having music lessons, and attending Yiddish theatre, concerts, and libraries. He belonged to the *Kulturbund*, and later the Labor Union of the Workers.

Abram explains that the Jewish Labor Movement in Poland always had to deal with anti-Semitism. Jews were unofficially banned from employment "in a janitor's job or a job in a government enterprise, or the heavy industry [such as] the gas company or the tramways." Abram's contact with non-Jews was restricted to a short apprenticeship in lacquer finishing. His boss was a drunk who made Abram work overtime on Yom Kippur. In Lodz, where Jews represented a third of the population, being called a "dirty Jew" was not uncommon. Abram remembers a pogrom in 1937 or 1938 that ended on his street "because the Jews resisted. They put up a fight."

Abram heard about the Nazi invasion of Poland on September 1, 1939. The president, Ignacy Moscicki, made a speech on the radio about resisting the attack but Abram says, "This was not really the case. It took only two or three days before they reached Lodz, with very little resistance. . . . The German population of Lodz (about one third) sympathized with the Nazis, and along with many of the Poles, helped the Nazis pick out the Jews."

Abram remembers, "There was always a Pole who would say, this is a *Jude*. They learned that word very fast."

At the time, Abram helped his aunt distribute bread from her bakery to a long line that assembled outside every morning. German soldiers pulled anyone they could identify as a Jew out of the line. Poles were particularly vigilant in helping the soldiers pick out "good faces," Jews who could be mistaken for non-Jews.

Before the ghetto was formed, Abram was arrested on the way out of a pharmacy and taken to Gestapo headquarters. He was put to work cleaning up the back yard and washing the Gestapo's cars. One of the rags Abram was given was a red silk flag of the *Po'alei Zion* (the socialist Zionist movement). At three or four in the afternoon, he and some other Jews were released and sent outside where they were forced to run around for thirty minutes while *volksdeutsch* boys hit them with "something like a baseball bat." Then the soldiers put them in a straight line and told them to sing. They sang a popular Yiddish song, "I want to go back home." Because Yiddish and German are similar languages, the Germans understood most of the song, except for one line the Jews had changed into "I don't want to be here any longer because those pigs are with us." The Yiddish word for pig, *nevelah*, comes from Hebrew and bears no resemblance to the German word *Schwein*. Remembering the courage it took to look the Germans in the face while singing out this line, Abram says, "I'm proud of my people."

Around this time, the Germans arrested the senior Jewish activists of Lodz, the leaders of the *Po'alei Zion*, the Bund, and the Textile Union, and held them in a temporary concentration camp outside of Lodz. Abram heard that the German soldiers gave them shovels and made them hit each other because the soldiers wanted to take pictures of them to send home to their mothers and girlfriends. The photographs were meant to depict the soldiers' "heroism." Abram tells the story of Morgenthal, the leader of the Textile Union, as an example of Jewish resistance. He refused to follow their orders. When the German took out his gun. Morgenthal said, "Shoot me. But you can't insult my community." For Abram this shows that Jews did fight back in order to save "the honor of their people in their own way."

In May 1940, the Jews of Lodz were confined to a ghetto. For some this was a good sign: "They decided not to kill us." But Abram had an inkling of what was at hand. He remembers seeing the headline of a German paper that read, " 'The Jews are finished. We have eliminated them.' That is when we realized."

The Germans installed a Jewish autocrat, Chaim Rumkowski, as the sole governor of the Lodz ghetto. Abram was forced to work in a woodworkers' factory. In 1941, Rumkowski discontinued the extra half-kilo ration of bread that the woodworkers received daily. Abram and his colleagues retaliated by going on strike. They barricaded themselves in the factory and were violently removed by Rumkowski's Jewish regiment. One striker died of his wounds. Four strikers, including Abram's brother Hirsch, were arrested. Two weeks later, the prisoners were released. The various ghetto organizations considered assassinating Rumkowski. However, they decided not to, afraid that the Germans would retaliate against the Lodz ghetto and that "another Rumkowski, maybe a worse one" would take over.

Occasionally, people disappeared from the ghetto on transports. Abram heard, via illegal radio, that people were being taken to concentration camps, where they were being killed in gas chambers and burned in crematoriums. "It was too much to believe. It was too much to absorb in our own mind that this is possible altogether, mass murder. It went beyond the imagination." After a while, Abram started believing it because nobody ever came back.

Abram's father died of starvation in the ghetto in February 1941. Before he died, he requested that Abram "make a picture of him" in order to document what happened to him. Abram says, "You look at the picture and you can see what this man died from." He was buried in the cemetery in Lodz.

Abram and his mother were now left alone. For ten days in September 1942, the Germans overhauled the Lodz ghetto, selecting children, women, and the elderly for liquidation and single workers for deportation to Auschwitz. Abram was caught in the roundup. A few Germans and a few unarmed Jewish policemen, "the servants of the masters," pushed those who had been selected onto a truck that was waiting outside. Noticing that there were only Jewish policemen and they had no guns, Abram jumped off the truck and starting running:

> I run, I don't remember for how long. I didn't realize the direction. I don't know where I was going, but when I stopped running, I ended up in my back yard.

Another boy, Leibel Kulmus, followed Abram in his escape and the two discovered they were both alone in the ghetto without any parents. Abram's mother had been taken in the raid, as was Leibel's father. Because they were both in "the same situation," they "started to live together like two brothers." Furthermore, Abram notes, Leibel's father was a cabinetmaker just like Abram's had been. Leibel survived the war and lives in New Jersey today.

Abram hid himself in the Lodz ghetto and evaded transports until the summer of 1944. At that time, Abram was hiding in a "double wall." "When we couldn't stay any longer—we had no more food—we decided to give ourselves up." Abram was taken to Auschwitz, along with his brother Mordechai who was married and lived in another part of the Lodz ghetto.

They arrived at Auschwitz in the middle of the night. There was a "terrible panic." The soldiers put them in a straight line. Dr. Mengele came over with other SS and made the selection. Abram went to the right. They were placed in a dark barracks. "We were up all night wondering, 'Where are we? What is this? And what are they going to do with us?'" In the morning, when they looked out the window, they saw that they were in a concentration camp. They were undressed, shaved, and taken to the showers.

Abram did not know if this was a "trick," because he had heard about the gas chambers disguised as showers:

> "Some *Kapos* told us: 'You see the smoke? This is a Jewish smoke.' We took it half as a joke to hurt you and half as maybe it is true. Maybe it is a Jewish smoke."

In October 1944, after five weeks in Auschwitz, Abram and Mordechai were taken to Gross Rosen-Gorlitz, a camp in Czechoslovakia (today on the Polish border of Germany). They were put to work in a factory that produced armored cars. For a few days they worked together with local Czechs: "Then we took over and we did not see them again." Abram says the job was "very simple." They worked twelve hours a day, six days a week, and were given soup and a portion of bread each day.

Abram remembers that one boy was caught stealing "the *Schweinen* food." As punishment, the boy was suspended from a post. "They pulled him up [not high enough] to hang, but not low enough to stand on his feet, so he was supporting himself on his toes." He stayed like this all night. In the morning the other prisoners were forced to watch as an SS guard said, " 'I want to see if he's ticklish.' . . . They tickled him; then cut him off the rope. He fell and died." Abram says, "This is more or less one of the pictures I can give you of what the treatment was like."

The factories of Gorlitz were evacuated in January 1945 because the Russians were advancing. The prisoners were taken out on one of the infamous death marches. On this march, a guard beat up Abram's brother Mordechai. The following day, Mordechai was unable to walk. Abram carried him for one day. That night, Mordechai died. He was buried in a hole that was previously dug as a latrine. After the war, Mordechai's body was exhumed and buried in the Jewish cemetery of Gorlitz.

The Russian advance stopped and, after four weeks of marching, the prisoners returned to the camp. They had been stationary for the ten or twelve days prior to the turning around. Abram believes that the soldiers did not know what to do with them. He thinks that the camp was reactivated primarily so that the German soldiers could avoid going to the front; "those SS needed that camp for their own survival."

Abram and the other prisoners were put to work digging ditches. Most of the guards were Ukrainians. The camp commander was a German convict who was sentenced to death after the war. Abram was a witness at his trial, where Abram discovered that the commander was placed in the concentration camp as punishment for two crimes. The first crime was forging money. The second crime, for which he got fifteen years, was for beating his mother to death.

On the morning of May 8, 1945, Abram and his comrades were called from their work. The commander told them that the Russians were advancing and that he and his staff were going to join the Americans and were taking all the supplies with them. No one volunteered to accompany them. Unsure whether this report was a trick, the prisoners spent the night in the camp. At 6 a.m. the next morning the Russians arrived.

Abram weighed thirty-eight kilos. The day after liberation he was taken to a makeshift hospital near Gorlitz. The doctor diagnosed a carbuncle on his shoulder as potentially lethal and operated on Abram without an anesthetic, concerned that either the fast-spreading carbuncle or the anesthetic could kill him in his weakened state. Abram recuperated for several weeks and then returned to Lodz.

After the war, Abram continued to be active in the Bund. However, in October 1948, Bund members were forced to join the Polish United Workers Party, a move that was part of the Sovietization of Poland. In order to help their fellow socialists, the Jewish Labour Committee in New York paid to smuggle Abram and other Bundists illegally through Czechoslovakia to Germany. In Germany, Abram renounced his Polish citizenship. "After a day of questioning I was recognized as a temporary émigré in Germany. I had no food stubs. The Jewish Labour Committee took care of that. I had to buy everything on the black market."

Because he had returned to Poland after the war, Abram did not have displaced person status: "I couldn't immigrate anywhere. But the International Ladies' Workers Union in Montreal and the president of the Jewish Labour Committee intervened with the Canadian government and they gave visas to twenty people." Abram obtained permission to work in Sweden as a cabinetmaker for ten months, while waiting for his Canadian visa. He set sail from Gothenburg, arriving in Montreal in June 1950 where he started work as a carpenter, joined shortly afterward by his brother Hirsch, the only other surviving family member. Their other brother Eli was arrested by the Soviet army, falsely accused as a "Nazi spy," and perished in a Russian concentration camp in 1943. Their sister was deported from the Lodz ghetto around the same time as their mother.

Abram was happy from the first moment he came to Canada. When the government official checked his passport and said, "Welcome to Canada," Abram says,

> I didn't understand English or French at the time, but I did understand the word "Welcome" and I did understand the word "Canada." I had tears in my eyes. I said, I am thirty-one years old and for the first time anyone tells me I'm welcome. I was never welcome in my own country.

He remains grateful to the Jewish Labour Committee and to the Bund.

Abram continues to have nightmares about his Holocaust experience "but it's not enough to resign, to say life is not worth living. Yes, it is worth living, for myself, for my family, and for my people." The war has left Abram with a sense of moral triumph:

> We came out—after we saw death and blood and mass murder—we came out clean. We came out human beings . . . [They] wanted to make an animal out of me and out of other survivors, but [they] didn't.

Abram F., age thirty-two, speaking at a conference in Montreal, 1951
Source: Used with the permission of the Montreal Holocaust Memorial Centre

Abram has not been reluctant to talk about his experience:

> I'm not afraid to think about it, to talk about it, to remember it
> twenty-four hours a day . . . . Even on *simchas*, on happy occasions, I
> talk about it. I spoke about this on my son's bar mitzvah. I wasn't afraid
> that people are going to cry or feel sad. I did on his wedding.

To explain the importance of talking about his experiences, Abram tells a
Chasidic tale about a Jew whose *kiddush* cup *(becher)* could not fill up until
an angel shed a tear into it:

> I don't want to free myself from making *kiddush* and I'm not going to
> free myself from that tear and that *becher*. It is my duty . . . . By nature,
> I'm a happy person. I get together with my friends and everyone knows
> that if F. is here then there's going to be laughing and joking and singing
> and so on. But not for one moment in my life do I ever forget that I have
> to include that tear in that *becher* of mine in order to make it full. And
> I make it full.

Rubin B.
November 19, 1991

Speaking slowly and deliberately to the camera, Rubin B. explains that this interview will be the first time that he has ever told his story. "It's not an easy task. It's not only memories involved, there's a lot of personal and human feelings attached." Throughout his testimony, Rubin is very loquacious about his suffering and reflective about his experiences: "It [the Holocaust] affects not only the Jewish people. It affects the whole human race. The rest of the world just sat by and let it go on."Rubin believes that humanity was abused not only by mass murder, but also by destroying the dignity of individual experience: "The Holocaust was not based on individual feelings. Individuals did not play a great deal of a role. Robbing a person of his or her dignity is the biggest crime. I felt I am just a pebble in the sand. People pass by; they step on it. Nobody ever paid attention to it." For Rubin, Nazis and inmates alike lost their humanity.

The first few days after Rubin arrived in Auschwitz he said to himself, "I am in a pit of snakes." He continues, "When I saw a uniform, I could see a devil, a monster, a person without human feelings. I could not understand: how can a country like Germany create these monsters?" Each of these "monsters" was programmed to act in the same way. "Something twinkled in my mind during that time. I just wanted to find out if those monsters were born monsters. I came to the conclusion that a lot of those monsters, when the chips were down and he removed his mask, were not the same person."

Rubin was born in Warsaw in 1923, the eldest of three children. He had a brother, David, and a sister, Gitel. His parents Elmer and Hannah owned an upholstery and furniture manufacturing business. He attended public school and then entered one of the five Jewish gymnasiums in Warsaw.

In order to survive, Rubin explains he had to willfully forget his prewar life: "I made peace with myself and said I could not live in a dreamland and think of my family, whether they are alive or dead. I myself can hardly recollect the mental ways which were going through my mind." It is only when prompted by the interviewer that Rubin touches upon his separation from his family and the chain of events that led him to Auschwitz. By contrast, he speaks freely about his time in the camp.

The Germans invaded Poland on September 1, 1939. The following day, Rubin's home was bombed. The family heard broadcastings that the Soviet border was open to refugees. Rubin's mother wanted to escape, but his father mistrusted the Communists and the family remained in Warsaw. In November 1940, the ghetto was sealed. In 1941, the government decreed that it was going to round up professionals and intellectuals. Shortly afterward, four Gestapo agents came to Rubin's home. They confiscated money, jewelry, and personal possessions. Rubin was identified as a student and was separated from his family, whom he never saw again.

Rubin was imprisoned in Nowy Dwor Mazowiecki (Neuhof), eighty kilometers northwest of Warsaw, for approximately six months. In September 1942, he was moved to Plonsk (Plohnen), where Jews from the surrounding area were gathered for deportation to Auschwitz. Rubin's deportation train consisted of passenger and freight cars, carrying approximately 4,500 people. Rubin was in a passenger car. There was no water or food and little ventilation. All doors and windows were locked. Of the sixty to seventy people in Rubin's car, ten died during the journey, many of them, babies held by their mothers. A variety of rumors circulated about what might await them at their destination, but Rubin found these rumors hard to believe. The train arrived at Auschwitz-Birkenau in the middle of the night.

Rubin was amazed by the infrastructure of the German organization: "The speed, the tempo was indescribable. There must have been four thousand people on the train and they liquidated them in half an hour. Women, children and babies they separated immediately. The whole process was done in such a discreet way, so that they themselves did not know what the final outcome would be."

Rubin was sent to the left. Despite warnings from other prisoners that he was going to his death, he did not run to the other side because he was afraid of being shot. The line in which he stood was chased toward a building marked "bathhouse," half a mile from the train platform. Rubin did not know if this was a gas chamber. However, looking over the fence and seeing people emerge from the other side, he ascertained that it was indeed only a bathhouse. Rubin and the others had to undress. Their hair was cut to an eighth of an inch from the skull. Entering in groups of twenty-five to thirty, they showered and were thrown a jacket, shirt, cotton pants, cap, and wooden shoes. They were then forced to run for an hour until they arrived at the main entrance of the camp. The sign above the gate read *Arbeit macht frei* (Work sets you free). An orchestra was playing.

A high-ranking SS officer addressed them: "You are all Jewish. This is not a labor camp. This is a *Vernichtungslager*, a 'destroying camp.' We destroy bodies here. Every one of you will die within six months." After this speech, Rubin's group of four to five hundred lined up and identified themselves to officers who were seated at tables. These officers handed each prisoner a slip of paper with their designated number, which was then tattooed on their arm. The tattooing was the work of non-Jewish prisoners in striped uniforms who used hypodermic needles filled with blue dye. The number was driven a quarter of an inch into the flesh, "like you puncture something in granite or steel." Rubin's number was 79635. His group was then quarantined for one week.

A triangle on the inmates' uniforms designated their category. Jews wore red triangles and homosexuals violet. Professional criminals wore green triangles. The latter were released from prisons and "shipped to Auschwitz where they were given high positions of torturing Jews. They were killing people with sheer strength." Rubin saw a prisoner ask one of these *Kapos* whether he could have a coffee. The prisoner received a fatal blow to his head with a sharp piece of wood. The *Kapo* shoved the body with his foot and it rolled down the stairs. Rubin resolved that vigilance, obedience, and keeping a low profile would be the only means of survival. Even so, he realized his "days were numbered."

Shortly afterward, an officer requested fifty volunteers who were *Schlösser* (locksmiths), metal workers, or carpenters. Rubin volunteered. He was taken to Buna-Monowitz, a sub-camp eight kilometers outside of the main camp. At Buna, the prisoners labored around the clock, building barracks for new inmates. Rubin was assigned to *Kommando 4*, which consisted of four to five hundred laborers who dug foundations. Some days as many as twenty-five people drowned in the pools of water that gathered on top of the lime earth. The exhausted prisoners had to carry the bodies away at the end of the shift.

For every body that was carried out, new laborers were brought in. Rubin remembers that a "shipment of Berliner Jews" arrived and that none of them survived. "They couldn't take it," he explains, "They did not have the stamina that a guy like me had. I took a lot of abuse, but I still had the stamina." He describes how one of them introduced himself to Rubin, who welcomed him "to the game," and asked where he might be able to get a cup of tea. " 'Ask the SS man,' I said, 'he has the power.'" The Berliner saluted and asked the guard for a cup of tea. " '*Mit Zitrone?*' " (with lemon) was the SS guard's reply. He then struck the new prisoner twice with a cable. The man fell to the floor "bleeding and gushing like a pig, while the guard yelled, 'Take him out. He's a *Schweinehund*.' "

Rubin recalls that prisoners in another *Kommando* of prisoners had to carry bags of cement between a train and a hangar, three hundred feet apart. If a prisoner dropped or split his bag, he was clubbed to death. This aimless work "doesn't make sense, but to the Nazis it made sense, because so many people died. Speaking of myself, many a time I came to a point where I wanted to get up in the middle of the night and grab the wires, 220 volt loaded. People don't grasp in a million years what it was like." Rubin's voice slows down and breaks:

> I have great faith in humanity. This Holocaust could have been avoided
> if people would stop hating each other. Get to know your neighbor. If
> a group of people possesses above normal power, they're dangerous.
> There's not enough water to extinguish that fire.

Rubin describes the time from his arrival in Auschwitz until February or March 1943 as "the worst months I ever lived through in camps. My life was always on the line. I never knew if they were going to carry me back [from work] or if I was going to walk back." Rubin befriended "a big, huge Greek [who had participated in the Olympics]. I liked the guy. We didn't speak the same language, I communicated with my fingers and shared some food with him." One day, an SS officer stopped them. He motioned to the

Greek and ordered him to shine his shoes with his tongue. Rubin's friend spat on the officer's shoe. He was shot. Rubin proceeded to lick the shoes himself. Rubin explains that always obeying orders was "one of the basic vocabularies of survival."

Every Saturday night, six gallows were erected. Six inmates were chosen at random to be hung. The purpose of these hangings, as announced over a loudspeaker, was "to prove that we can do with you people whatever we want and nobody can stop us." On one occasion, Rubin thought he had been selected. However, the guard was pointing to a friend of his who was standing next to him.

Rubin realized that "something had to be done if I ever wanted to survive." He approached a *Kapo*, a German Jew, Jakob Günther, and asked to be transferred to his *Kommando*, where there was rumored to be less torture. Günther's *Kommando 34* worked for *Steffens und Nulle*, a Berlin-based steel construction company (*Hochbau und Tiefbau*) in the industrial park, entirely under the jurisdiction of I.G. Farben Industries. Rubin's task was to sit on a horizontal beam in the scaffoldings and hook it up with a beam brought by a crane. Although this was "treacherous, dangerous work," it was also "the best I could have gotten at the time."

It was here during a lunch break that Rubin made the acquaintance of Mr. Beisel , the president of *Steffens und Nulle*. He questioned Rubin about his life before Auschwitz. "At that time I was eighteen, eighteen and a half. As it happens, I was the youngest." Beisel was in his early sixties: "He says to me, you know that war crippled a lot of industries in that country. He says, I have two grandchildren, a boy and a girl, in Berlin. All the toy factories were turned into arsenals. Why should they deprive the kids of their toys?" Beisel then asked Rubin if he was interested in a work assignment of building toys for his grandchildren. Rubin quickly agreed because the work would take place in a shack, and each shack was equipped with a stove.

Beisel arranged for Rubin and his friend, David Herschkowitz, to begin work. "At that point the wheel turned a bit in my favor." Beisel furnished Rubin with extra supplies of food. Toward Christmas, he offered to smuggle him out of the camp. "He says, I've got a suit. You put it on. At six when I leave at night you come with me. No one at the gate has the nerve to stop me." Beisel went on to explain that his wife would be waiting outside in the car; she would take him to Berlin, where Beisel's son and daughter would look after him. Fearful of the Nazi power, which was at its height, Rubin declined the offer. He told Beisel, "I trust you. I know what's ticking underneath your uniform. How can I trust the others?" He was afraid that in Berlin he could be uncovered and liquidated.

After Christmas, Rubin offered to make a cabinet for Mr. Beisel's office, in order to stay longer in the shack during the winter. One day, *Sturmführer* Rakasch, a "notorious killer," walked into the shack where David and Rubin were working and ordered them outside. Beisel arrived at this point and sent Rakasch off his territory, but not before Rakasch had caught a

Rubin B. in the fall of 1945

glimpse of Rubin's number. Because of the numbering system, Rakasch could tell that Rubin had far exceeded the six months that inmates were supposed to survive in Auschwitz. This marked Rubin as someone who knew how to work the system and who had obviously received preferential treatment: "he put two and two together. You had to be in the camp a certain length of time to get to know what gives." A few days later Rakasch returned and asked Rubin to get him a cigarette. Rubin promised to bring a pack of Salem Six, which he knew that Rakasch smoked because he had once noticed the brand of an empty packet that Rakasch discarded. When Rakasch, having taken one, told Rubin to keep the remaining cigarettes, Rubin protested that the other inmates would steal them. Rakasch looked at Rubin's number and replied, " 'nobody steals from you.' That's how the strange relationship started with one of the most brutal killers in Auschwitz."

Rubin, age twenty-two, in early 1946

Late in the fall of 1943, Rakasch asked Rubin if he could procure four kilos of *Knackwurst* and two bottles of cognac by Christmas. Rubin worked in the same area of Buna-Monowitz as French, Czech, and German civilians, and was able to trade illegally with them. Rakasch offered to give Rubin money to carry out the transaction, but Rubin told him that money was useless. Wool blankets were the only means of barter. In order to smuggle Rakasch's goods back into the camp, Rubin rolled the sausages around his body, and shoved the bottles down his pants. Rakasch stood at the gate when the prisoners returned to camp in the evening. He pulled Rubin out of the line and brought him to a shack, where he retrieved the items.

After Christmas 1943, Rubin had to return to his old construction job. As time went on, familiar inmates slowly disappeared and "new faces" arrived. Rubin felt alone. "You keep on talking to yourself because no one would ever listen to you. You end up like a nut. But I always had the vigor, stamina, and determination to survive."

The next year, 1944, was the most difficult for Rubin. "My life was getting weaker; I lost a lot of weight. I was never a cry baby but I cried a lot." Hunger led to extreme isolation: "People under normal circumstances have a tendency to cover up their character. In Auschwitz, no one covered up his or her character. Normal people could be converted in such a short time into beasts. The basic reason is hunger and few people in the world really know what hunger is. When I was a kid I read a book by a Swedish [sic] author called Knut Hamsun, it was called *Hunger*. When I got into Auschwitz, I thought about that book. I could understand much better the philosophy of that book *Hunger*. Hunger forces the human being to become an animal."

Marching through the camp in the winter with only a thin layer of clothing to cover his body, Rubin felt "something cold and metal in my pants." He touched it and found that it was his penis, which "had frozen like an icicle." At the end of 1944, Rubin fell ill with pneumonia. He did not go to the clinic because patients never returned. Rubin's memory of this period is vague. However, he sensed certain subtle changes. There were fewer SS officers. The food also improved somewhat.

One day in January 1945, the prisoners did not go to work. Instead, they were assembled in groups of five hundred. Each prisoner was given margarine, a loaf of bread, and one blanket. The Soviet Army was reported to be fifty kilometers from Krakow. The Nazis were evacuating Auschwitz and its satellite camps. Rubin and his fellow prisoners rode for two weeks in open freight cars, covered with snow, with only that loaf of bread to keep them alive. "After about a week, I looked out and I see Prague. We had taken the long way around. There was no way we could go directly to Germany." By this time, twelve people out of the fifty in Rubin's car had died. The train stopped in Prague and a commanding SS officer called for volunteers. Rubin came forward and was sent to carry bread from a nearby bakery. "It's difficult to describe how the inmates in my car felt when I gave them a hot loaf of bread. There is no item in the world they would have been more appreciative of." After giving each inmate one loaf, Rubin guarded the leftovers and divided them throughout the remainder of the journey. One night, Rubin witnessed a young man sitting on top of an elderly person, choking him to death. The young man said, "I have a right to do it. He's my father, he lived long enough." The son strangled his father for a piece of bread.

The train ended up in Buchenwald. The camp was so overcrowded that Rubin had to sleep outdoors. After a week, Rubin was sent to Dachau by train, where there was a typhus epidemic. There were "people dying every minute of the day." Rubin volunteered to go to Spaichingen in Southern Bavaria, where he lived in a nearby camp.

At the end of March 1945, the Americans were approaching from the north and the west and the Soviets from the east. The prisoners were marched westward from the camp for ten days to the town of Schongau. Here the SS seized a farmer's barn and said that they were going to get food for the inmates, addressing the Jews as "*Freunde*" (friends). This seemed ominous: "I spoke to my friend Felix and said, 'We have to go. They couldn't spell *Freunde* all these years.' " Afraid that they were about to be liquidated, Rubin and Felix escaped from the barn. They found that an elderly German peasant was the sole guard of the sixty inmates. Rubin took the peasant's gun and the inmates walked to a nearby bridge, where they were liberated by the American Army on the night of April 28, 1945.

Rubin talks of his overwhelming sensation of liberty and freedom: "You have to love life, especially liberty and freedom. Do not take liberty and freedom for granted."

He weighed seventy pounds. During the previous fortnight he "had become a connoisseur of grass. For four days I lived on sheer grass. I can detect which grass has a sweet taste."

In 1949, Rubin and his girlfriend Louise, who later became his wife ("a terrific person, she's one of the greatest"), came to Canada where he began a restaurant business in Montreal. They have three sons and, at the time of the interview, three grandchildren.

Until now, Rubin was never able to share these memories: "I couldn't open up. I've got three sons. They never asked me really. I couldn't come to it. I thought about it many times. When I came to it I got cold feet. I couldn't open up . . . . It was hell. H-E-L-L."

Of his experiences he says, "Those are items, which will remain with me for the rest of my life. A drowning person will grab a razor to save his life, even though he'll cut himself up. What I said was not just a story, fiction, non-fiction. It was a true-life happening . . . It's very important for our children and grandchildren to realize that life is not a lollipop. Life is a treasure. People of the world should at least try to protect that treasure."

CHAPTER 4

Hiding on the Run: Perspectives of Child Survivors

Leah K.
February 11, 1992

Leah and her family, consisting of her mother, father, three brothers, and three sisters, were deported from their home in Herta, Romania, and sent on a death march through the Romanian countryside. By the time they had crossed the Dniester and got to the Ukraine, only Leah, her mother, and her sisters were still alive. They were kept in the Kopajgorod ghetto under Romanian guards. Leah's sisters and her mother died of starvation and Leah was left alone, keeping herself alive by going into the surrounding towns pretending she was a little Russian girl, begging and working for food. She was only nine years old. Her testimony describes how she fought for survival all alone during the war and in the years following the war. She also describes the many people who saved her along the way and the extraordinary circumstances that enabled her to overcome the odds against her.

"When the war caught up with me, I was living in a small city called Herta," says Leah. Her parents Samuel and Bracha had seven children. Leah is younger than all of her brothers, Nathan, Chaim, and Benzion, and her three sisters, twins Rifka and Liba, and Devora. Leah says she does not have a clear memory of either of her parents before the war broke out "because they changed so drastically as events overtook us."

Her father was a clothing merchant and her mother was a midwife and healer. They were orthodox Jews, but they had a great deal of contact with the gentile population because her mother's skills were well known throughout the community. She was always willing to help both Jews and non-Jews alike. Leah remembers accompanying her mother on several occasions when she was called upon for help. Her mother used leeches to draw out the "bad blood" and Leah says "they always horrified me but I was fascinated by how my mother knew which ones were right and how quickly people would get better." Memories of her father are more vague because when he was not working, he was often at the synagogue studying. Leah explains that she was very attached to her mother: "She was a person who would wake up every morning [thinking] 'who can I help today?' and she's lived with me forever. I've never said good-bye to her. . . . I've mourned her always."

"I had no idea that things were coming to such a bad end." Leah describes herself in retrospect as a "pampered" and "careless" little child. Growing up, she was often sick, always falling ill with whatever diseases came into the city. This, she says, prepared her for the war because her friends who had always been healthy were more susceptible to sickness and often died. Leah, on the other hand, was strong.

"The war for me began suddenly . . . it is like . . . the sky came falling down." In 1941, Leah, age nine, was about to begin the fourth grade. She was an excellent student and very determined and excited to begin another year of school. Instead, bombs were falling, and her family had to escape the Romanian Iron Guards who came looking for Jews to kill. This was a very shocking transition from her prior "happy cocoon of Jewish family life." She says, "I don't think my parents believed that the day will come that we would be driven from our homes, never to come back."

Leah's family did not live in a Jewish district. At school, gentile children were among Leah's close friends. However, on one occasion, when she was four, she was assaulted by a group of children who accused her of "killing Christ." Still, nothing in her mind prepared her for what would happen.

One night when the family was sleeping, neighbors woke them to warn that Leah's brother, Chaim, who was a known communist, was on a list to be killed the next day, along with his entire family. Leah's family fled in the middle of the night. From that moment on, their lives were in danger.

Leah and her family sought refuge in another city. One evening, a loud knocking at the door interrupted their shabbat dinner. The children hid while the parents stayed "to face whatever they had to face." The Romanian Iron Guards who had barged in knew by the table setting that the children were hiding. They called everybody out. Then they took them outside and lined them up to be shot. One of the guards recognized Leah's mother as the woman who had brought him into the world and healed him when he was sick. He halted their execution.

Leah's family was temporarily safe until an order came out that all Jews had to return to their cities of origin. Back in Herta, Leah remembers her mother was busy digging holes around the house to hide things. Leah does not remember what went into these holes but recalls that her mother used to say, "This will come in handy when we come back." Leah says, "It didn't occur to us that we will never come back."

Eventually, Leah's family was told to go outside and line up in the middle of the night. They dressed themselves feverishly with as much clothing as they could and congregated in the market place to begin what would be their "death march." They marched aimlessly for months on end with no protection from the elements and no food or water, aside from what they could scrounge along the way.

One of Leah's earliest memories of this march is of German soldiers summoning her to the window of their passing car. Remarking on her long blond hair, they told her they were going to take her away because she could not possibly be a Jewish child. Leah's mother became hysterical. The Germans drove off, leaving Leah scared and confused. This incident, Leah says, planted a seed in her mind for a survival strategy: she realized she could pretend she was not a Jew. As the one family member who could pass for Christian, she became the provider for her family. Later on, when she was left all alone, it gave her the idea that she could go into hiding.

Jews on the death march were deported into the Ukraine. Near the border, Leah remembers a night of mass killings. Both her father and her brother disappeared. Benzion, her brother, was never found but Leah's mother saw her father's murdered body. Because her two older brothers had been caught earlier by the Romanians—Chaim had been shot and Nathan sent to Russia—Leah, her mother, and her three sisters were the only family members who remained on the march.

When they reached the Dniester River, the guards threw many of the weak and the sick into the water. Leah says the screams of these drowning people have followed her the rest of her life. The ones who were spared crossed the border to the Ukraine. "On the other side, it was the most horrendous sight. The Ukrainians took good care to clean out the Jews. Rows and rows of Jews were sitting with their children in their arms. Dead. Shot. They hadn't buried them or taken their bodies away."

First they stopped in Mogilev-Podolskij but then they were driven on further to Kopajgorod. Everywhere they stopped to rest, Leah begged the villagers for food. Sometimes she worked in exchange for food. In Edinet, Leah received a loaf of bread each time she helped the baker's daughter with her homework. She shared whatever she could with her mother and her sisters. Her mother, however, always gave away her portion to the other children; she only ate what she could pick up in the fields, such as frozen beets. Because each of the girls had gold earrings, they were also able to buy bread from local Gentiles who were willing to exchange food for valuable items, especially gold. Leah remembers they had to drink water from mud puddles, down on all fours. At night they slept in open fields, exposed to the elements and huddled together for warmth. Along the way to Kopajgorod, Leah's sister Devora died of starvation:

> I felt totally dehumanized, it felt like a punishment but I had no idea for what. I felt that I must have done something bad and every time something happened worse and worse, I thought the end was going to come. People were dying all over the place.

Leah's mother, who was deeply religious, believed the world had become totally evil, one of the conditions that would bring about the end of the world and hence the arrival of the Messiah. To help accelerate this process, she fasted every Monday and Thursday, "on a death march," adds Leah: "By fasting she was hoping to bring about the coming of the Messiah, she absolutely believed it."

When they arrived in Kopajgorod, they were placed in a ghetto compound and assigned a big room that might have been a stable. Leah explains that everyone had just enough space to sit down or lie down. The entrance area was reserved for "the bodies that died."

"Don't ask me how but somehow I knew how to sneak in and out of the ghetto, who to watch, when it was safe . . . ." Outside the ghetto, Leah went from door to door, posing as a gentile orphan girl, begging and pleading for food. Sometimes she was put to work helping farmers in their fields or sometimes they just gave her some of the little food that they had. Leah brought it back to share with her mother and her sisters.

Even so, her twin sisters Rifka and Liba, like so many others in Kopajgorod, died of starvation.

Leah continued to venture outside the ghetto to keep herself and her mother alive. Recognizing that Leah had figured out how to survive, two other little girls attached themselves to her. The three of them together started going into the villages for food. The local population was violently anti-Semitic so the three girls always split up to avoid the suspicion that they might be Jewish children from the ghetto. She remembers local children would stop her and demand that she say "cucuruza," the Ukrainian word for corn. For the Ukrainians, the inability to pronounce the rolled "r" correctly was a telltale sign that one was Jewish. Leah, however, quickly mastered Ukrainian so this test was not a threat to her.

One evening, instead of going back to the ghetto with the other little girls, Leah decided to spend the night in one of the villages because she had not managed to get enough food. That night, the other girls were gruesomely killed by some local children. The news of their deaths reached the ghetto. Leah believes her mother found out and, thinking that Leah had died too, lost her will to live. When Leah returned to the ghetto several days later, she found her mother's body among the pile of corpses. "I didn't cry. I wasn't sad. It was a question of time that I knew I too would be on that heap of bodies. It was inevitable."

Leah decided to run away and find her mother's sister in the Mogilev ghetto. Along the way, she knocked at people's doors, asking for food and for them to take her in for the night. On several occasions she remembers being bathed and deloused by strangers who would then put her to bed in the haystack. Leah explains that sleeping inside the houses would have been too dangerous. Above every door of every house there was a sign posting the number of people who lived there. If an extra person was ever found, everyone was immediately shot. One man she met along the way, to whom Leah revealed that she was Jewish, told her that she was very lucky because the day after she left Kopajgorod, the ghetto was liquidated and all Jews were taken into the forest and burned alive.

Somewhere along the way to Mogilev-Podolskij, Leah became sick and fainted. She does not know what happened after that but someone must have taken her in and cared for her. She says it was not until the spring of 1942 that she found herself on the road again. She made it to the Mogilev ghetto and found her aunt in terrible shape, left with only one sick child. Instead of staying with the aunt, Leah went to the ghetto orphanage. Here she quickly realized that children were frequently disappearing. She knows now that the Jewish police were collecting them and sending them to their deaths. At the time, her instinct was to find something outside the ghetto walls.

Escaping the ghetto was not difficult for Leah because she knew she did not look Jewish. She created a little living space for herself with straw in a bombed out building. Soon she found other Jewish children like herself who wanted to survive and they formed a little pack.

Leah encountered a woman who ran a small café that served vodka and sandwiches. She observed that this woman's café had no sink and that in order to wash her dishes she had to use a pump in the yard of the restaurant across the street. Leah offered to take over the dishwashing duty for this woman, Mrs. Bukowska, and soon Leah was performing other tasks for her as well, such as sorting through the garbage, making sure that nothing useful was wasted.

After a few days, Mrs. Bukowska offered to take Leah in. They pretended she was a relative and went by the name of Lydia Bukowska. The first night she slept there, Leah had "a very big nightmare": "[Mrs. Bukowska] woke me up and said, 'you spoke in a very strange language. What are you hiding?' I said, 'It's nothing. It's nothing. 'And she saw that I was very frightened and said, 'don't be frightened. I won't give you up. Whatever you say to me, I will protect you. You are like my child.' I said to her that I was a Jew and that my whole family died. She said, 'Not a word of this to anyone,' and after that she was really very good to me."

During the year Leah lived in Mogilev with Mrs. Bukowska, she discovered, consciously, her will to survive; she felt like she was "the last one left." She was determined to be a witness to everything that happened. Because of her appearance and what she describes as her quality of being very observant and therefore able to imitate Christian customs, she was confident in her abilities to pass as a non-Jew. She was going to survive and tell her story.

One day, two unidentified Jewish police officers came into Mrs. Bukowska's café; they were not wearing the armbands they usually did so Leah did not know they posed a threat. Instead, when they struck up a conversation with her, Leah felt it was safe to reveal that, like them, she was Jewish. "In my naïve stupidity," says Leah, "I thought they wanted to help." Instead, they kidnapped her and dragged her off to the ghetto where she was placed on a transport to Pechora, which Leah describes was notorious as a "place of no return"—"They didn't kill you. They just threw you in without food or water."

She was stuffed into a wagon and the journey lasted for days. When she arrived at Pechora, Leah encountered people who "looked as though they came out of a cemetery." They were "completely mad. They didn't look like humans." Leah went into the compound and "[she] was absolutely horrified. Corpses, dead, the living together, the stench, the filth, the flies, the lice, it was absolutely incredible." Leah ran out and slept close to the gate. She decided that there was no way she would stay there. "If I can get out and live, so be it. If I am caught and killed, so be it. I didn't want the slow death of this compound." She started to observe the activity at the camp's gate to see how she might manage to escape.

One day, she saw her chance when the only guard on duty diverted his attention to a beautiful woman as he was opening the gates for an entering vehicle. Leah just walked out and quickly blended in with the crowd of Gentiles who were always hovering around the gates trying to sell bread to the Jews in exchange for valuables.

By now it was winter of 1943. Leah tried to get back to Mrs. Bukowska. On her journey to Mogilev-Podolskij, she relied on the help of people along the way who believed she was a poor Russian orphan. They gave her clothing, fed her, and deloused her. Her journey was slow and it took her months to finally arrive.

Soon after Leah's return, Mrs. Bukowska, who made frequent trips into the ghetto to "buy things off of the Jews," found out that there was an arrangement to send orphan children back to Romania. It was now the beginning of 1944. Leah presented herself to the committee in the ghetto in charge of returning children to Romania but they did not believe she was Jewish. It was only on her third attempt that she succeeded. An old teacher recognized Leah and was able to confirm to the committee that she was a Romanian Jew. Leah was given food and clothing and was transported back to Romania in a luxury train car.

Back in Romania, Leah's struggles began anew. She was placed in an orphanage in Dorohoi, where she and the other children were mistreated. They were beaten and used as laborers for the local wealthy population, instead of going back to school as Leah had hoped. A relative of her mother's found out that Leah was alive and made arrangements for her to live with them in Bacau. However, the orphanage decided that it was too dangerous to send her because the war had broken out in Romania between the Russians and the Germans. Leah was not deterred so she ran away and hitched trains to Bacau on her own. Along the way, she remembers seeing fields littered with the bodies of dead soldiers.

Leah stayed with her relatives until the end of the summer in 1944, when she decided to go and live in a Jewish orphanage in Bucharest. There, Leah says she was happy until Russians came to the orphanage to claim all the children who had previously lived under Russian occupation. Herta, where Leah had lived with her family, had been under Russian control. Rather than going with the Russians, Leah attached herself to a dressmaker in Bucharest, for whom she performed various menial tasks. Meanwhile, Leah began having attacks of appendicitis. "I did my thing. I did my throwing up and my crying and screaming. When it passed, I figured this was the new me. I didn't have anyone to tell."

After a while, Leah returned to the orphanage but this time under an assumed identity, Surica Furman, which would protect her from the Russians. Surica Furman was the name of a friend of hers who had died. The orphanage arranged to send a group of orphan children to Palestine and Leah was part of this group. Before their departure, Leah went to the infirmary because she was not feeling well. Then, her appendix burst and Leah went into a coma. The hospital thought that they should not bother to operate on her because she would surely die either way. A surgeon, however, wanted to save her life. By some miracle, he succeeded. In the meantime, the boat left for Palestine. Somewhere between the Black Sea and the Mediterranean, the boat was blown up and it sank. Ironically, Leah says, her burst appendix saved her life.

Living at the orphanage, Leah began nurse's training at the hospital. Even though she was only fourteen, a nurse who had known Leah when she was a patient faked Leah's age on her papers. Leah also explains that she looked older than she was, partially because she was fat and partially because her experiences during the war had aged her. In 1945, Leah found out that her oldest brother had survived in Russia. He sent for her at the orphanage. Leah abandoned her nurse's training and went to live with her brother and his family.

"This was the beginning of much pain," Leah says. Her brother Nathan had changed drastically during the war. He was cruel to Leah, beating her often. Against the wishes of her brother, she eventually left him and went to an orphanage in Strobl, Austria, under the auspices of the Joint Distribution Committee. There, she went to school and began preparations to emigrate to Canada. Leah says that the Jewish community in Canada was split on bringing children orphaned during the Holocaust because they thought that they would have to support them in asylums. But in February 1948, Leah, now fifteen, was among a group of children that left for Canada. Leah was placed with a family who lived in Calgary.

The Hubermans, her family in Calgary, "had good intentions but they didn't know what to do with me." She stayed with them for six months and then went to study Hebrew in Montreal, with the intention of becoming a teacher. She rented rooms and lived off the scholarship she received from the Seminary she attended and the little extra money she earned from babysitting. Leah eventually married, had children, and went on to complete a B.A. in History and an M.A. in Jewish Studies from Concordia University. In Canada, Leah says that she struggled with feeling ashamed of her pain. "Books saved me," she says, because they left her no time to think. Leah now lives with her husband just outside Jerusalem, near two of her sons and their large families.

❧ ❧ ❧

David G.
February 18, 1992

David G. spent most of the war as a child, hiding in a barn in Poland. As he sought refuge from the Nazis, he was betrayed time and again by people claiming to offer help. Eventually, he and his family found a farmer who agreed to hide them for the duration of the war. But their hardships were not yet at an end. Soon after they ran out of money, the farmer stopped feeding them almost entirely, and they had to survive in a cramped shelter on a starvation diet. Following his liberation by the advancing Russian army in January 1945, David moved to Canada and eventually established himself in the Toronto needle trade.

David describes his wartime experiences as a series of small miracles that always allowed him to stay just one step ahead of his persecutors—"one step ahead of the Devil." One day after the war had broken out, when he was already on the run, David went to pray in a synagogue. When the Rabbi saw David, he went over to the young boy, asked him where he was from, and shook his hand. David cannot forget how this Rabbi looked him in the eyes and said, "I hope that you survive." Later on, David often recalled these miraculous words, because "you hang yourself on anything when you are in that situation, so maybe that Rabbi gave me a good wish."

David was born into a well-to-do traditional Jewish family in Pinczow, Poland, in 1930. The family owned a wholesale tobacco business as well as a wholesale-retail grocery. Both of his parents, Yehuda and Hanna, had been Zionists since World War I. In the mid-1930s, his father planned to emigrate to Palestine, but a cousin who already lived there persuaded him to postpone the move. David's father was a self-educated man who was well liked by both the Jews and the Poles; he sat on the city council while simultaneously maintaining a friendship with Yitzhak Greenbaum, a deputy for the *Po'alei Zion*. His family led a "very nice comfortable life" and even built a new house between 1937 and 1938.

Life in prewar Poland had its troubles. Although about half of the population of Pinczow was Jewish, on many occasions Poles physically harassed any Jew they found walking around at night. Since some of the younger Jews were already beginning to "hit back," there were many fights in the streets. The Poles even created an organization, *Endek*, whose express purpose appeared to be bullying the Jews. Members of *Endek* sometimes paraded outside Yehuda's grocery store with signs that read, "Don't buy from the Jews."

The antagonism was not limited to anti-Semitic Poles. With pressures mounting, some members of the Jewish community began to fight amongst themselves. As the situation grew worse, especially in neighboring Germany, some Zionist Jews became even more fervent in urging their fellows to move to Palestine while there was still time to do so. But the Chasidim of Pinczow were vehemently opposed to any human (as contrasted to divine) initiative to reestablish the Jews in their homeland. David recalls that on a particular Saturday, some Chasidim hired thugs to intimidate the Zionists, threatening that if they did not stop preaching, "we will knife you."

The Germans invaded Poland on September 1, 1939, not long after the Polish government rescinded the special concession allowing David's family to own and operate a private business. He was just nine years old at the time,

David G., age eleven, in Pinczow, January 1942

but David clearly remembers hiding in the basement of his family home while, on September 7, the *Wehrmacht* marched through his hometown and burned everything in sight. Taking revenge on the Poles, who had fiercely resisted the invasion, they killed one out of every three prominent members of the community.

Shortly thereafter, a group of armed soldiers who "looked like murderers already," stood at the entrance to the cellar in which the family hid and yelled "*Heraus!*" (Get out!). The family was then taken to a churchyard in the center of the village, where they met up with all the other Jewish inhabitants. As he arrived in the churchyard, David saw the corpses of Polish soldiers and their horses, lined up neatly in a row. The *Wehrmacht* had intended this display as a warning to the villagers of the consequences for those who resisted. Next, the Jewish men and women were lined up while a soldier aimed his machine gun at them. At the last moment, a brigadier ordered the gun to a different location and David's family was allowed to return to their home. When they got home, all that they found was their cat meandering over the rubble that lay where their house had once stood.

Since the *Wehrmacht* had burned nearly all of Pinczow to the ground during the invasion, it was impossible to build a ghetto for the Jews. David's family rebuilt their home and Yehuda even opened a small grocery store again. For a while things "were so good" that they could regularly send parcels of foodstuffs to his aunt and uncle in Warsaw. The only German in Pinczow ran the local jail, and the Jews were even able to pray, in secret. But at times, German soldiers came into Pinczow from Kielce to "take out" certain Jews and kill them. In addition, the Jews had to wear armbands and were prohibited from walking on the main streets.

On October 4, 1942, the *Wehrmacht* surrounded Pinczow and issued a decree that any Jew who left his home would immediately be shot. Since the Jews of the neighboring town had already been "evacuated," David's family knew this probably meant they would soon be sent to Treblinka. While his family was hiding in their house later that evening "awaiting whatever happens," a local farmer knocked on their door under the pretence of buying some yeast. This farmer, Marian Wilczynski, was a bachelor who regarded David almost like a son. He told David to take off his armband and follow him home. Since both the Poles and the Germans would have shot Wilczynski if they had discovered that he was helping a Jew, Wilczynski asked David to keep a safe distance. Frightened to walk through the streets alone at night, the young David turned back and went home. When Wilczynski returned for a second time, David's father insisted his son follow the farmer all the way to the safety of his home, and David complied.

While David was hiding under a heap of straw in Wilczynski's barn, his two sisters, Shoshana and Esther, came looking for him. Wilczynski then agreed to hide them too, as well as their mother Hanna, who joined them shortly thereafter. However, when the farmer went looking for David's father Yehuda, he had disappeared. David never saw his father again.

David, his sisters, and his mother hid at Wilczynski's farm throughout the two days that the Germans searched the village for Jews. For the time being, they were relatively safe there, because Wilczynski's brother, who lived on the same farm, was a commandant of the Polish police. Wilczynski knew the Germans would not search his home because it would have been an insult to his brother, who collaborated with them. At the same time, however, David's family knew they could not remain there indefinitely, because Wilczynski's brother did not know of their presence in his home. According to David, "God only knows what he would have done" if he had found out.

This is why Wilczynski took David's family to a farmer in Srebowice as soon as the Germans left Pinczow.

Within two hours of their arrival at the new hiding place, the second farmer chased them away, saying that Germans had come to the village and that they would kill him if they found out what he was up to. As it turns out, there were no Germans in Srebowice. Instead, a mob of villagers quickly surrounded the young family chanting, "let's get the Jews." The mob sought the two kilos of sugar the German's promised to anyone who turned in Jews. They robbed David's family of their coats and sweaters. One man even stabbed David in the hand.

During the attack, two Poles emerged from the mob and persuaded the villagers to spare David and his family. These two appeared "out of the blue moon" and said, "listen, are all of you crazy—we just came back from Germany—do you know what the Germans are doing to the Poles?" This roused the villagers' sympathies, and they spared David and his family.

In exchange for pay, the two men who had saved David's life agreed to take the family to Dzialoszyce, a nearby town where Jews could evade Treblinka by submitting to forced labor. David's cousin lived there, and the family hoped that he would agree to hide them. But the two men who had saved them in Srebowice disappeared in the middle of the night, and David's family soon discovered they had been led in the wrong direction. The next morning, David's family convinced an old Polish man to lead them to Dzialoszyce. Since they had not had anything to drink in days, they asked for some water when they passed by a farm on the way. A woman at the farm responded by calling them "dirty Jews" and shouting "you will not get water, you'll get stones" as she threw rocks after them.

When they arrived in Dzialoszyce, the family hid in a crawlspace at the house of a cousin who himself had lost his wife and children at camp Plaszow. It was not long until someone informed on them. The Jewish police forced David's family out of their hiding place and beat them. David recalls that the Jewish police "were ugly, as ugly as anyone else." He believes that they tried to show the Germans how well they could cooperate—thinking they could better their own position by preying on those who were weaker. David particularly remembers one Jewish policeman named Bialobroda, who wore black boots and often walked through the town with an SS officer and his German shepherd.

After the Jewish police discovered him, the Germans immediately put David to work crushing stones on a nearby highway. For about four to six weeks he and over a thousand other Jews like him had to get up at five every morning and walk to work through the fields. The prisoners were closely guarded by the Polish *Junacy* (young policemen who wore the blue uniforms of the *Granatowe*, but carried batons instead of guns). One day David stood up to straighten his back. A guard came over and beat him until his baton broke in half.

Polish farmers regularly thrashed the Jewish laborers with pitchforks as they walked back through the fields in single file at the end of the day: "It was a good deed to beat up a Jew in those days. Probably somebody would give the guys a medal, or they would go to heaven for it. Like the Hezbollah, you know, if they get killed doing such a deed they get right to heaven. These guys may have thought the same way."

On November 9, 1942, David did not go to work because his mother had a nightmare. She had a vision of David's grandmother telling her that it would be a terrible day. Her premonition that "it's going to be hell today" came true, as the Germans had surrounded Dzialoszyce to deport all of the Jews. While David and his family hid in their apartment, a Jewish woman came and asked them, "You have money, don't you?" After agreeing on a price, the woman led them through the sewage system to the outskirts of the town where her husband stood waiting for them with a horse and a wagon.

While they were fleeing from Dzialoszyce and headed for Kolkow, David's family found out that the Jewish woman and her husband, a cattle dealer, had conspired with some farmers to kill rich Jews and take their money. Luckily, David's sister convinced the Jewish couple to take them to another farmer whom they could bribe to hide them. David's family made a deal to pay the couple in return for sparing their lives, even as they realized that the couple would now start looking for another Jewish family to kill.

On a "cold and windy night" in January of 1943, they arrived at a farm owned by a man named Stronczyk who agreed to hide them for 7,000 Zloti per month. Stronczyk built a special compartment under a pile of straw in the barn in which they hid for the next twenty-four months. For the first seven months he fed the family three times a day and even gave them a light and some books to pass the time. After their money ran out, however, things quickly changed for the worse. For the next year and a half, they had to make do on no more than one piece of bread and a small portion of thin soup every day. The husband of another couple who hid in the barn with them eventually went "berserk" from hunger and beat his wife so she would give him some of her food. When the farmer ran out of bread, they survived for six months on raw cabbage, oats, and wheat kernels they found on the ground.

Since Stronczyk's barn was adjacent to the main road, David's family and the other couple had to remain silent at all times. They did not dare go outside except for a few rare occasions at night. As the Russian army pushed westward in 1944, a pair of German soldiers searched the barn for anyone who might be in hiding. David remembers seeing the tips of their bayonets as they prodded the straw for Jews. When the front had arrived in Kolkow, where they were hiding, a German commander planned to set up a howitzer cannon in Stronczyk's yard. This would have meant certain death as German soldiers would have been in and out of the barn all of the time. By another stroke of good luck, the command decided that a better vector was available at another house just down the road.

The Russian army liberated David in January 1945. He remembers hearing heavy shooting as the front moved further and further westward. Stronczyk came and told them not to go outside unless he opened the barn door and slammed it again. This signal meant the barn was on fire and everyone inside must run for their lives. Three days after the Russians had broken through the German front the family felt safe enough to go outside: "I remember we were kissing each other. You can't describe it. We were numb. We didn't know how to react." David's family immediately returned to Pinczow and to their home, which the Poles had occupied throughout the war. After three months of living in fear of the Polish Secret Police, the family moved to Lodz where David attended school and learned how to drive.

Not long after, he and a friend from his class left Lodz because of their teacher's anti-Semitism. They agreed to go to Szczecin (Stettin), a town near the German border, where they bribed some Russians to put them on a truck full of other Jews headed for East Berlin. In Germany, they met up with David's mother and sisters, who had left Lodz as well. After six weeks in East Berlin, the whole family crossed into the western zone of Germany. The German police apprehended them and told the Americans that David and his family were Russian spies. The Americans sent them back across the border to the Russians, who jailed them as runaway Polish spies near the German town of Hof.

By a final stroke of good luck, the Russian judge presiding over the trial was a Jew and therefore sympathized with them. During the interrogation, he uttered the secret phrase "*amchu*" which literally means, "your people," with the implication, "are you one of us?" David replied that he was, and the judge put David and his sisters on a train headed for Dresden while his mother stayed behind. Since Dresden was still completely bombed out, the three returned to Berlin, where they remained for six weeks. Subsequently, they traveled to the British zone posing as German refugees. While in transit, some Germans realized that David, Esther, and Shoshana were Polish Jews and they informed the Russian soldiers escorting the train. The Russians ordered David and his sisters off the train and they had to walk the remaining forty kilometers from Halle to Heiligenstadt. Upon arriving in the British zone, a tall officer asked them for their papers. Although they did not have any documents, the officer, having learned that they were Jewish, put them on a train to Munich. From Munich they traveled to Föhrenwald, a DP camp, where they were reunited with their mother Hannah.

David immigrated to Canada by ship in 1948. He was assisted by the Canadian Jewish Congress and, along with other Jewish refugees, was given a grand welcome in Montreal. He convinced his mother to move there from Israel in 1953. His sister Shoshana also joined him from Israel, in 1959. Esther left Germany for the United States, where she opened her own business.

In Canada, David first worked as an auto mechanic in Winnipeg. Not much later, he moved to Toronto and established himself in the needle trade. He is happy that his new country welcomed him, but feels disappointed that the Jewish community in Toronto shunned the influx of new refugees streaming out of Europe.

According to David it is important to tell his story as an expression of his Jewish identity. He also found it important to visit Poland after the war.

David G. (right) in Germany in 1946

Although for forty years David did not want to talk about his experiences during the Holocaust, he has now joined the Child Survivors/Hidden Children's Association. This has given him the sense of belonging to a family and reinforced his decision to give his testimony.

⟫⟪ ⟫⟪ ⟫⟪

Stefanie S.
December 7, 1992

Stefanie was a young child during the Shoah. She and her mother lived in hiding in Warsaw, sometimes together and sometimes apart. Following the war, Stefanie did not discuss the Holocaust with her mother. As a result, Stefanie's memories of the war are like "vignettes [suspended in] space and time." Her experiences are only loosely arranged into a chronology. According to Stefanie, these vignettes emerged after she sought therapy following her immigration to the United States in the 1950s, and began to dig into her own memory.

Stefanie was born in Lodz, Poland in July 1938. She is the only child of Dunka and Isaac, a middle-class Jewish couple. Their household was neither Yiddish speaking nor religiously observant. Her paternal grandparents owned a glass foundry and a retail store in Radomsko, a small town near Lodz. After the outbreak of the war, Stefanie's family, along with many other relatives on her father's side, moved into her grandparents' apartment in the Radomsko ghetto.

Stefanie has early memories of her family's life in the ghetto. She vividly remembers the doctor coming to the house to apply leeches to her grandfather's temples as a treatment for his high blood pressure. She also has an image of her grandmother "sitting on the edge of her bed each morning and [wrapping] bandages over and over around her leg." The bandages were supposed to help her bad varicose veins. An uncle fascinated her as well, with his habit of "nervously handling bread" at the table, rolling it between his fingers into little balls.

Stefanie remembers little of her father, except that he was "very tall" and had to duck to get through the gate in the ghetto. She perceived him as the "kinder parent" of the two. After the war, Stefanie struggled with wishing that her father had survived instead of her mother. Her mother was "the nervous wreck type" and "quick with her hand." She recalls, for instance, her mother beating "the living daylights out of [her]" for tripping near the open sewers in the courtyard and landing in the raw sewage. Now she understands that her mother "was the one who was coping with everything," and was much more preoccupied with how to survive. Her father, on the other hand, was an "idealist" and not a "planner."

Stefanie's father was killed early in the war. One night when her cousin Bronka was very ill with meningitis, Stefanie's father went out past curfew to get the doctor. A Polish man saw and betrayed him. Stefanie's father was shot by the Gestapo. The circumstances of Stefanie's father's death were always concealed from Bronka. No one wanted her to feel guilty because he died while trying to get help for her. Stefanie herself did not know how her father died until another cousin told her in 1955. Her mother, she explains, never talked about her father; "it was as though it was [an] Immaculate Conception; I didn't have a father."

Shortly before her father's death, when Stefanie turned four, plans were made to get her out of the ghetto. Her mother bleached her already dark blond hair. She was tutored in Catholic prayers, and instructed that outside the ghetto she could "never talk about what goes on in the house [or] say the names of anybody," or reveal information that might betray her Jewish identity, such as her grandfather having a beard. "This had been very carefully drilled into me," she says. Stefanie remembers her mother and cousin made a doll out of sawdust and straw for her to take with her when she left.

A woman named Wanda collected Stefanie from the ghetto and took her to a small town outside Warsaw. There, Stefanie remained in hiding with Wanda's mother for about three months. Neither Wanda's mother nor Wanda's son, who lived with them as well, treated Stefanie kindly. In fact, the son terrorized her. Even when they were having "good times," like boating on the lake, Stefanie was always afraid that he would drown her. The worst thing the boy did was burn the doll Stefanie's mother and cousin had made for her. She explains, "That was the one thing from home that meant the most to me." Stefanie did not even realize how much it meant to her until years later. Through art therapy, she connected this doll with her obsession in adult life "to find the perfect doll."

Not only did Wanda's mother inform Stefanie about her father's death; she also lied and told her that everybody in her family had died. That night, Stefanie says, "I cried terribly. I sobbed and carried on and [Wanda's mother] spanked me and told me that I was keeping them up during the night and that I was not to make any sound crying." Then, "as a way of suppressing the sobs that were coming out," Stefanie chewed her nails "to the quick, down to the blood," ripped off her cuticles, and "with my teeth tore the skin off my fingers." Until the end of the war, Stefanie says that she had terribly bloody nails; "I just mutilated my nails during the war."

One day, Stefanie unwittingly revealed her Jewish identity by mentioning to some townspeople that her grandmother used to exclaim "*Oy vey*." Wanda's mother got in touch with Stefanie's mother, who at that time was living in Warsaw, and insisted that she take the child away.

Wanda took her back to Warsaw. Stefanie did not recognize her mother at the train station: her dirty blond hair was dyed pitch black and she was extremely thin. "I said 'this isn't my mother,'" but the woman grabbed her hand. They walked up and down the streets because, as Stefanie realizes now, her mother had no place to take her. They spent the night in the staircase of an apartment building.

The two of them remained together at the home of Adela, a relative from Stefanie's father's family. Adela was a Jewish woman who converted and married a Polish scientist. They lived in Zoliborz, a suburb of Warsaw. Adela took very good care of Stefanie's mother, Dunka, who was confined to bed with a bleeding ulcer. When Dunka recovered she got a job as an operating room nurse even though she did not have nurse's training.

Stefanie and her mother had false documents that a priest had procured for them. These were the actual birth certificates of deceased people who were born at about the same time as Stefanie and her mother. As a result, they could not go by the same name. She remembers that her mother claimed Stefanie was her illegitimate child, named Maria. When Adela's eighteen-year-old daughter, Krysia, was caught working for the underground, Stefanie and her mother fled from Adela's home because they feared the Gestapo would search the house.

Next, Stefanie remembers going to a *mleczarnia* (dairy store) with her mother and leaving with a woman who took Stefanie to her place in the country. During the days, Stefanie was left alone. However, she does not recall ever feeling scared, particularly because the woman had a friendly goat that became her companion. After a while, Stefanie had to leave this hiding place, possibly because this arrangement became too expensive for her mother.

Upon returning to Warsaw, Stefanie hid in a villa with her mother, only three houses away from Adela's home. The gentile woman who owned the villa was hiding seventeen illegal Jews (Jews without Christian papers). Among them was a boy with curly dark hair and big black eyes. His name was Rysiek. Like Stefanie, he was about five years old. In order to protect him, Rysiek was taught to pretend he was a girl, and wore Stefanie's dresses. They became friends.

Two secret hiding places were constructed in the house in order to conceal the seventeen Jews in the event of a search. One was a hole behind a water closet in the basement, which extended into a tunnel that went several houses down. The other was in a small bedroom on the second floor. There was a cabinet built into the wall with shelves that could be removed. From there, people could crawl into the eaves of the house.

According to Stefanie, the woman who owned the house was having an affair with a high-ranking Gestapo officer, who knew that she was shelter- ing Jews. He planned to warn her if the house was going to be searched. Stefanie does not know what happened because one day, without warning, the Gestapo were at their door. Even though Stefanie and her mother were supposed to "act normal" and not go into the hiding places because they had false papers, they panicked and with all seventeen others, crawled into the eaves of the house. When they heard boots going up the stairs, Stefanie remembers that some people began laughing and making noise because they thought it was the end. They were saying "do whatever you want, finally it is over." But nothing happened and they heard "the boots going away." Time went by and eventually the woman let them out. She told them that their laughter had been audible to the Gestapo but that for whatever reason, they ignored it.

On another occasion, the Polish underground barged in with guns, robbed everyone in the house, and locked them in the dining room. Stefanie and Rysiek hid together under the table. She remembers seeing one member of the Polish underground shoot a little puppy and another beat an old man for making noise. When they left, Stefanie escaped the dining room via the "silent butler" and opened the door for all the others who were still locked in.

Stefanie spent the longest period hiding in the home of "Auntie Lucia," a poor woman who lived in an old house in Warsaw with an adopted daughter who played guitar, her niece, and her son. At this point, Stefanie says she no longer had her papers so she could never go out of the house.

Aunt Lucia had a brother who worked for the Gestapo and would occasionally come by to visit. When he did, Stefanie had to remain quiet and crouched beneath the table, hidden by a tablecloth, for up to two days. Because she had nothing to occupy her time, she tried to relieve her boredom by pulling the hairs out of her head and arranging them into pretty patterns.

During this time, Stefanie remembers that her mother was working as a housekeeper. She sometimes brought food to supplement Stefanie's diet. At Aunt Lucia's, they only ate black bread dipped in dark oil and potato latkes. Once her mother stole a piece of sizzling meat for Stefanie, as she was cooking it, by throwing it down her bra. It burned her badly and left a scar on her chest. On another occasion, her mother had received some butter for working as a private duty nurse. She gave it to Stefanie on a piece of bread. Because her digestive system was not used to butter, Stefanie threw it up. Having gone to such great lengths to obtain this butter, her mother beat Stefanie with a shoe.

In Warsaw, Stefanie remembers passing by the ghetto on the tram and seeing the jagged glass on top of the surrounding wall. When Stefanie asked what it was, nobody wanted to talk about it. Aunt Lucia's house was close enough to the ghetto that during the ghetto uprising in April 1943, she was able to see the smoke of the burning ghetto from the window.

During the Warsaw uprising of August 1944, Stefanie's mother feared she might never see Stefanie again and came to get her from Aunt Lucia's. At this point, Stefanie was so malnourished she could barely walk. She also had infected wounds from the "armies of bed bugs" in Aunt Lucia's house. She remembers that each night they threw boiling water on the walls to try to kill as many bed bugs as they could.

After leaving Aunt Lucia's, Stefanie remembers being transported in a rickshaw through the streets of Warsaw while grenades were falling all around her. She and her mother took shelter with Gypsies in an old fortress that was very near the villa where they had been hiding earlier. For days, their only source of food were the pumpkins they found growing in other people's gardens. To this day, Stefanie has an aversion to pumpkins.

Stefanie and her mother marched out of Warsaw with the Poles. Along the way, they met up with Rysiek and his mother who were also leaving the city. As Stefanie watched, a German soldier executed Rysiek and his mother without explanation. Dunka forced her to walk on, without looking back. They never spoke about the incident again.

At the end of the march, they were packed into cattle cars bound for Krakow. While in the cattle cars, Stefanie remembers that her mother bribed a Polish passenger who had surmised that she and Stefanie were Jewish. She gave him a ring she had found so he would not betray them.

In Krakow, her mother was hospitalized because of her ulcer. Meanwhile, Stefanie hid in a town outside of the city. They were reunited shortly after the Russian liberation and emigrated to the United States.

After the war, Stefanie had a recurring nightmare of going to the store with her cousin Bronka and being followed by German soldiers in a vehicle. In the dream, the soldiers are laughing and trying to run them down. Stefanie says she never reaches safety and wakes up screaming. Because of these nightmares, Stefanie realized how difficult is was to resume a "normal life." She also remembers being at parties and feeling overcome with a sense that she did not belong. She felt abandoned and not worthy or entitled to live.

When Stefanie went into therapy in the 1950s, she says, "Not even therapists wanted to talk about it." Two therapists turned her away, insisting she was fine. " 'I don't know why you need help,' they said. It was hard to find someone who was willing to listen." More recently, Stefanie has been active in organizing groups of child survivors, and she now plays a leading role in the International Network of Child Survivors. She lives just outside Philadelphia, Pennsylvania.

꒐꒐ ꒐꒐ ꒐꒐

Leslie S.
July 19, 1990

By 1944, when he was not yet twelve years old, Leslie had lost both of his parents. Through the intervention of Raoul Wallenberg, he and his younger sister Emmy narrowly escaped execution by the Hungarian fascist police. They survived the war in a series of orphanages that offered them only the scantiest care. When the war was over, Leslie began a new life in Israel; he lived on a kibbutz before starting his own family and having a successful career. Thirty-two years later, Leslie, his wife Veronica, and his children Gabriel and Yael moved to Canada. They settled in Ottawa in order to be near Leslie's sister Emmy, who had emigrated there in 1956.

Leslie was born on November 12, 1932, and before the war he lived with his parents and younger sister Emmy in a small one-bedroom apartment. They were a family of assimilated Jews in a poor and predominantly gentile neighborhood in Budapest. Leslie did not attend a Jewish school; his "sole connection to the Jewish religion" was the Hebrew classes he attended in the afternoon. He also adds that the anti-Semitic "environment" in Budapest gave him the feeling he was Jewish. As the only Jewish boy in his class, Leslie was ostracized. "Elementary school was a nightmare," he says, recalling that the gentile boys refused to socialize with him. Leslie describes this discrimination as "the beginning of the suffering."

In 1941, Leslie's father Gabor, a baker, was called for forced labor duty and sent away to work in the salt mines of Atmanslatina. He was gone for ten months, during which time Leslie's mother began working in her father's business. Leslie remembers that his maternal grandparents, who were better off and lived outside the city in a big house, often helped them financially, even before his father left Budapest. While his father was away, Leslie's mother was allowed to correspond with him, and to visit him occasionally at the salt mines.

Leslie's father returned home at the beginning of 1942, but was then sent away for another term of forced labor in Natka, USSR. In January 1943, Leslie's family received a notice from the International Red Cross informing them that he was "missing." He was thirty-eight years old. The family never received further news of him.

In March 1944, the Germans invaded Budapest. The Hungarian population welcomed them, and Leslie remembers a celebration in the streets. The Nazis soon imposed a curfew on the Jews of Budapest, allowing them to leave their homes only between 11 a.m. and 5 p.m. As a result of these restrictions, and the limited supplies in Budapest, it was difficult for Jews to

Leslie S. in Budapest, age nine, 1941

buy food. Leslie explains that stores stocked their shelves in the morning, and by the afternoon were empty. It was hard for Jews to get work or go to school. They were also deprived of access to telephones or radios. Leslie remembers that some neighbors were helpful during this time, bringing them food and sharing their radios, but most of them avoided contact.

Soon all the Jewish families were forced to move to houses designated by a yellow Star of David. Such housing was scarce and overcrowded. His mother was lucky enough to make a connection with a family who lived in one of the designated houses and who agreed to take them in. Leslie, Emma, and their mother left their belongings behind and moved into an apartment with three other families. Like Leslie, many children in their building did not have a father. He does not quite remember how they were able to feed themselves but he knows that his mother always managed somehow.

On November 15, 1944, the Hungarian fascist police (*Csendörseg*) came to their apartment, rounded up all the adults, and took them away. His mother, then forty years old, was arrested and he never saw her again. Leslie does not know what happened to her. He says that after war he did not make any effort to contact others who had been there at the time. He never found out where any of the adults were taken, or how they died.

After his mother's disappearance, he and his sister waited a few days in the hopes that she would come back. Finally some non-Jewish neighbors took Leslie and Emma to the Red Cross in Budapest. Leslie recalls that

Leslie in Budapest, 1943

there were many Jewish children there, living in poor conditions and nearly starving. Not having enough food caused much suffering for the children. He recalls that the children were always thinking and talking about food. Because of this deprivation, he says that today he never leaves a single crumb on his plate.

Under the auspices of the Swedish Embassy, a Zionist organization brought the children to a rented house, which served as a shelter for five hundred children. Here, the accommodation was somewhat better and the children received slightly more food. Leslie was twelve years old, and his sister Emmy was eleven.

On Christmas Eve of 1944, a group of "fascists with armbands and rifles" took all the children to an army camp on the other side of the Danube River. There the children were stripped of their identification papers and family photographs (so that their bodies could not be identified after the killing), and lined up against a wall. Just as the soldiers were aiming their machine guns at the children, a Swedish man, who Leslie later learned was Raoul Wallenberg, arrived with papers authorizing the children's release. All five hundred children were taken to the ghetto.

In the ghetto, every street was fenced off and heavily guarded. The living conditions were miserable and Leslie remembers nothing but sadness. A group of adults organized food for the orphans, but Leslie has no recollection of how or where it came from. He does not believe he would have survived without the kindness of other people in the ghetto.

In January 1945, the Russians liberated Budapest. During the air raids and fighting in the streets, the children hid in the basement for safety and listened to the cannons and rifles. A Russian soldier found them, and brought them food. Leslie remembers that he and the other children were so happy to see the soldier that they each hugged and kissed him.

Later, a Jewish organization took the orphaned children to a big house, far away from the city. Adults arrived to claim many of the children, but nobody claimed Leslie and Emmy. Leslie could not return to Budapest to search for any remaining relatives because it was winter and there was no transportation. He later learned that his maternal grandparents had paid Gentiles to hide them, but were killed after a neighbor betrayed them.

At the orphanage, the conditions were terrible. There was no school and not even water to wash themselves. Leslie wore the same clothes he had been wearing the day his mother was arrested. Most of the children were ill and there was no medical attention. In February 1945, the children were taken to the countryside by train where there was a better food supply. A Jewish family in a small village in the east cared for Leslie and his sister until the fall of 1945. Then Leslie and Emmy went back to Budapest, where they continued to live in a house under the care of the Jewish community. Shortly thereafter, Leslie learned some relatives had survived. Two of his aunts had been sheltered during the war by another aunt who, prior to the war, married a non-Jew and converted to Catholicism.

Leslie and Emmy left the orphanage in November 1945. They were separated and each went to live with a different aunt. Leslie lived in an older neighborhood in the north of Budapest, in a growing community of Jews who had survived the war. Hostility toward the Jews endured in Budapest and Leslie encountered it, even from his teachers in school. His experience of anti-Semitism led him to develop an interest in the Zionist movement. Fellow Jewish students brought him in contact with *Hashomer Hatza'ir*, which he joined.

At the age of seventeen, Leslie left for Israel with a group of fifty other youths. Leslie says, "it was a wonderful trip, it was the beginning of my new life." Leslie arrived in Israel in July 1949. He lived on a kibbutz for two years. He remembers it as his "first home." He and the other people on the kibbutz "made such a connection." "We felt like a family," he says. Leslie kept in touch with his sister who stayed inside communist Hungary. Emmy married in 1955, and left for Canada after the Hungarian revolution in 1956.

On the kibbutz, Leslie studied for half the day, and worked the other half. In 1951, he was drafted in the army. He completed three months of basic training and then moved onto a kibbutz in Northern Israel, near the Golan Heights. In August 1952, Leslie began work to establish a new kibbutz, along with Yehuda Bauer, who would go on to become a prominent Holocaust historian. Leslie remarks that there were harsh conditions, such as a shortage of water, but he says, "It is easy to take those harsh things when there is a goal to achieve." They built up a new settlement, which still exists today. Leslie is very proud of this accomplishment.

Leslie said this for him, life on a kibbutz was a good way of living: "I believe I am such a person who can live in a kibbutz. You have to give up your privacy. Living in a group, you are involved in everybody's life." Leslie left the kibbutz in 1958 when it became bigger and there were more people coming and leaving. Then, he moved around Israel, working in all kinds of occupations. He completed a course to become an electrician. In the 1960s, Leslie was trained to operate a nuclear reactor; he worked in nuclear research for nineteen years. Because he loves Israel very much, Leslie is proud that he was able to give something back to the country as a pioneer in the field of computer programming and nuclear research.

Leslie met his wife Veronica in May 1963 and they were married one month later. Leslie and Veronica have two children. They first adopted Gabriel, and two and a half years later they adopted a daughter, Yael. In December 1981, after living in Israel for thirty-two years, Leslie and his family moved to Ottawa, where his sister Emmy had settled.

Through living in Israel, Leslie learned more about the Jewish religion and what it means to belong to the Jewish nation. From this he says that he learned to respect all religions: "I respect all people's beliefs, and I don't compare religions, I believe that Jewish people survived because we stuck to our religion, but religion shouldn't divide people." Instead, Leslie says he is invested in finding ways to tolerate all religions and all beliefs.

Leslie gives his testimony out of an "obligation to history." He believes his contribution will be valuable to people who want to learn and understand this period of time. The Holocaust has been a regular subject in his home and Leslie says he has tried his best to explain this difficult moment in Jewish history to his children. He also adds that he has previously given lectures to school children in Israel about his experience. "I hate generalizations. Good people and bad people include all kinds of nations and races. Most people are good and helpful."

CHAPTER 5

Evading the Nazis

Margot S.
July 4, 1990

Margot's father was born in Poland, but settled in Germany after the World War I. In Berlin, he raised a family and assimilated to life in the Weimar Republic. When Hitler came to power and began persecuting the Jews, the whole family made plans to leave Germany through official means. Before they could do so, however, they had to flee in secret to Poland. Although they managed to evade the German army after the 1939 invasion of Poland by moving even further east, they were eventually deported to a Russian labor camp. When the Molotov-Ribbentrop pact failed and Germany attacked Russia, Margot and her father were released and she lived out the war in the Soviet Union, at one point even working for the communist government. After the war, she returned to Germany where she met her husband and gave birth to her daughter. Afraid that the Soviets would eventually overrun all of Europe, the young family immigrated to Canada in 1951.

Margot says she survived the war because she had been prepared for the worst and could subsequently adapt to any situation. "I would say that my survival is partly due to my parents' awareness of what humanity can do to one another. They did not play around the bush: they knew what was coming and they talked about it . . . my survival was due to knowing I would perish. I knew it." This knowledge imbued her with an incredible sense of self-reliance. She learned to take matters into her own hands, and did whatever was necessary to outlast Hitler. At the time of her interview, some forty-five years after the war, her outlook on life has not changed. Confronted with the present situation in Israel, all she can say is, "*Die Menschheit ist nicht zum Retten*" (mankind cannot be saved).

Born in Berlin on September 1925, Margot was the only child of Ruth and Simon. She remembers her childhood near the Alexanderplatz as "very happy," and she got on well with her German neighbors, who treated her as "the darling of the building." Because her mother had failed to enroll her in Jewish school early enough, Margot attended the public Catholic school. Her teachers and classmates were "very nice," and she "never heard a word about being Jewish, until Hitler came to power."

Margot's parents were "very liberal-minded, very interesting people." Her father Simon had fought for Polish independence prior to 1918. After World War I, he fled from Poland to Copenhagen and then to Berlin, to which he was drawn because it was such a cosmopolitan city: "It was the Weimar Republic, liberalism was flourishing." Neither of her parents was very religious, and she describes her father as a "Volk Jew," who would nonetheless visit Lodz every year to "breathe in the air of . . . Mecca." He worked as a well-respected sales representative, buying fabric from German-owned textile mills and selling it to Jewish tailors.

After Hitler came to power in 1933, Berlin suddenly became perilous for Jews. Margot remembers that right away, "groups of hooligans" made it dangerous to walk the streets at night. People were assaulted frequently and at random, and Jewish children began to disappear from Margot's class. Sometimes, the SS took Jews to the *Kneipe* (the beer hall) to have a drink and "amuse themselves." The Jews usually returned with an eye out, an ear cut off, or several broken bones. One night, Simon witnessed some Germans cutting the beard off an orthodox Jew. When Simon returned home that night, he got sick and ran a fever.

The general hostility against the Jews greatly surprised Margot and her family who had put a good deal of faith in their German neighbors, because Hitler was never actually elected to the Reichstag. "These were under-handed politics that brought him into power," she says. Simon grew increasingly nervous, he was afraid to walk the streets or fall asleep at night. He read Hitler's *Mein Kampf* carefully, and often spoke about the fate of European Jewry at home. Sometimes people asked him how he could speak so candidly in front of his daughter. He replied, "I'm sorry, I haven't got the luxury not to say what I think is going to happen. I cannot put her under a glass—she has to know."

Simon had already begun the process of securing false papers so that his family could leave Germany for another Western country when the SS came knocking on his door one night in July of 1935. The officers were looking for Jews, but luckily a cousin who was a dancer and "didn't look Jewish" answered the door, and "flirted [with them] a little." The SS guards left without suspecting anything, but the next day Simon packed some suitcases and announced that the family had to leave. He told his wife, "If you want to stay here longer then you will have to stay by yourself, I'm going and I'm taking Margot with me."

Simon called on Mr. Bucholz, a German mill owner with whom he did business, and asked him to help the family move. Mr. Bucholz tried to persuade Simon to remain in Germany, saying that the German people would not continue to follow Hitler much longer. Simon replied that based on everything he knew about human nature and politics, Hitler would remain in power "until the next World War, and you will march in a uniform." Mr. Bucholz who, like Simon, belonged to the SPD (Social Democratic Party), agreed: "You are right," he said, "dreaming is not good."

A few days later, in 1935, the whole family fled to Poland, taking a train to Gdynia, by way of Danzig. Because he did not want to lose the papers that allowed him to live and work in Germany, Simon did not tell anyone that he had left. He had Mr. Bucholz pay the rent on their apartment, and returned to Berlin about every six months to renew his visa. Margot says that her father never actually thought he would return to Germany perma-nently, but her mother "was always dreaming that she will go back to Berlin." When Simon visited Berlin in 1938, he witnessed *Kristallnacht* and decided never to go back. Margot says that when "he . . . saw what was going on, he just turned around."

On Margot's second morning of school in Poland, the whole class prayed. After the prayer, a girl sitting next to Margot asked her why she had not crossed herself. When Margot answered "because I'm Jewish," the girl replied, "I'm not going to sit next to you." After that, "everybody was looking at me like a Christ-killer, and they would tear my clothes apart. I came home crying and I said 'we have to move.'" When her mother complained to the principal, he told her, "You people of the Old Testament, if you want to live here, this is what you have to endure because we want this city to be free of Jews."

A few months later, the family relocated to Torun [Thorn], where they remained until Hitler invaded Poland in 1939. In Torun, Margot's parents opened a clothing store and things were "not too bad," because "people were poor in Poland, so when you had money it was okay." Although Margot was fair haired, she could not pass for a non-Jew. "The Poles knew the Jew better than the Jew knew himself," she explains.

Before the war started and Hitler invaded Poland, Simon had managed to acquire the papers to immigrate to Montevideo, Uruguay. He booked a departure from Torun for September 29, 1939. He said, "'let's get out, I don't care what will happen then.'"

Less than a month before they were going to flee, however, Germany invaded Poland. This thwarted their plans to leave and made life "impossible." Margot recalls that, immediately after the invasion, she saw two SS men approach a Polish woman and order her to give them her baby. The SS men threw the baby back and forth, "like a ball." The mother "went crazy," and scratched one of the SS officers in his face. "Instantly," the SS men's dog attacked the woman and her child. The dog tore them to pieces.

Margot says that, although she was only fourteen years old, she was "much more aware" of what was happening than other Jews, and decided she had to leave the German occupied zone of Poland. "It came to me that we can smuggle to the Russian part of Poland." Her parents told her that they were "too old," and would not survive. She replied, "I want to survive, so you will have to come with me."

Not long thereafter, the Germans made an announcement that Torun's Jews would be "relocated." Margot's family managed to secure special papers from the *Bürgermeister* (mayor), because he was one of a number of *Volksdeutsche* with whom they were friendly. These papers allowed them to make the journey to Warsaw by train on their own accord, rather than having to march there with most of the other Jews. Later, Margot learned that most of Torun's Jews had been herded into a synagogue and burnt alive.

At Zychlin, on the border between the Third Reich and the Polish Protectorate, the Germans ordered the Jews off the train. Margot's family pretended not to hear them and remained seated, but some of the other people on the train reported on them. Simon knew that his family would be shot along with everybody else if they got off the train, so he made a last-ditch effort to survive as he disembarked from the train. He looked at the German officer and said, "*Was kann ich dafür das meine Mutter eine Jüdin war?*" (Is it my fault that my mother was a Jewess?). The German was stunned by Simon's Berlin dialect; he "was hit like somebody would hit him over the head, and he said 'fast, into the train, before I shoot you.'"

Margot and her family arrived in Warsaw in November 1939, before the ghetto was officially established. Simon contacted sources to find someone who could arrange to smuggle them to Bialystok, which was in the Russian zone. His contact was a Polish farmer who would lead Simon and Margot to Bialystok in return for payment. Margot's mother stayed behind in Warsaw, so that they would have a place to return to if they did not succeed. She intended to join them later. They did not know that they would never see her again.

Margot and her father met the smuggler at the train station in Warsaw. He told the whole group of ninety Jews fleeing from the Polish Protectorate that they would have to jump from the window of the moving train before it pulled into Malkinia station, at the border of the German and Russian occupied zones. Once they had jumped out, they followed the smuggler, running underneath five lines of stationary trains while the Germans shot at them. "This was like the movies," Margot says. "If I would see it, I would say, 'only in the movies these people could survive.'"

After they made it to the other side of the trains, the refugees had to run eleven miles through the snow-covered "no-man's land," to get to the Russian side of Poland. Before they made it to the zone controlled by the USSR, the whole group was captured by the Russian border patrol. They were confined in a barn, along with hundreds of other captured Jews, and left for three days without any food or water.

Eventually, the Russians asked everyone whether they would rather go on to Bialystok or return to Warsaw. Often, they sent people in the opposite direction they had asked for. Margot remembers a group of young Jewish women with babies who asked to go to Bialystok so they could be reunited with their husbands, who had preceded them. The Russians ordered these women into the line of people destined for Warsaw. When some of the women refused, the Russians shot at them, until they agreed to return to where they had come from. According to Margot, many people returning to the German-occupied zone of Poland froze to death in no-man's land because the Germans would not let them back in. "This is what the Russians did," she says, "and they knew exactly these were Jewish people running for their lives."

At the border, Margot and her father met a Russian Jew who told them that he would trick the Russians into letting them go on to Bialystok. He told them to "make themselves look stupid," as he spoke to the Russians. The Jewish man addressed the border guards in Russian, and told them "this old man and this stupid child, they want to go to Germany and bring their mother to Russia." The guards laughed at Margot and Simon, saying, "we have so many women in Russia, you'll find a wife," and sent them to the line destined for Bialystok. Margot admits that "it's hard for me to understand this here, it's a Russian mentality."

In the summer of 1940, after spending six months in the Bialystok area, Margot and her father, along with 350 other Jews considered "politically unreliable" by the Russian government, were shipped north. They traveled by cattle train to Kotlas, and then by boat to a work camp called Poshekhon'ye Volodarsk, in Arkhangelsk, "near the North Pole." The journey took more than two weeks on a train that was not equipped with any toilets. "You knew that you were going to go through such hardships that hell couldn't think of it, but then again in comparison to what the others went through in the concentration camps, it was nothing."

The people on Margot's transport were the first inhabitants of this camp, which consisted of three barracks in the forest, and was guarded by the NKVD. Although the prisoners were not deliberately starved or beaten, life in the camp was difficult, with hunger and cold an ever-present reality. The prisoners worked every day, walking ten miles through "neck-high snow" to and from work in winter and through swarms of black flies in summer. Margot, aged fifteen, labored in the forest cutting and burning tree branches. While in the camp, Margot received one letter from her mother. Ruth wrote that she was glad Margot was not in the Warsaw ghetto like she was.

Margot remembers that life was extremely difficult in the camp. A Jewish lawyer from Warsaw and his son both hung themselves in the forest because "they just couldn't take it any more." "We were hungry all the time, and cold." Margot attributes her survival to the fact that she was young and strong, but more than anything,

> I wanted to survive the war and I wanted to see the downfall of Hitler. We were dreaming about it, this was our whole goal. We survived everything, all the hardships, only because we had this hope that we will one day come back and see Germany destroyed. The Russians tried to take away this hope.

In 1941, when the Germans invaded Russia, Margot, her father, and the other prisoners were released. When Margot asked an NKVD officer where would be a good place to go, he answered, "everywhere is Russia," which meant, "there are no good places." Ironically, freedom left them with neither food nor shelter. Margot and her father wanted to go to Asia, but never managed to because all the trains were full. "Every time you tried to go on a train that brought you nearer to the place [you wanted to go], you were knocked down." When their journey took them to Kirov, their documents were stolen. This made it impossible for them to travel any further. In Kirov, Margot and her father spent many long September days in the train station. At night, they had to sleep in the street.

On the verge of starvation, Margot and her father went to a Russian social agency to look for help and food. They were sent to work on a communal farm, a *kolkhoz*, near Kirov. Upon her arrival, a group of Russian villagers approached Margot, asking her who she was. When she replied that she was Jewish, the villagers did not believe her and said "you cannot be Jewish, you haven't got any horns."

Within a year, famine struck the area and everyone on the farm was starving. Margot and her father returned to Kirov, where Simon died of scurvy. Margot is extremely reluctant to describe the experiences that surrounded her father's death. "It's too much to tell, it would take five years," she says. When prompted to speak about her feelings at having lost the last remaining member of her immediate family, she adds: "I was in the hospital. I saw him dying. The doctors and the nurses, they were stealing bread from the sick people. He died, and I was alone."

Margot had found work in the Polish delegation, which was run by the anti-Communist General Sikorski. One day after her father's death, everyone at the delegation was taken to jail on the grounds that they were enemies of the state. Margot, who was not at the delegation while the arrests were taking place, ran away and had to live "underground," without any papers, money, or food.

Before long, Margot heard that the government was sending Polish Jews to "better places." In 1944, she was sent to Voronezh, to work in a government-run factory. Margot believes that these factories were a way to indoctrinate Polish Jews: "they already prepared Polish people for a Communist Poland."

In the factory near Voronezh, the NKVD called Margot into their offices and, "because I was more educated than the others," asked her to read "Communist propaganda" to the Poles, Jews, and Ukrainians who were working there. The people to whom she read declared that the Russians were no better than Hitler. "They were right," she adds. Even though she desperately wanted the Allies to win the war, she "hated the Russians like poison."

After reading for a week, the NKVD commandant asked Margot to see him in his office the next day and report how the workers responded to the propaganda. After thinking about her answer all night, Margot went to see the commandant and said, "to be honest, it's a waste of time, as much as I like to read, a war is going on and we should work for Russia to win the war. We should not waste time, because they are not listening to what I am reading, they are using this time to sleep." The commandant was pleased with her report, and said, "you are a patriot, you are wonderful, you stop reading."

When Germany was defeated in 1945, the NKDV called the Polish Jews together, and "showed us pictures from the ovens" and the camps. "They told us 'you will be going to Poland, and Poland will be Communist, and you will work for us there. But be very careful because Poles are killing Jews again.'"

In 1946, Margot was repatriated to Poland. She was appointed Political Commissar of Legnica (Liegnitz), a high position she was reluctant to accept. On the train to Legnica, she heard three young Jewish men say "*amchu*" near Posen. She replied in kind, and followed them off the train. Two of the men were partisans and the third was from Palestine. The men instructed Margot to go to Lodz where a group of young Jews lived together in a sort of kibbutz. From there, she would be smuggled into Germany and then to Palestine, or wherever else she wanted to go. The three men gave Margot some money and told her to wait for some boys at the next station, whom she would recognize when they said *amchu*.

Back on the train, Margot went up to Aron, a fellow Jewish traveler who had also been promised a political position in Poland, and asked if he wanted to go to Lodz with her. Aron said, "you must be crazy, when could I have such a career going for me?" She told him that it was he who was crazy, "you don't know the Russians, you have no business to tell the Poles how they should run their country." Aron did not listen to her, and when she saw him later on in Munich, he was running for his life.

After Lodz, Margot was twice arrested while attempting to sneak over the border into Germany, and was sent to a Polish jail. Fearing that she and her comrades would be sent back into Russia, two Polish Jewish partisan men from Margot's group called the Polish guard and asked him to trade some vodka for an expensive watch they had. When the guard returned with the alcohol, the partisans asked him if he would like to have a drink with them. They killed the guard when he opened the gate, and escaped to Warsaw. The Jewish Committee in Warsaw paid 100,000 Zloty per head to get the others out of jail. Later, Margot and her companions disguised themselves as "East Germans" so they could go to an East German *Flüchtlingslager* (refugee camp). From here, Margot managed to sneak into West Germany, where she lived in the DP camp Leipheim, near Munich, which was administered by the Joint Distribution Committee.

Margot recalls that the postwar climate in Germany was hostile to Jews. One day while riding on a streetcar in Munich, Margot overheard a German girl telling her companion, an American soldier, to bully a group of Jewish passengers. The soldier began to push the Jews around. At this point, an American Jewish chaplain showed the soldier his ID and ordered the soldier to get off the streetcar with him.

Margot met her future husband in Munich, and in 1947 they married. Their daughter was born in Munich. In 1951, out of fear that the Russians would overrun Western Europe, the couple immigrated to Canada. In Munich, they had proved to a Canadian embassy official that they had money in an account in Switzerland, and under the "capitalistic quota" obtained a visa in three hours. They arrived by boat in Halifax, Nova Scotia, and went to Montreal from there.

Margot has had a good life in Montreal. She has two granddaughters, and has spoken about the Holocaust in their schools in California. At the time of the interview, she is very troubled by what she perceives as a recent resurgence of anti-Semitism, especially in the Middle East: "I think it's coming back, something very bad." She says that Jews need to take matters into their own hands and become more militant, since history shows that nobody will help them.

⁊⧸⧉ ⁊⧸⧉ ⁊⧸⧉

Irene B.
March 23, 1994

Irene says that she feels she is giving Holocaust testimony under "false pretenses." None of the predominant aspects of Holocaust experience are applicable to her: she was not in the camps, she did not have a number, she was not starving, and most notably she was not even in Europe for much of the war. However, as a Jewish woman born in 1916 in Bedzin, Poland, the Holocaust was undeniably a formative experience in her life.

Because of her involvement with the Irgun movement, Irene was able to leave Poland for Palestine on January 3, 1940, but due to economic hardships, she did not remain there. Instead, she lived in Africa for nearly two years before emigrating to Canada in 1943. Irene became a successful hat designer. Later in life, she tried her hand at writing and published a collection of short stories, Picking Up Pearls, in 1997. Irene had two sons, Peter and Tom, with her husband Ignace. At the time of her interview Irene also had three granddaughters.

Irene's parents Frieda and Abram were divorced, and her mother, worried that she might be "badly influenced by the atmosphere," sent Irene to school in Krakow. Irene felt abandoned and alone, and wished that she had at least been sent to a boarding school in Switzerland. Instead, Irene was stuck with "other Polish girls from the provinces." They were housed, fed, and supervised by a professor who boarded students for extra income. Switzerland would have been much more glamorous. She was also a little bit resentful because her younger sister stayed with their mother. It occurred to her that this was because her sister was blond and pretty, "a little Marlene Dietrich." Irene was not blond and did not consider herself pretty and became the official ward of an aunt and uncle. Although she grew up not even having her own room or a bed, Irene thinks that she nonetheless survived her childhood very nicely.

Her life became very interesting when she was in her early twenties. She moved to Warsaw and became involved with the *Irgun*, a Zionist organization. The members of Irgun were part of an underground army preparing to establish a Jewish homeland in Palestine. They envisioned each Jew as a citizen-soldier, willing and able to take up arms, to fight, and to die for the country. To Irene, the whole idea was beautiful, like creating a "Sparta of the Middle East."

Two members of the *Irgun*, "Cookie" and "Sascha," came to Poland to train soldiers. They recruited Irene's first husband, Dr. Jacob Bauer, who was an officer in the Polish army. Jacob was a perfect recruit because he was a Polish patriot. The *Irgun* philosophy was that patriotism could not be learned or created later in life; it was easier for existing patriots to switch their allegiance, which Jacob did in the course of an afternoon.

Irene was not a member of the *Irgun* because she was not a soldier. Instead, she was an auxiliary who performed whatever tasks were requested of her, always in strictest secrecy. She had to be invisible and untraceable, and she often did not even know what was going on. Irene felt honored when she was able to see all the nebulous underground work that she had done culminate in a trainload of newly trained soldiers leaving Poland. As they were leaving, the soldiers were singing, *sotto voce*, the *Hatikvah*, which was so deeply moving and so gorgeous that Irene says, "I wanted to die."

On September 1, 1939, proclamations glued to every wall in Warsaw announced that Poland had been invaded. Over the radio, the city's mayor instructed everyone who was mobile to evacuate Warsaw for the east, and throughout the night many citizens obeyed. Jacob left to join his regiment but Irene decided not to leave their apartment. For those who stayed, the only thing they could do, as the mayor suggested, was fill every tub with water, in anticipation of German strikes on the water supply.

When the bombing started, it was continuous. Glass shattered as windows caved in from the abrupt changes in air pressure. Doors also caved in, sometimes blown off their hinges to lie flat on the floor. Then the incendiary bombs began to fall so thickly that the city started to burn. Irene, along with other women, took little pails and filled them with sand from the courtyard and then ran up the stairs to the tops of buildings from which they poured the sand to extinguish the fires below.

Warsaw was in a state of complete collapse. People were forced to cope by themselves, so "we were building barricades mostly at night under the cover of darkness," using just about anything, "things out of attics and cellars: old bedsteads and washstands, and baby cribs. God knows what was dragged out." They also piled on huge slabs of ripped up sidewalk; today it is not clear to Irene how she even managed to lift these. Ultimately their efforts would not deter the German tanks but "[they] did it because [they] had to do something."

The siege ended on September 28 and the Germans took control of the city. They had a phobia of typhoid fever and so they immediately established clinics where every available doctor in Warsaw, including Irene's stepfather, was made to work. In exchange, he was given rations of bread, the only food that the Germans provided, although Irene recalls that this bread was not really food. It seemed to be made out of clay and it could not even be cut because "clumps of it would immediately adhere to the knife." Still, if it had not been for her stepfather, Irene would not have eaten at all because she absolutely refused to stand in line for the bread or chase after the trucks from which German soldiers tossed loaves into the hands of the hungry.

In defiance of the German occupiers, Irene did not wear the armband with the Star of David. Instead, she walked the streets of Warsaw in a hat with long pheasant feathers, jodhpurs, and riding boots, trying to stare the Germans down. Irene also carried a handbag that openly contained a big ball of wool in which she had hidden her money and her mother-in-law's diamond jewelry. From the ball of wool, Irene had made a few rows of knitting in order to make it seem less suspicious. During this period of occupation, she coped as well as she could. In fact, Irene says she coped beautifully.

On a cold and miserable day, a contact from the *Irgun*, Mr. Berman, came to her apartment and told her that she was on a list to be taken out of Warsaw. Mr. Berman would let her know when she had to leave, emphasizing that she would have to be ready to depart immediately. She would travel from Poland to Trieste, and then from Italy to the Middle East. Mr. Berman was going to arrange for her passport and the other documentation, including the *Ausweisschein* (identity card) the *Entlausungschein* (proof of delousing), the train permit, the express train permit, and Aryan papers. Irene told Mr. Berman that she did not want any of the extra documentation. He thought Irene was crazy but she told him that the passport would suffice. The *Irgun* had made her so confident in herself, so proud, and so seemingly invincible that it seemed demeaning to need so much documentation to prove that she was the person she said she was. Mr. Berman warned that she would not be able to buy a train ticket without such documents, so Irene called two Italian friends who were employed as engineers at the Fiat automobile factory. They agreed to help her get a ticket when the time came.

During this time, Irene was not really aware of the danger Jews faced in Poland, aside from the risks of war. For this reason, she was not concerned with getting her family out of the country. However, in the midst of her plans, Irene's mother decided that she wanted to leave for Palestine as well and she paid Mr. Berman for papers, using diamonds she had hidden in the seams of her corset. Then Irene's husband returned unexpectedly from a Russian camp and Mr. Berman arranged for him to accompany Irene to Palestine. One morning, Mr. Berman came to their apartment and handed them their passports. At the train station, they waited for the Italians to arrive and purchase two train tickets to Trieste. Without saying a word, or even acknowledging them, the Italians carefully slipped the tickets into Irene's hand.

Irene and Jacob went down the stairs to the train, entered the wagon, sat down, and hung up their coats on a hook. They were on their way to Vienna

and Irene soon realized that it had been unwise to decline the papers from
Mr. Berman. The conductor came through the train calling out for tickets
and Irene watched the other passengers reach into their pockets for their
passports and all their other documents. She was not sure what she was
going to do so she started riffling through her purse for documents that she
did not have. The conductor approached her husband, who sat with his eyes
closed, his complexion grey, and perspiration running down his face. He was
seventeen years older than Irene was and did not seem to have her "stamina"
in this situation. She wondered if men might be in more danger somehow; or
she thought that maybe he had endured more in the Russian prison. At any
rate, the conductor turned to Irene and she took out their two little passports,
stood up, and backed the conductor into the corridor.

Irene told the conductor that she had no documents because she had
completely forgotten them at home. The conductor was speechless, perhaps
because he believed her. Next she requested his help because she was
traveling with more money than the ten shillings per passenger that were
allowed. This was not a bribe (the sum of money Irene had was too small
to be a compelling bribe); rather, she wanted to make him a partner in
crime. Irene asked him to get off the train at the next station and go into
the restaurant to buy her something small (a paper, a bar of chocolate, or
candy) in order to make change from the two extra ten shilling notes that
she and Jacob had. Irene told the conductor that she wanted to hide the
smaller bills by stuffing them into various pockets. Needless to say, this was
an odd request and the conductor was completely baffled. Irene coaxed him
off the train at the next station and watched him enter the restaurant. Then
the whistle blew, and the train was off, leaving the conductor behind.

After successfully dispensing with the conductor, Irene and Jacob made
it to Vienna by seven in the morning, fifteen minutes too late for their
connection to Trieste. This was a terrible situation: it was very wet and cold
and they did not know what to do with themselves. They also felt very
exposed because it was so obvious that they were not Viennese. Irene and
Jacob walked around the city, which was "a very dreary way to spend the
day." All the storefronts were covered in butcher paper with the message
Nur für Arien (Aryans only) and Nazi flags hung everywhere they looked.
When night fell, they found a cold and damp hotel room with a naked bulb
hanging from a string and filthy grey sheets on the bed. They slept in their
coats and shoes until 6:45 a.m. the next day.

The next morning they boarded the southbound train. It moved slowly
as it approached the Italian border. The guards got on at Treviso and
began inspecting passports. When the Italian passengers saw Irene's Polish
passport, they asked her many questions about Warsaw, wanting to know
if things were as bad in Poland as they had heard. They even bought her
oranges and Chianti from the local vendors who came up to the train
window to sell their wares. By the time they arrived in Trieste, Irene felt very
welcome. In turn, she adored the Italians. She says she even liked Mussolini

just because the Italians loved him so much. Irene and her husband stayed with a woman, Torre Biana Decci, whose husband was a bookkeeper in the army.

Irene's journey to Palestine began after Italy joined the Axis. At this time, she approached the Greek Consul in Rome who immediately gave Greek visas to her and five other Jews (including Jacob and Ignace, the man who was soon to become her second husband). From Greece they went on to Turkey and met up with Mr. Brot who was aiding the movement of Jewish people from Turkey's neighboring countries into Palestine. They spent some time with Mr. Brot in Istanbul, helping him take care of some of these Jewish refugees and then at Mr. Brot's request they agreed to lead a group of Jews into Palestine on the Orient Express.

As they traveled through Turkey everybody grew more and more on edge, especially Irene's husband, whose nerves were shot to pieces. After a quarrel with Irene, he was so beside himself that he got off the train in the dead of night somewhere in the middle of Turkey. The next morning, Irene was in the dining car about to have coffee and melon, when the police boarded and took her off the train, accusing her of being a spy. Irene aroused suspicion because she was a woman traveling with a separate passport from her husband (not the custom in Turkey). They also found it quite mysterious that her husband had jumped off the train in the middle of the night. Then they told her, in all seriousness, that spies were to be shot at dawn.

The train went on without her and Irene was left in Bilejic, Turkey, waiting for her execution. The town featured a winding dirt road, half-naked

Irene B. in Tel Aviv, 1941, with Ignace

children, mangy dogs playing in the dirt, mud huts, and very old oak trees. The police station was a room on stilts and the chief of police, at his generally boring post was happy to see Irene and Ignace, who had decided to stay behind with her. The hours passed while the chief of police waited to connect with Istanbul. In the meantime, Irene's husband was caught by Turks and brought to Bilejic. Jacob vouched for Irene and she was released from police custody. Irene, Jacob, and Ignace continued on their journey through Syria and Lebanon, where they were put on a series of buses and taxis until they arrived at the Palestinian border.

Palestine was very beautiful and very inspiring but they had nothing to live on. There was no money, no work, no place to live, and no institutions to help. Irene divorced Jacob. She explains he was a "very gorgeous person to look at," and "he played jazz, he played the piano, and he was such a good doctor, he was wonderful but he was not husband material." Shortly after, she married Ignace, who joined the British army.

Irene's mother, her stepfather, and her sister had already arrived in Palestine and were working in Tel Aviv. Her mother was a beautician and her sister did menial labour at a pharmaceutical company. If it had not been for the little money the two of them earned, Irene would not have eaten at all.

Irene in a bazaar in Cairo, 1941

Irene's stepfather, like other doctors in Palestine, had nothing to do. Each day he spent time at the Polish Consulate hoping for news about what was happening back in Poland. One day the Polish Consul was looking for a doctor. A group of Polish VIPs, (among them a senator and a superior court judge) had arrived from Cyprus. The people in the group were "guests of His Majesty the King" [of England] for the duration of the war, so they were being sent to a special camp settlement in Africa. The British did not want to send them without a Polish-speaking doctor. Irene's stepfather offered to go to Africa on the condition that his whole family could go with them. It was agreed.

It was an excruciatingly hot day and the air felt as hot as fire. There was sand in the air, on their lips and in their nostrils. The entire population of Tel Aviv sat outside on little balconies, trying not to expire from the heat, and for this reason, there was very little privacy. Whispering, Irene's step-father told them that they were all going to Africa. Irene was absolutely elated because it seemed as though in Palestine they were going to starve.

They traveled via Cairo all the way to Durban where they were treated to a beautiful breakfast in a lovely hotel. Then they boarded trucks for the inland trek to Rhodesia. They arrived at the site of the camp covered from head to toe in red dirt. The camp itself was nicer than expected. The British had gone out of their way to hire cooks and boys to keep the camp clean and arranged, and every bungalow had a plot in front for a little garden. Some of the people already living there were prisoners released by the Russians as a result of a pact made between Britain and Russia; as Irene recalls, they were thieves and prostitutes. The British governor invited the new arrivals for tea, an invitation that became the mark of Cain in the eyes of the Russians, who had not received a similar invitation. When Irene and her family returned from having cucumber sandwiches and cake with straw-berries and whipped cream at the governor's mansion, they were completely rejected by the Russians, who were so anti-Semitic that they thought it was better to get sick than have anything to do with a Jewish doctor.

Because the camp proved to be a bit of a nightmare, they moved out as soon as possible, or "even five minutes before." They bought a small tobacco farm where Irene became pregnant and gave birth to her first son, Peter. For the most part, though, Irene felt isolated and miserable. Once they had sold their first tobacco crop they had a glimmer of hope that they could get out of Africa. But as soon as she left Africa and came to Canada, Irene realized that she had not appreciated how beautiful the African continent really was. In retrospect, the experience had been phenomenal: "To have a leopard at the bottom of your patio, to make your own frigidaire, to make your own drinking water, to eat rotten meat, those were absolutely fantastic things." Not to mention that "defending yourself from the ants, the bats, the mambas, and the monkeys," were all fascinating things to have experienced.

Irene arrived in Canada on March 29, 1943. She, Ignace, and Peter traveled by boat from Cape Town across the Atlantic Ocean to Brazil, and up through South America and Mexico to the United States. Irene's testimony does not cover her long journey to Canada. Nonetheless, when she displays her passport with its twenty-five to thirty visas, it is obvious that like her other experiences, her journey was arduous and extraordinary.

〉〉〈〈 〉〉〈〈 〉〉〈〈

Harry F.
June 7, 1991

Harry F. is a gifted storyteller, with fantastic powers of recollection and a splendid talent for infusing the past with a lively immediacy. His testimony is unique, not only in that he is the only Sinti survivor included in this volume, but also because he covers a great deal of ground besides the familiar wartime territory (the Sinti, as well as the Roma, are a subgroup of the Romani people, who are often, inaccurately and pejoratively called Gypsies). For Harry and his family, as indeed for so many others, the end of World War II did not translate into a life free from discrimination, racism, or even violence. At the same time, Harry also speaks lovingly and at length about his family's traditional puppet theater. Harry gave his interview in German; all quotes are translated into English by the editors.

Harry's testimony begins on a moving and reflective note. Asked what life was like before the war, he says it was "pleasant, different than now." Before he catches his breath, Harry continues, "of course I was a child, but my parents also said that things were better before the war." "People were not as wicked," he says, "and there wasn't any xenophobia—this hatred of non-Aryans—in Germany. That did not start up until it all got going with the Jews; it happened to my people shortly thereafter."

Harry elaborates on these memories, and describes how he saw the Nazi plan of annihilation unfold very slowly. It was around 1937, he remembers with a characteristic flair for understatement, when his people began to get consistently "slapped on the wrist." For example, his uncle was arrested, "without reason," only because he went to town and forgot to bring all the right papers. This uncle had left home to purchase some materials for the puppet theater—among other things, black string from which to hang the marionettes—and he never returned. Shortly thereafter, Harry's grandfather went to town with hopes of discovering where his son might be. The grandfather was told that Harry's uncle had been sent off to Oranienburg, a concentration camp near Berlin. Eventually, the family received a postcard from Harry's uncle. It read that he was being put to work building a camp that was to become Oranienburg-Sachsenhausen.

"At the time, then, we realized we Sinti were being targeted," Harry says. He comments on the now famous German anthropologist Robert Ritter and his female assistant, Eva Justin. During and just before the war years, these two eugenicists went all around Germany taking a census of all Sinti and Roma, hoping to develop a comprehensive genealogy with which to trace the purity of each Romani's ancestry. "There was this woman going around that called herself Lolitchai [an affectionate Romani name], but now we realize that she was Eva Justin," recalls Harry. "Back then, none of the Sinti thought such a thing was possible; that someone like that could speak our language, look up all of our people and ask them, 'you have a sister, where does she live, does she need anything?'" According to Harry, Justin claimed to represent a welfare agency. So, naturally most people trusted her. Unwittingly, they told her everything: how many siblings they had, where each one of them lived, and so forth.

At first, Harry's family managed to escape persecution because they traveled about a great deal, performing with their puppet theater. He describes them as "major plays," Hamlet, Faust, and the like. Before the war, before there was a cinema in every town, villagers flocked to see a puppet show, so Harry and his family found plenty of work in almost all parts of Germany. This period constitutes one of Harry's fondest childhood memories. However, very soon after his family settled near Dessau, a town not far from Leipzig, "things started up with my uncle."

It was not long until they received similar news about other relatives. A few had been locked up and then sent to Oranienburg-Sachsenhausen. At this point, Harry's grandfather realized something must be conspiring against his people. As his family witnessed what was happening to Jews—Harry specifically mentions *Kristallnacht*—they decided they had no choice but to flee Germany.

Flight was not only difficult but also treacherous because Harry's family had been forbidden from traveling. Nonetheless, the family piled into an automobile and sped off to Nuremberg, where they had been told they could procure fake passports. They paid 500 *Reichsmark* each, got the necessary papers, and by January 1940 the whole lot were headed for the Italian border. "At that time, we already had large trailers and we were therefore what you would call a real theatrical enterprise, some might describe it as a circus, a circus without any animals," Harry explains.

German military border patrolmen stopped Harry's family at the Brenner Pass before they could cross over into Italy. Although everyone had a passport, the group had not received written confirmation from the *Reichstheaterkammer* [the German theater guild] stating they had been authorized to perform in Italy. Even though Harry's grandfather was a member of the guild, they were told to turn back with all their equipment and trailers in tow. Just as the whole troupe was about to turn around, a well-known Italian movie actress from Rome came over, threw her arms around Harry's grandfather, kissed him, and said, "how lovely to see all of you again." Apparently, this Italian actress overheard the discussion between Harry's grandfather and the German *Wehrmacht* soldiers and realized exactly what was going on. "Why, do you know these people?" the border patrolman asked. "Of course," she replied, "we worked together once." "Why don't you want to let these people cross?" she continued her interrogation of the dumbstruck soldiers. "This is such a rare treat for Italy, these are spectacular artists, please let these people cross," she entreated. "All right," the border patrolman conceded, "if you are willing to vouch for these people everything is in order, the trailers can pass." Harry explains that this actress had never met any members of his family before. "She had probably worked with other Sintis," he says, and so she seems to have understood how much was at stake in the discussion she overheard.

Harry's family was overjoyed to enter Italy and it was not long before they could draw a large crowd. As none of them spoke any Italian, they could not stage their puppet plays but performed music, as well as some acrobatics, instead. Harry recalls one incident in particular. He and his family thought they heard members of the audience chanting "*Mist*!" (shit), so they all climbed out a window behind the stage and ran off. The next day, Italian policemen asked Harry's family why they had cut the previous evening's performance off prematurely. The entertainers explained what had happened, at which point it was revealed that the audience had not been chanting the German word "*Mist*" at all. Rather, they had been shouting the Italian word "*Bis*," which translates into "encore."

Unfortunately, after a relatively unproblematic two-year stay in Italy the authorities discovered that Harry and his family's passports had expired and they were once again forced to flee the country. At the border to Yugoslavia, Italian patrolmen working under German orders arrested several members of Harry's family. As of the time of the interview, Harry still does not know exactly what happened to them, though he believes many were sent to work at a concentration camp near the Brennner Pass.

The remaining members of the group knew they could not cross the border by legitimate means, as they did not have proper authorization papers. On top of that, they had been forced to "extend" the expiration date on their passports, but the forgeries were crude and nobody pretended the papers would pass serious scrutiny.

Harry does not give a clear account of how he and his family eventually did manage to cross into Yugoslavia. He simply explains that his mother and aunt were gifted musicians with beautiful voices, and that they sang for the Italian border guards. "They sang in such a way that the Italians were fond of them," he says rather enigmatically, and the border guards "said they [i.e. Harry's mother and aunt] should return early the next morning with their horses and trailers." "Then we came to Yugoslavia," he concludes rather abruptly.

Somewhat later in the interview, Harry returns to this section of his long journey. He reiterates that their stay in Italy was relatively comfortable: "The Italian is not a bad person, but when he gets an order he must obey. So, as long as our passports were valid, there was no need to have fear." Once their passports expired, though, they all became officially wanted criminals. Thus, when the group found itself surrounded by the police one day, "everyone bolted." Especially vivid is Harry's memory of his uncle who, with tears streaming down his face, dismantled his new car and lamented, "all that we must leave behind us, only because they can't leave us alone."

Life in Yugoslavia proved to be a great deal more difficult than it had been in Italy; Harry describes it as "very, very, very bitter." "We couldn't show our faces anywhere," he explains, because "we didn't have a residence permit." Necessity constantly forced them to remain on the move. They had to beg for food, "whether we wanted to or not," because they were prohibited from earning a living through legitimate means. Sometimes, and if they were lucky, a member of the group managed to steal a chicken, but most of the time they went hungry. Another difficulty that kept them from earning some money, besides not having any official papers, was their ignorance of Yugoslavia's terrain and demography. Whereas some parts were safe enough to pass through, others were so dangerous that Harry's family did not dare cross inside: "Here were Partisans, there were Chetniks, and here were German military, and here were *Ustashe*, which were especially terrible to the, what you would call the Gypsies."

In fact, things were so bad in Yugoslavia that Harry's family decided to move on to Bulgaria, only to find the place crawling with so many Germans that they were forced to return. At the Romanian border, they were once again confronted with guards who would not let them cross back into Yugoslavia. Again, Harry's mother managed to make a deal. "My mother was an extremely beautiful woman," Harry explains. "The border patrolmen looked her over and thought to themselves, 'what a thing it would be to have such a woman.'" Harry recalls his mother saying, "yes, I'll go out with you, but first we must get rid of my old man; and this trailer must be allowed to cross to the other side, as we plan to perform over in the next village." What follows is a farce so surreal it could have come out of a movie. Apparently, after Harry's mother had left briefly to fetch the family's horses, the two border guards proceeded to fight with one another. As one might expect, the dispute concerned which one of the guards would sleep with Harry's mother first. At the same time, Harry's father hid his entire family inside the trailer, strapped himself into the horse's harness and pulled the whole affair back across into Yugoslavia. All the while the guards were so busy exchanging blows they failed to notice what was happening. Harry describes how, inside the trailer, he and his grandmother lay hidden underneath a bed. "My heart was going like this with fear," he says as the palm of his hand pounds quick, fluttering beats onto his chest.

Back in Yugoslavia, Harry's family began to perform for German *Wehrmacht* troops, pretending to be a part of the Nazis' *Kraft durch Freude* (KdF: Strength through Joy) campaign. The only reason they performed was to escape undue suspicion, for they rarely earned wages in exchange for their efforts. Every now and then, a few farmers came to see their performances and they had to pay an entrance fee. But of course the soldiers gave nothing, as actual KdF performances were financed by *Wehrmacht* central command in Berlin. "Even today I am still amazed to be alive," Harry says. He remembers performing traditional Romani and Jewish songs for German soldiers and even the SS: "God stood by us, otherwise we would all have been arrested," he reasons.

It was not long until Harry's family was forced to flee once again, but this time they were caught. While the troupe was getting ready for the evening's performance, Harry overheard some soldiers tell local farmers that there would not be a show for that night. When the young Harry told his family what he had overheard, the whole group escaped through a small window backstage. They ran, aimlessly, into the night with what little they could carry. It was not long until they found themselves surrounded by German soldiers in a nearby forest. After beating every adult male, the German soldiers proceeded to hurl a barrage of invective at the whole group: "Didn't I tell you lot that you shouldn't take off?" "You wanted to join the Partisans, eh?" the soldiers shouted. The *Wehrmacht* men then ordered the female members of the group to climb into the back of a truck. The men were forced to run alongside of the truck with all their belongings under both arms. Harry complained about the weight of his suitcases, to which the German soldier responded, half-joking: "you carried them all the way out here easily enough, now you can carry them back."

Harry's family spent the next ten to fourteen days in jail, the men in one cell and the women and children elsewhere. One night, an SS *Oberscharführer* came to Harry's cell and announced that all the married men could go up and sleep with their wives one final time. The next day, everyone was herded into a cattle train and began a long journey back to Germany. "It was terrible inside of this wagon," Harry says. "The women had to relieve themselves, the men relieved themselves, and the wagon was only a few meters long," he remembers. In an attempt to reduce the shame of exposing their private business in public, when a woman relieved herself all the other women stood around her in a circle, thereby blocking the men's view.

In Zagreb, the whole group was deloused, so as not to bring vermin into Germany. Harry remembers how everyone had to disrobe and stand together naked. "For us this was especially terrible," he explains, "because for us there is a tremendous . . . let us say etiquette." Harry goes on, "With us it is terrible to disrobe in public. Even to go to the toilet is a terrible thing for us, a degradation of our humanity: your dignity is just KO [knocked out]. A grandfather saw his grandson, the grandson saw his grandmother; everyone had to stand there nice and naked for delousing."

After delousing in Zagreb, the group was taken by train to Germany. Harry remembers one instance along the way where the soldiers allowed one person from each family to go and purchase some food. "If one of you doesn't return," the soldier warned, "I'll kill the rest of his family." Harry's mother gave a piece of bread to her son. She had pressed a small nugget of gold inside of the bread and encouraged Harry to escape, but he was unable to do so: "I couldn't leave my mother, my parents, and my brother alone there, so I returned."

Back on the transport, Harry's mother began to cry. "Alas, what will I do?" she asked her son desperately. "I have gold teeth, two gold teeth," she lamented; "They won't smash them out of my mouth, will they?" Harry tried to reassure her: "Mama, such a thing can't possibly happen. They can't possibly be like that. They can't kill people like cannibals, and they won't smash your teeth out of your mouth."

In private, Harry was less self-assured. He often spoke with an SS guard who was close to him in years, desperately searching for a measure of reassurance. "Why must we die now? Why must we go to the KZ?" he asked the young man. "Oh no, it's not at all as you imagine it will be," the German replied. "You will only be called on to work," he went on to explain.

Harry remained unconvinced: "But I already have an uncle in there. And already we don't hear from him anymore." The young guard only managed to say "oh no" before Harry pressed on: "I'm far too young to die. Why must I be taken away to that place?"

Despite his pleas, the whole group was soon loaded up onto cattle cars once again, destined for the Mauthausen concentration camp. At the Austrian border, an SS officer inspected the train. "Mauthausen; what did you do over there [in Yugoslavia] anyhow?" he asked. "We performed for the German army," one of Harry's relatives replied. After they explained that they never took money from the German soldiers, the SS officer decided, "in that case, there's no need to send you to Mauthausen. You might just as well work here."

With that chance decision, Harry's family just barely averted disaster once more. They were taken to work for an aeronautics factory at a labor camp. Harry remembers his time in the camp with remarkable clarity. He was given a number, he says, but it was not tattooed on his arm. Rather, it was marked on a plaque that he pinned to his shirt. The camp was populated by prisoners, mostly French and Italian POWs, but also members of the German resistance. Most of the time, Harry was put to work digging ditches to slow down the advancing line of Soviet tanks. Alternating between the day and the night shift on a weekly basis, Harry recalls how he and his fellow laborers had to work through air raids. Although surely these moments were extremely dangerous, and indeed several prisoners were killed, Harry was pleased to know that the fighter planes of what he calls "the Partisans" were up there winning the war against Germany. Harry also makes a point to say that he and the other prisoners were fed regularly at the camp. His mother, however, had a much worse time than her son did. At times, the hard manual labor proved too difficult for her, so a supervisor painted a white cross onto her back. This was to advertise her noncompliance, and from then on out, she was forced to work knee-deep in freezing cold water as a cruel form of punishment.

After about eight months in the labor camp, Harry's family escaped. Apparently, one of Harry's uncles had met some fellow Romani traveling through the area around Christmas time. These people had trailers and all of the right papers. Somehow, they had managed to escape classification as Romani, and thus were exempt from the so-called "Gypsy Ordinance." In any case, shortly after Christmas, Harry and his family took off. Knowing each and every one of them were destined to end up either as "cannon fodder" for the *Wehrmacht* or execution victims at KZ Mauthausen, they took their chances and escaped. Miraculously, they made it out of the camp and joined up with the group of Romani that Harry's uncle had met a few weeks before. These people agreed to hide the whole extended family in their trailers until the end of armed conflict.

"And then came liberation," Harry says. And he continues: "One beautiful day, the Americans arrived and since then we have been free. And that is the story."

But of course, the story does not really end there. "After all," he says, "we were all hunted together." At the very beginning—just after leaving Dessau—the whole group of performers numbered almost eighty people. When they entered Yugoslavia, they decided that it was impossible to keep up an undertaking of that size, given the conditions that obtained at the time. So, they split into two groups; one included Harry and his grandfather, another included Harry's uncle.

After the war ended, one of Harry's uncles—a man who had joined the group not including Harry—returned to Germany to meet up with the surviving members of his family. "When he came," Harry says, "we all asked, 'where are the others?' " " 'They are all dead, they were all murdered' " the uncle informed them.

Then, the uncle told them the whole sad story of what had happened. Apparently, the second group of performers had set up shop in a small town in Yugoslavia, near Zagreb, called Marija Gorica. They got hold of a barn, in which they all lived and performed. One night, at one, two, or three in the morning, the *Ustashe* drove them all into a small shack. There, they proceeded to beat them all ruthlessly. Harry goes on to recount the rest of the story in vivid detail:

> My people were taken to an out-of-the-way farmhouse. The farm stood empty because the farmer had been with the Partisans. There was a small shed—let's say eleven or twelve meters long and eight meters wide—on this property. That's where [the *Ustashe*] led them, and there they were brutalized, terribly mistreated. We know this because of what

was left behind: many were beaten to death. Next, [the *Ustashe*] drenched the place in gasoline and the whole shed went up in flames. All the people inside—with their kids, old men, young men, both young and old women . . . At that time, I had a bride, and she was part of this group. My fiancée was sixteen years old then. Her and I, after the war we wanted—after we had lived through it all and it was all over—we wanted to get married. She was there with them, and [the *Ustashe*] did her in too.

Many years later, Harry went to Yugoslavia to verify what had happened to his young bride. He spoke with the local farmers, who told him everything. They told him how they heard his people scream as the *Ustashe* tortured them inside that shed. "My God, those beautiful people, they murdered all of them," he remembers one man telling him. They also told him that the fire was not strong enough to burn all the corpses completely. So, after they stole all of the victims' jewelry, the *Ustashe* buried the human remains beneath a pile of manure. Later, after the *Ustashe* had left, the local farmers dug up the corpses and buried them all in a mass grave, near the back of the Christian cemetery. As they exhumed the corpses, the townspeople came across a pregnant woman. When they lifted her out from under the pile of manure, a dog fell out of her abdomen. Someone had cut open her belly, removed the child, and replaced it with a dog. Her husband, who had tried to resist, had his face beaten in with the butt of a rifle.

"And now?" Harry asks rhetorically. "Now it is many years later, but I could never forget that. It's all still inside of us," he says. "I could talk for three days," he continues, "but who is still interested in what we lived through today? And we, we were upstanding people. We didn't steal from the Third Reich. We only played puppet theater. We did nothing, but we still had to bleed."

CHAPTER 6

Rescuing: A Danish Perspective

Hans M.
April 26, 1995

Hans M. was born a Lutheran Protestant in Copenhagen, Denmark, and was active in the underground resistance to the Nazi occupation during World War II. As a member of the resistance, he helped smuggle over 7,000 Danish Jews to safety in Sweden. At the time of the interview, he was Director of Libraries at McGill University in Montreal, and taught Scandinavian literature and Danish at McGill.

Hans fondly recalls growing up before the war in an apartment in downtown Copenhagen, where he lived with his mother, stepfather, sister, and two brothers. The family lived comfortably and had many discussions about life, literature, and politics. His mother, who was a warm and generous woman, particularly loved to have young people in her home. His stepfather, Gunnar, was a medical doctor "of the old type" who frequently made house calls on his bicycle. Hans remembers thinking that his father must have been a very prominent person because he owned two bicycles. Gunnar was also "a very bright and highly principled, idealistic person."

Both of Hans' parents were most supportive of his educational pursuits when he enthusiastically entered university in 1937. He recalls that his step-father refused to "hear anything" about the idea that Hans take a job and earn a bit of extra money, saying that academic studies are far more important than a few Kroner. Hans also never joined the military, though he did serve in the Civil Police, which was intended to help extinguish fires, provide order, and help with crowd control during the war.

At university, Hans "worked like mad," studying Danish literature and German. His stepfather, a Francophile, had a strong antipathy towards Germans and "wasn't too keen" on the young man's decision to study German. He was very upset to learn that Hans wanted to go to Hamburg on a student exchange because he could not "stomach" the thought of his son visiting Nazi Germany. While he was in Germany during the late 1930s, Hans "witnessed some of the rising Nazism."

Gunnar's perspective typifies the vexed relationship the Danes had with Germany. Hans explains that while the Danes loved German art and music, they also feared the nation's brutality and military power. Furthermore, they deeply resented "the German autocratic, bureaucratic type of attitude." Better than any other European country, however, the Danes understood the Germans because they had had a great deal of interaction throughout history. Hans is convinced that this ability to understand something of the German mindset played a major role in Denmark's capacity to subvert certain aspects of its own occupation during the war. The Danes managed to evade the fate of most other European nations, and eventually saved almost all the Danish Jews from the death camps.

Hans M. in Sweden, about 1938

For Hans, a significant part of Danish national identity is a fierce defense of the rights of minorities and individuals. According to Hans, this constitutes basic Danish values that are reflected in everything from literature to music and philosophy to politics and find their most eminent representation in the religious thought of Søren Kierkegaard. For example, Grundtvig, another important Danish religious and political figure, is remembered for his maxim "the majority is always wrong." Although this is "a shocking statement to make in a democratic system," it clearly shows how much Grundtvig feared the tyranny of the majority and understood the need to protect minorities at any cost. To further illustrate this point, Hans says that just before the war there was a great deal of unemployment in Denmark and that this caused a surge of interest in Communism. Even though many people were "a bit afraid" of the Communists, the thought of discriminating against them "was unheard of." This liberal attitude would also manifest itself when the Danish population came together to defend the rights of its Jewish community.

As a child, Hans never paid much attention to who was a Jew or a Christian, despite the fact that he associated a great deal with Danish Jews. This, he explains, is because as early as 1814 the Danish government had given the Jewish population complete civil rights and therefore they were "a strong, vibrant, cheerfully Danish group." In fact, he even remembers that after the Nazis took control of the German state his family was more frightened than most people in the Jewish community. While his father and uncle were petrified of how the events south of the border might affect Denmark, "the Jews were absolutely convinced that the Danish government would protect them."

Hans clearly remembers the German invasion on April 9, 1940. He says that even now he feels goose pimples on his skin and in his spine when talking about it. At about 3 a.m. his mother came into his room and said "Hans, they are here." The entire family went to the window and saw troops marching through Copenhagen. Since the Danes had never been deprived of their freedom before, the sudden shock of total occupation was overwhelming and the whole affair is "still so unthinkable."

Germany claimed to liberate Denmark from the British. They even dropped leaflets that read, "'we came to liberate you, so stay calm.'" The Danes "thought it was hilarious" and treated it as a joke because they needed no protection from the British. They were also amused "because [the Germans] didn't know proper Danish: there were a lot of spelling mistakes" on the leaflets. Denmark officially remained a neutral country, but it capitulated on three conditions: 1) that Germany respect Danish integrity and sovereignty, 2) that it not conscript Danish citizens, and 3) that it not touch the Danish Jews.

This marked the beginning of a detested policy of collaboration that lasted for the next two years. The rationale for collaborating was the protection of Jews, but many Danes felt their government was engaging in a dishonorable policy. In retrospect, however, Hans admits that collaboration probably saved a number of Jewish lives because it allowed the Danish government to manipulate, at least in part, the terms of its occupation.

At the same time that the Danish government was capitulating, an underground resistance movement formed. At the beginning, resistance was limited and mostly staged by various communist cells. By the time Danish industry was poised to make a serious contribution to the German war effort in 1942, the underground had grown tremendously. All at once, sabotage units sprang up everywhere. These units mostly targeted industrial-manufacturing plants: "as soon as [factories] could produce for the German army—that's when they exploded." Hans, too, involved himself in the underground, although he did not have the courage and stamina to become what he calls a "front-line saboteur." Instead, he participated in the distribution of illegal newspapers and the transportation of weapons. When walking down the street in Copenhagen with his library books, he often carried a couple of hand grenades and a Sten gun in his briefcase.

The resistance movement was very complex and nobody really understood the intricacies of how the network operated. Hans did know that some of the weapons used by the resistance were dropped by the British and Americans in Jutland. This kind of first-hand information is significant because although historians are now looking into these things with growing interest, "it is difficult because there was no documentation being kept." Transporting weapons was very risky, and therefore extremely secretive, since being caught by the Germans meant an automatic jail sentence and the possibility of torture—or even execution. Hans was in a comparatively safe position, though, because he always wore his Civil Police uniform. He explains, "There is nothing that Nazis respect more than a uniform."

Hans never exited a bathroom, an office, or the bus without leaving behind a copy of the mimeographed underground newspapers. These newspapers contained mostly news about the war from England and Sweden. In fact, some of the sea routes and contacts that would later be used to smuggle Danish Jews to Sweden were initially set up for the purposes of information exchange. Because of these illegal newspapers, Hans knew about the Final Solution and the death camps long before 1945.

Hans believes that the resistance in Denmark grew so large and efficient in 1942 and 1943 because the population as a whole was behind it, "literally 99.9 per cent." Things came to a head when "practically the whole country" went on strike for several days late in 1943 to protest the German infringement on Danish sovereignty. He recalls the situation vividly:

> I remember how in the streets of Copenhagen [the Germans] tried to impress us with a lot of heavy equipment. In the central square they lined up a whole series of tanks and because people were not working they had a picnic in the square to see the tanks. There are wonderful pictures of people with strollers and baby carriages parading around, and the Germans were of course offended and horrified that we were not more afraid of them.

This event marked the complete collapse of the policy of collaboration. This was also when Werner Best was asked to "put the screws on Denmark." From then on, the situation changed drastically. All of a sudden, word came that the Germans planned to capture all the Jews and deport them to Germany. Hans rushed home and warned every Jewish person he knew. Returning from his lectures the following day, Hans found his parents' apartment filled with Jewish friends and acquaintances. He remembers "the anxiety, the nervousness, on the faces" of his guests before his family could figure out how to get them out of the country. He also recalls a famous episode where the former prime minister of Denmark told the head of the Jewish community of what the Germans were planning to do. The Jewish community leader only said "'you are lying, I don't believe it.'"

At this point, Hans went from transporting weapons to smuggling Danish Jews. He remembers that everyone was busy rounding up or warning anyone who might be Jewish. He stresses that the whole rescue was "a spontaneous, almost universal, all-embracing action of the Danish people: it was everyone." For example, on the first Sunday following the announcement that Danish Jews would be deported, the Bishop of Copenhagen sent a letter to every church around the country. All of the pulpits then denounced the German action as un-Christian, undemocratic, and "totally unacceptable from a humanitarian point of view," which made it very easy for "the whole population to join the ranks." The "tremendous willingness" of everyone to hide people and then transport them down to the ships was instrumental to the success of the rescue operation that followed.

The rescue operation lasted for about four weeks in October and November 1943. In Hans' case, someone usually came to the hospital, where he worked as a guard, and told him that there were some refugees he needed to transport. He would then go to meet them at the Central Station, where he recognized his party by the colored piece of paper they held in their hand. Since it was important to make things appear as natural and normal as possible, he usually pretended that they were just going to the coast for a picnic. When they got to their destination, usually the train station of a town called Nivaa, another rescuer met up with the party. The whole group would then go for a walk, and shortly thereafter, Hans disappeared: "you never knew who they were because you didn't want to know."

Altogether, over 7,800 people, mostly Jews and some of their Christian spouses, were smuggled out of Denmark in this way. The Germans only managed to capture 480 Jews. There was only a single case of a Danish informer tipping off the German authorities. Unfortunately, this resulted in the capture of a group that was hiding in a church in Northern Sjaelland.

All of the 480 Jews who failed to escape Denmark were sent to Theresienstadt. Apart from those apprehended in the church, many of them were elderly Jews at a nursing home in Copenhagen who had been overlooked by the underground. The rest of the 480 were people who refused to leave because they thought it was an illegal act. Hans says that although it is hard to understand today, "at that time some people felt it was dishonorable" to go underground.

Hans continues to have strong feelings about the 480 people who did not escape, and he is "very moved" by the thought of them going to Theresienstadt. He still grapples with "the thought that they went down there." Fortunately, Svenningsen, a deputy minster of the Danish administration, kept in touch with them: sending questionnaires, making telephone calls, and dispatching delegations. He continually asked for reports, creating a great deal of red tape that let the Germans know that he was following their actions closely. He knew the Nazis' bureaucratic weakness, and was able to keep the 480 out of the death camps. Although the prisoners did not live in comfortable conditions, they were relatively safe.

The Danish Jews in Theresienstadt were eventually rescued by the Red Cross and were bused to Sweden via Denmark. Hans remembers seeing those buses make their way through Copenhagen and how "excited" this made him. After Denmark was liberated on May 4, 1945, many of the Jews returned to Copenhagen to discover that their rents had been paid by the city. Some of them even "found that their apartments were clean and well-organized—there were even flowers on the tables when they came home."

For Hans, the liberation brought with it a sense of "elation, but also a certain fear." He recalls that "when the news broke, it was a lovely evening, warm, and people were just hilariously happy." However, he also saw "a couple of ugly incidents" where freedom fighters arrested the so-called German girls: young women who had relationships with the soldiers. Some Danes shaved the heads of these women and paraded them through the streets in pickup trucks. For Hans, this was too close to Nazi behavior, "very un-Danish," he says.

While working for UNESCO a number of years later, Hans became "enamored with the situation in Canada" and moved to Montreal, where he produced documentaries for the National Film Board. He emigrated because there was too little room for professional advancement in Denmark after the war. At the time, he aspired to academia, wanting to be a head librarian or a full professor, goals he eventually achieved at McGill University where he rose to become Research and Development Librarian and Head of Libraries, and teach Danish language and literature. He refers to these years in Montreal as "the best of my life."

For many years Hans felt that people should not dwell on the past, that they should look more to the future. However, recently he has come to realize that if people like him fail to tell their stories, then younger generations might forget what happened. It is important that we remember what happened in the past so that we can "look optimistically and positively toward a future that is more fair and reasonable."

CONCLUSION

Ghostwriters: The Hidden Children of Living Testimonies

Anita Slominska

"[T]he writing of the Shoah must involve a continuing discourse about the inadequacy of the act of that writing . . . As Levinas argues, sincerity involves not only an exposure of one's thoughts and motivations before the other but also an exposure of that exposure. In this vein, one is obligated as an historian not only to engage in a discourse about the Shoah but also to engage in a discourse about one's discourse . . . [1]

James Hatley

I know that I must live with an experience that has scarred me forever. I am a captive of history. I speak from my need. I cannot understand [the] Holocaust; I can only live with it.[2]

Renata Skotnicka-Zajdman

Over the course of putting together this collection of survivor testimonies, the editors agreed that the final chapter should pay tribute to the contribution of founding members of *Living Testimonies*, Yehudi Lindeman and Renata Skotnicka-Zadjman. Yehudi and Renata, child survivors from Holland and the Warsaw ghetto respectively, have had an important presence throughout each aspect of the writing of this book. Their reflections and observations, as well as personal initiative and courage point to some of the links between the testimony process and subjective experience that have informed and conflicted with the shaping of the final text. Their voices, as survivors, interviewers, and writers/editors provide an urgent counterpoint to the objective tone, or "ghostwritten" quality, of the summaries in this volume, and offer a starting point to reflect on the dilemmas of Holocaust representation and healing.

Breaking the Silence

Renata Skotnicka-Zajdman grew up in Warsaw. During the war, she escaped the Warsaw ghetto and went into hiding, posing as a gentile girl. Her personal story of survival is a hidden but pervasive subtext to the Living Testimonies project. Her involvement also reveals the personal motivations that often inform the process of Holocaust documentation. In Renata's case, these motivations are related to her own experience of Holocaust remembrance:

> I tried to tell my story 30 years ago, even 40 years ago when I came to Canada, but I was brushed off. People thought I was trying to indulge in something and I was very hurt I didn't get any understanding. Maybe because Canadian people didn't understand themselves, there was an atmosphere that if you were murdered in the Holocaust you were a victim and if you survive you're scum . . . I always felt that people would not understand and they would rip me apart, so I was very quiet about it. They asked me, "How did you survive? You must have been flirting with some Germans because you were such a young pretty girl." So they shut me up for so many years because I realized that they think that I did something wrong in order to survive; [they didn't] realize it was a question of luck or because other people helped.

Even her family was completely silent about the Shoah; it was treated as a "black hole." Renata's late husband, Adam, a survivor from the Polish city of Radom, refused to acknowledge the catastrophic events of the past: "I would cry and scream at night and he said, 'please don't cry don't cry'; but he never asked me, 'why are you crying?' He was afraid to ask . . . I understand now that he was afraid to learn from me how his mother and the rest of his family perished, while he was deported to Siberia." For thirty years, until Adam's death, the Holocaust was "a wall" between them.

Renata's daughter, Sharon, from the age of ten was aware of her mother's sadness and asked her many questions. She once wrote about the family secrets in a story titled "The Yellow Basket." Her son Michael's interest in the Holocaust was only revealed to Renata later in her life, which contributed significantly to Renata breaking her silence, and "going deep into my own history."

Renata never spoke about her Holocaust experiences until 1989, when Sharon introduced her to Yehudi Lindeman, who was interested in interviewing survivors. Renata recorded eight hours with Yehudi on audiotape, and later made a three and a half hour videotape as well. Renata identifies both of these experiences as a "catharsis." She realized there were other survivors like her who needed a similar catharsis and wanted to help people who were afraid to talk. Renata now describes this as an "obsession" to help others break their silence. "The more I learned about survivors, the more I felt I can help," she says.

As a survivor, Renata believes she has more empathy and understanding than other interviewers who do not share the Holocaust experience.

She considers her subjective involvement with the survivors' stories an asset: "I am not detached, I mean I try to be professional, very calm but after it's over I am not calm, I am part of their experience and they know they can trust [me]. I think that's important." She believes survivors are more trusting of her because she is a survivor herself. She establishes a relationship with interviewees, based on a "special bond," that lasts beyond the interview itself. For example, Renata always stays in touch with interviewees following the interview and insists on giving them her phone number. Even if they never call, it is not uncommon for Renata to run into them in her Montreal neighborhood of Côte St. Luc where much of the survivor community lives. Renata also experiences the solidarity of the survivor community and their families through her volunteer work at the Holocaust Centre in Montreal.

By eliminating her sense of isolation, Renata's perspective on her survival has shifted. Now when people ask her how she survived, Renata says confidently, "I was lucky, people helped me, and my own courage . . ."

The need to overcome the silence and isolation following the Shoah is a motivation Yehudi Lindeman attributes to many survivors. He explains, "They have lived with that silence and the silence had been so long and so loud." Yehudi, a retired professor of English at McGill University and founder of Living Testimonies (1989) experienced the silence first hand as a child survivor. After the war, he found himself in the same elementary school as Sophia, whom he describes as his "little sibling" because the two of them were hidden together in four different places in the east, and north of the Netherlands. He and Sophia were liberated by the Canadian First Army in the same village on the same day. Yehudi says,

> I came back to elementary school in January 1946 in Amsterdam into second grade and there was Sophia. It was the only day that I was early, the first day that I came to school, and so was Sophia. We were the only two in the schoolyard and I remember standing there with my funny little leather bag . . . I was totally stunned to find her there. I said, "That's strange to find you here," and she said, "yeah that's strange," and those were the last words we ever spoke about our shared experiences during the war! We didn't avoid each other, but there was an awkwardness about us that had to do with our common past. We certainly were careful never to talk about it.

The ubiquity of silence following the Shoah, the "black hole" as Renata calls it, relates to the massive trauma of the event as an inexpressible experience. Holocaust scholars and psychiatrists alike contend that traumatic memories or memories of destruction and loss exist outside the range of comprehension and expression, and account for much of the silence among survivors following the war. Yet this "unspeakability" of the Holocaust is contradicted by the strong inclination many survivors have, and the initiative they take, to talk about their experiences.[3] In instances when survivors no longer want to be silent, as Renata was for example, the silence can still be perpetuated by the absence of a willing and sympathetic listener. Yehudi explains,

> Maybe because the trauma itself was so great on the part of survivors and because the pain that even telling the smallest story of survival incurred on the part of the listeners, the bystanders, was too great. I myself was such a bystander for 30–40 years . . . I think my aunt, my mother's older sister who survived Auschwitz, really tried quite hard in her own family, but we were never open to her story, not her two daughters and certainly not me, her [nephew]. Those are about the only surviving members of that whole extended family . . . I remember my aunt more than once tried to tell her story of how at one point in Auschwitz she and several hundreds of other women stood in line for the gas chamber and stood there through the night and nothing happened. They stood there hour after hour waiting to be gassed and when it was close to morning, they were told, "okay you can go back to your barracks," and when they asked one of the people in charge, who was a Jew, [what had happened], they were told, "they were out of gas." Now I remember my cousin Rifka and I, Rifka's older than me but not by that much, we used to hear the story and sort of giggle about it, "yeah, yeah nice story: they were out of gas," but that was about it. I believed her but it didn't touch me; it was like a weird story and I wasn't ready. Probably just letting in that . . . degree of horror was way beyond what we were able to invest in emotionally.

Two incidents significantly changed this resistance on his part. The first occurred while Yehudi attended a conference of psychologists and other health professionals in Jerusalem during the mid-eighties. It was at this conference, after giving a paper on Etty Hillseum's attitude to her impending deportation and death, that Yehudi was "unmasked" as a child survivor. It unnerved him. When he came back to Montreal, he began to look for a connection with other Holocaust survivors. The second incident was viewing Claude Lanzmann's film *Shoah*.

> I think I saw *Shoah* in '86 or '87 and there is a moment in *Shoah*, it's actually Treblinka, where women are standing in front of the gas chamber and they're waiting to be gassed and they're naked and they stand there for hours and eventually they're driven into the gas chambers and they're all gone . . . I thought of my aunt who just stood there, standing there in front of the gas chamber in Auschwitz-Birkenau, and I don't know, something clicked.

Yehudi was compelled to find out more about his family, and the fate of Dutch Jewry as a whole. Drawing on the work of Emmanuel Levinas, Yehudi describes this epiphany in terms of an encounter with the Other, that is, an affective proximity, a state of being profoundly touched by the Other, and his/her mortality and defenselessness.

James Hatley in *The Suffering Witness* similarly uses Levinas as the basis for his understanding of the role of the listener in Holocaust testimony. He equates listening with being "summoned to attentiveness" whereby the listener registers the gravity of the violence not only as an "objective fact" but a "subjective blow." He explains, "The witness [listener] refuses to forget the weight of this blow or the depth of the wound it inflicts."[4]

There is a tension however between the obligation/duty of the listener and the way that Holocaust testimony, as noted by Dori Laub, can trigger the listener's full range of defensive feelings. According to Laub, possible defensive reactions are: paralysis ("fear of merging with the atrocities being recounted"); outrage and anger directed at the victim; withdrawal/numbness or awe/fear (keeping the survivor at a distance "to avoid the intimacy entailed in knowing"); and an obsession with fact-finding ("an absorbing interest in factual details of the account which serve to circumvent the human experience").[5]

Interestingly, Yehudi and Renata's own stories feature some of these very defense mechanisms—Renata experienced the Jewish community in Canada's inability to appreciate survivors as victims; and Yehudi, as a listener, experienced the need to protect himself. In both cases, silence became a structuring aspect of their lives after the war.

The Role of Testimony in Holocaust Representation

In referring to the Yale Fortunoff archive as an "archive of conscience," Geoffrey Hartman points to a crucial distinction between documented historical data and retrospective personal testimonies from witnesses of the Shoah. In this vein, Annette Wievorka argues that Holocaust testimony does not only have the sole purpose of "[increasing] knowledge" about a historical event. Instead, testimony should also be understood as a "means of transmission."[6] Henry Greenspan even more specifically identifies the "process" of "[entering] into survivors' struggles for words" as the best means to understand the Shoah. He explains, "it is only as we learn to follow survivors' accounts *as* they become disfigured and finally fail [cease to fully and adequately represent traumatic experience]—because the destruction is too vast, because the loss is too unbearable, because meaning becomes undone, because stories fall apart, because voice starts to struggle, because death again invades the recounter [survivor]—that we begin to approach the Holocaust itself."[7]

Even though the memories relayed through testimony might misrepresent what "really" happened in the past, the substance of memory, as Irving Howe has pointed out, is not "made up." Individual witness testimonies offer a crucial perspective as well as a wealth of information about the relationship between the instance of remembrance (the present) and the past.[8] At the same time, survivor testimonies can also be valued, in a more traditional sense, as a source of evidence and facts that would otherwise not make their way into documented history. However, when survivors are exclusively seen as repositories of evidence and facts, there is no room to consider how memories are themselves a part of history. As Renata points out, the valorization of "facts" over personal recollection results in too much emphasis on the correspondence between one's own story and "historical truth." Thus, any misrepresentation of known facts may threaten to undermine a survivor's entire testimony, or worse, put into question the veracity of the Holocaust and play into the hands of deniers. She believes that people might say, "what's the matter? This is not right. What's right?"

Yehudi explains that when discussion first began about starting a Holocaust video archive in Montreal, in 1987–1988, there were immediate questions about the role of testimony as historical documentation of the Jewish tragedy. The committee in charge of preparing the ground, representing Canadian Jewish Congress and the Holocaust Memorial Centre (through Federation CJA) brought together a number of academics (including historians), health professionals, and lay people. The historians on the joint committee saw its primary purpose as obtaining historical data to see, as Yehudi puts it, "how they tally with the documented record." For this purpose, historians were in favor of doing audio interviews because they perceived the use of video as merely a distraction. Yehudi thinks that since Living Testimonies was established as a video archive at McGill University in 1989, the decision to use video recording, as opposed to audio, has been more than vindicated because in addition to facts, video testimony also records the powerful visual nuances of the survivor's reactions and emotions. The immediacy of video, which offers a specific corporeal referent to historical testimony, is essential to what Yehudi calls compiling the "history of the victims." He says, "The victims of history are not known so there is a sense that we should name them."

Video is able to bestow individuality on each interviewed survivor. In this sense, Yehudi sees the emergence of this and other video archives as part of an ongoing attempt to "put into context" the "assault on the individuality" of Jewish victims of the Holocaust, and the attempt to annihilate their identities.

For this reason, a video testimony archive is distinct from historical documents and sources that are only concerned with recording the facts of the genocide. However, Yehudi emphasizes, one of Living Testimonies' principal endeavors is to place testimony in a complementary relationship with documented history. This means that on the one hand, testimony can be measured by what is known, or accepted as historical facts. On the other hand, by including a personal voice that is otherwise lost in traditional documented history, Yehudi thinks one can "make certain connections that you otherwise cannot get." This corresponds to what Claudia Eppert calls the "past as memory": "Remembrance is emphasized as a 'living entity' that consolidates linkages between past and present. While history is out there, apart, and unaffecting, living memory suggests a personal, emotional, and meaningful relation to past events."[9] In this vein, Yehudi says, "By watching these videos, people can get an insight into what it was like ... it's fragments, it's bits and pieces here and there but taken together it represents something more than just these pieces."

As the intensely personal "bits and pieces" or shards of memory emerge from testimony, survivors, at the same time, are also called to be witnesses to the "bigger picture," and to leave a record of their experiences to future generations. Thus, the structure of each interview in the Living Testimonies archive is oriented to giving survivors a chance to tell their stories, not only for themselves, but for others. For pragmatic reasons, Living Testimonies has relied on chronology in the elicitation and presentation of each testimony, which Yehudi describes as "bending in the direction of the reader." A uniform interview structure and chronological presentation effaces the presence of an individual subject in the narrative summaries to some extent, but it also helps to provide accessibility for present and future generations and to ensure that survivors will not be forgotten victims of history,

On the downside, Yehudi has observed that for survivors themselves the method of following a chronology can have the effect of interrupting them and the working of their memory. Ironically, he says that by sticking closely to a chronology "you will succeed, except for the most tenacious, you will succeed in getting [the interviewee] off track." Nonetheless, Yehudi believes that the listener benefits from the guidance of a "chronological plot": "Otherwise you could get very, very lost ... it has to have some kind of form, some kind of coherence."

In Yehudi's observation, survivors often enter a "bubble," re-living certain episodes and experiences that "are connected not necessarily by chronology but by association." The task of the interviewer is to keep order and flow to a narrative that covers prewar life, the Nazi period, and postliberation experiences. He believes that testimony "needs a narrative strategy that firmly anchors it, otherwise the reader or the listener is going to go berserk."

Presented in the form of written summaries, which are narrated in the third person singular, oral testimonies are subjected to a layer of retelling that brings them closer to conventional/standard historical narratives. The movement from the oral process to the written product involves synthesizing, paraphrasing, and clarifying; in short, turning an unrehearsed oral account of deeply personal events and experiences into an ironed-out story. Yet, we are also aware that treating testimonies as "finished texts" or "stories" runs counter to the notion expressed by Greenspan that the "fullest significance" of survivor accounts are their "unfinished, contested, and nondefinitive character."[10] In this vein, we have concerns about the degree to which the interviewers and the writers of the summaries in the book have intervened in the survivor's own narrative. Collectively, as an editorial team, we are aware that the final presentation of the third person narrative obfuscates the degree of interpretation that is going on and have therefore tried to limit editorializing as much as possible.

All the same, a degree of editorializing is inevitable as we transliterate the oral/video testimony into a written document. As discussed in the Introduction, the third person pronoun has been a source of some conflict in this regard, as it is responsible for the "ghostwritten" qualities of the text. At best, if not invariably, Yehudi believes we have succeeded in "getting closer in our third person singular description to the voice of the individual speaker," and bringing out their individuality, even if this sometimes involves a "sleight of hand."

In this light, it is important to bear in mind that in both oral and written form, testimony points to a gap between the "story" (language) and the "person" (experience), and the unrepresentability of the Holocaust as a historical event. Hayden White contends that the Holocaust marks a "new actuality" because it is unlike any event in history. As such, he argues that it does not readily fit with preexisting and available categories; and the Holocaust is therefore incommensurable with our modes of understanding.[11] Renata expresses this point of view: "As a human being, I will never understand [the Holocaust] . . . There are so many things which you can't say: obscene, brutal, cruel, grotesque. I mean there are no words; you can't even say it . . ."

At the same time, critical reflections on the status of the Shoah in historiography should not overshadow the way survivors feel a very real need to talk about their experiences, and to externalize their memories. Neither should we lose sight of the courage it takes for survivors who attempt to make their Holocaust experiences accessible to present and future generations. Dominick LaCapra has pointed out that in focusing on the limits of language, a survivor may face the threat of finding oneself "at the point of irrecoverable loss and empty silence."[12] Because the alternative is that their stories will never be told, Renata insists that giving testimony is a "positive experience" for survivors.

On the whole, this book has been a challenge as it faces the unresolved problem of "translation," including how to describe emotions, moments of silence, the difficulties survivors have in talking about their experiences, or even a survivor's very specific use/command of the English language. Even the medium of video more effectively depicts the inadequate means survivors have to describe their experience, or what Elie Wiesel describes as the "unbridgeable gulf" between "the survivor's memory and its reflection in words, his own included."[13]

The gap between experience and narrative however can allow survivors to detach themselves from the trauma. Survivor Paul L. says that when he externalizes his experiences in a narrative, he does not "choke himself" with his story. Renata echoes this sentiment, explaining that when she gives talks to groups of schoolchildren, she detaches herself and thinks, "it wasn't me, it was that girl Renata." When her memories are condensed into something contained like a narrative she protects herself from being affected too much and undergoing "open-heart surgery." Even though she knows she is censoring herself, Renata says it is "the only way I could function."

Yehudi also explains that for him the process of converting memories into a "plot" or "narrative trajectory" serves the purpose of "validating" his memory. He says, "memory is just that little fragment, but plot amplifies memory" because it involves "external knowledge" and other people. Narrative reconstructs the past in a coherent and meaningful way that can lead to shared understanding and consensus. Renata likewise acknowledges the importance of narrative form in making a survivor account more intelligible; it not only provides coherence but also makes one's past analyzable. In retelling her experiences to herself and to others, she says, "Many times I start to analyze why it happened. I start to analyze my behavior and someone else's behavior." This hermeneutic quality emphasizes narrative as a mode of understanding and further distinguishes it from the experience itself.

However, it is worth emphasizing that oral testimony, by its very nature, is frequently marked by an unexpurgated quality. Yehudi and Renata have noted this, especially when someone is "breaking their silence" or actively digging into their memory. They observe that the "drama" of testimony occurs in the emergence of a narrative, not its repetition. Even though the actual facts pertinent to a survivor's testimony have already been shared in a "preinterview" some days prior to the taping, the video testimony itself frequently offers the opportunity to witness an unrehearsed account of the survivor's experience. As an interviewer, Yehudi says a crucial aspect of grasping the survivor's point of view is being attuned to the way the act of giving testimony produces new and shared insights and realizations between the survivor and the listener; in Laub's words, "the creation of knowledge de novo."[14] The spontaneities of memory are paramount to this interpretative aspect of giving testimony.

This drama of encountering the ways that memories are articulated, and narrative structure unfolds, is one of the reasons why it is more effective and instructive to watch a video testimony rather than to read a written "story" based on that testimony. Secondly, nonverbal communication, including postures, gestures, and facial expressions, has an immediate and somatic impact on the viewer that is less available to readers of a summary. Indeed, for both Yehudi and Renata, one overriding purpose of the book is to make the readers (lay people as well as scholars, educators, and documentary film makers) want to see the video testimonies of the survivors for themselves. Renata says that with the visual component, "I think you get more emotional; you have more empathy when you watch that person, you see more feelings I think."

To compensate, she thinks that the summaries should aim to emphasize the individuality of the survivor, "the real person," though this strategy also has its pitfalls. She says,

> You have to be very careful. It's a very thin line between taking liberties in describing that person's feelings and [letting] someone who's interested see for themselves.

It is also worth noting that video testimony is likewise a limited medium—it only allows survivors to talk about certain experiences. Time is a serious constraint; Renata says, "I can't go deep into every experience with them." For this reason, Renata believes that oral testimony is to some degree, superficial. What enriches testimony is an understanding of what is unspoken, especially because silences often stand in for some of the most significant moments. The ineffability of Holocaust experience is also evident in Renata's observation that survivors are notably stoic when talking about horrors. In this light, it is crucial that the reader/viewer has the sensitivity to consider what is not being said, while at the same time recognizing that attempts to make survivors' stories communicable works toward a "healing process" of collective memory and shared understanding.

History, Community, and Healing

For Yehudi, Living Testimonies has had the primary historical motive of restoring the "lost voice of the survivor." Geoffrey Hartman, cofounder of the Yale Fortunoff Holocaust archive, writes that the purpose of compiling individual testimony is "the documentation of a collective fate," that is, documenting the way that survivors' stories are "disastrously alike."[15]

From Renata's perspective, sharing one's individual story with a community is a constituent part of the healing power of giving testimony. That is, not only does testimony establish the veracity of a collective past trauma, Renata explains that it is a "validating experience" for survivors: "It's not [only] my tragedy . . . it is the tragedy of that person I am interviewing, it's our tragedy, it's a Jewish tragedy so it really took away the edge from my own." She believes that in participating in a testimony project, one's own survival is crystallized as a shared experience.

Furthermore, in recognizing her own story of survival in other people, Renata also emphasizes that her feeling of guilt disappeared completely. In this sense, the definition of the healing aspect of testimony includes overcoming the trauma of having been silenced in the years following the Holocaust, and the "collective fate" of survivor guilt. She says, "Now the more I talk to other survivors, I see there is nothing wrong with me, there is something wrong with the society here because I hear the same story, the lack of understanding, even brutality, emotional brutality to survivors."

Renata's perspective sheds light on how a significant healing aspect of giving testimony and "breaking the silence" lies in its capacity to restore a sense of community. More so than bringing concrete resolution to the traumatic experience of the Holocaust itself, giving testimony serves to validate and edify the survivor community. Renata says: "I feel a bond with the survivors. I feel we are members of a secret society. I found strength and comfort in a group that shares a common past." Creating a sense of collective experience through Holocaust documentation is an important part of the healing process.

Giving testimony, however, has only been part of Renata's personal struggle to attain a sense of comfort and inner peace after suffering the catastrophe of the Nazi "killing machine." Initially, she says she wanted to forget what had happened to her. She left Europe "to just stay away . . . from the blood, from the horror." Only after her daughter's birth in 1955, and 1961, the year of the Eichmann trial, did Renata begin to seek help for the recurring nightmares that haunted her. However, her doctor advised her not to seek therapy. He said, "They'll rip you apart and won't be able to put you back together."

Renata explains that the notion that therapy would cause further rupturing is indicative of a society unable to come to terms with, or even acknowledge the Holocaust, particularly in the case of her doctor whose own wife, Renata later discovered, was a Holocaust survivor.

At the same time, "putting oneself back together" is an apt explication of the healing process. The magnitude of the loss can never be erased but confronting past trauma in a therapeutic or testimonial setting is part of an attempt to achieve a sense of wholeness. In this regard Dori Laub, a psychoanalyst and cofounder of the Fortunoff Holocaust Video Archive at Yale, emphasizes the vital role of the listener to aid the survivor in building linkages to the past and his/her memories into present-day life. In the act of giving testimony, both the survivor and the witness become engaged in a process of acknowledging the reality of the events as they occurred. Instead of the survivor experiencing, through "ceaseless repetitions and reenactments," the uncanny return of trauma in actual life, he or she works at assimilating his/her memories into present day life.[16]

The orchestration of "past discords into present and future harmonies"[17] is expressed by Renata as she describes her healing process, particularly as it was set in motion by her first return to Poland since the war. In 1973, she and her husband were on their way from France to Hungary via East Berlin when Renata had the impulse to go back to Poland, just for twenty-four hours. Her husband was hesitant and concerned for Renata because she showed signs of instability: "We never had one night where I wouldn't scream practically, it became like a routine I would scream he would make me hot tea, make me a hot bath, put on nice music just to calm me that was his job practically every night."

Renata felt courageous. The two of them went to Warsaw, and from there Renata insisted on going on a day trip to Sochaczew, a little town thirty kilometers away where her father was born. The whole time, her husband was petrified. That night back in the hotel room in Warsaw something changed dramatically:

> My husband was sitting on a chair practically all-night and crying, and he said, "You know you slept like a new-born baby, like after a bath,

you didn't even move" ... He couldn't believe it. So I guess that was very therapeutic. It was the first time that I faced my past and realized something. I don't know what happened to me. The whole trip was fantastic. I was very relaxed and I guess the healing process started. It took a long time but that was the beginning of the healing process.... After all, even the worst memory—being torn from a parent, deportation and disappearance—is not only a tragic memory, but also a very precious memory. It is a fragment of identity, a tiny bit of what once was.

Since then, Renata has returned to Poland every year, which fulfils a need to reconnect with her childhood. She says,

When I am in Warsaw you can't recognize anything there, everything was destroyed and yet I am able to go there and I walk in that part of Warsaw where I was brought up. We used to live across the park and I sit there for hours and I don't see the tramway running; I just see myself as a little girl and I go back to my childhood. You know it gives me certain peace. It brings pain but also I like the feeling of sitting there.

Yehudi also believes that a testimony project operates in concert with an underlying "need to talk," or the "need to make whole." At an intuitive level, he thinks survivors experience "not just the need to tell the story" but also the need for liberation, healing and completion, which they strive for "with the telling of the story."

For Yehudi, the idea of "making whole" has strong resonances with the Jewish tradition of *tikkun olam*, the reparation and transformation of the world. In this regard, therapy does not only have meaning on an individual level but concerns, on a global scale, "setting the world right." After the war, new hope for repair and healing was partially experienced through the return to Zion, symbolized by the new state of Israel, following 2000 years of diaspora that culminated catastrophically in the Nazi extermination camps. For this reason, the mere existence of Israel takes on a profound significance for survivors and indeed for all Jews in the post-Holocaust era. But the breadth of *tikkun olam* extends even further. Embracing a cabalistic notion of the world being in a delicate balance, affected, for good or ill, by each gesture and action, Yehudi believes that inherent in *tikkun* is the commitment to putting yourself in the place of the Other and taking responsibility for his or her suffering.

The cabalistic concept of *tikkun* can also be applied directly to the importance of a Holocaust testimony project. That is, "making whole" can be positioned as an orientation toward history. Such an orientation is seen in Walter Benjamin's philosophy of history. For Benjamin, history is fragmentary; it cannot be made whole without a kind of messianic intervention: "to make whole what has been smashed," and to "heal and restore the original being of things."[18] By bringing together the "shards of memory" in this volume, Living Testimonies hopes to contribute to the process of restoration and repair, and to move in the direction of establishing what Benjamin described as a "redemptive relationship to the fragments [of history]."[19]

Notes

1. James Hatley, *The Suffering Witness: The Quandary of Responsibility after the Irreparable* (Albany: State University of New York Press, 2000), 112–113.
2. Renata Skotnicka-Zajdman, unpublished memoir.
3. See Geoffrey Hartman, "Introduction: Darkness Visible," in *Holocaust Remembrance: The Shapes of Memory*, Geoffrey Hartman, ed. (Cambridge, MA: Blackwell Publishers, 1994), 6.
4. Hatley, *The Suffering Witness*, 3.
5. Dori Laub, "Bearing Witness, or the Vicissitudes of Listening," in *Testimony: Crises of Witnessing in Literature, Psychoanalysis, and History* (New York: Routledge, 1992), 72–73.
6. Annette Wieviorka, "On Testimony," in *Holocaust Remembrance: The Shapes of Memory*, Geoffrey Hartman, ed. (Cambridge, MA: Blackwell Publishers, 1994), 24.
7. Henry Greenspan, *On Listening to Holocaust Survivors* (Westport, CT: Praeger Publishers, 1998), 16.
8. Irving Howe, "Writing and the Holocaust," in *Writing and the Holocaust*, Berel Lang, ed. (New York: Holmes and Meier, 1988), 192.
9. Claudia Eppert, "Throwing Testimony against the Wall: Reading Relations, Loss and Responsible/Responsive Learning," in *Difficult Memories: Talk in a (Post) Holocaust Era*, Marla Morris and John A. Weaver, eds. (New York: Peter Lang, 2002), 51.
10. Greenspan, *On Listening*, 169.
11. See Hayden White, "Historical Emplotment and the Problem of Truth in Historical Representation" and "The Modernist Event," in *Figural Realism: Studies in the Mimesis Effect*, Hayden White, ed. (Baltimore: Johns Hopkins UP, 1999).
12. Dominick LaCapra, "Representing the Holocaust: Reflections on the Historian's Debate," in *Probing the Limits of Representation: Nazism and the "Final Solution,"* Saul Friedlander, ed. (Cambridge, MA: Harvard UP, 1992), 127.
13. Quoted in Greenspan, *On Listening*, 5.
14. Laub, "Bearing Witness, or the Vicissitudes of Listening," 57.
15. Geoffrey Hartman, *The Longest Shadow: In the Aftermath of the Holocaust* (Bloomington: Indiana UP, 1996), 134.
16. Laub, "Bearing Witness, or the Vicissitudes of Listening," 69–70.
17. Lawrence L. Langer, "Remembering Survival," in *Holocaust Remembrance: The Shapes of Memory*, Geoffrey Hartman, ed. (Cambridge, MA: Blackwell Publishers 1994), 73.
18. See Walter Benjamin, "Theses on the Philosophy of History," in *Illuminations*, Hannah Arendt, ed., Harry Zohn, trans. (New York: Schocken Books, 1968); Ronald Beiner, "Walter Benjamin's Philosophy of History," *Political Theory*, vol. 12, no. 3 (1984), 423–433. Gershom Scholem, "Walter Benjamin" and "Walter Benjamin and His Angel," in *On Jews and Judaism in Crisis: Selected Essays*, Gershom Sholem, ed. (New York: Schocken Books, 1976).
19. Ronald Beiner, "Walter Benjamin's Philosophy of History," 424.

MAPS

Europe 1918–1933
Source: Printed by permission of the Center for Holocaust Studies at the University of Vermont

Map by Katherine Quimby Johnson

Europe 1918-1933
Key:

1 Denmark	4 Luxembourg	7 USSR (Ukraine)
2 Holland	5 Switzerland	8 Bulgaria
3 Belgium	6 Czechoslovakia	9 Albania

Major camps and cities
Source: Printed by permission of the Center for Holocaust Studies at the University of Vermont

map by Janet Sobieski

CHRONOLOGY

Barry Stahlmann

GERMANY

January 30, 1933	Adolf Hitler is appointed Chancellor of Germany by President von Hindenburg.
February 27, 1933	The *Reichstag* [German parliamentary building] is set on fire in Berlin.
March 22, 1933	*Konzentrationslager* [KL—concentration camp] Dachau is established.
May 10, 1933	Before a crowd of 40,000 people in Berlin, the Propaganda Minister Joseph Goebbels presides over the burning of books that are judged to be un-German and decadent.
July 14, 1933	The sterilization law is enacted, "for the Prevention of Progeny of Sufferers from Hereditary Diseases."
August 2, 1934	President Paul von Hindenburg dies at the age of eighty-six. Adolf Hitler becomes the *Führer und Reichskanzler* [Leader and Reich Chancellor].
August 19, 1934	In a Plebiscite, 89.93 percent vote yes to endorse Adolf Hitler as the Leader of Germany.
September 15, 1935	In Nuremberg, the "Reich Citizenship Law" and the "Law for the Protection of German Blood and German Honor" (a.k.a. the Nuremberg Laws) are promulgated. The Jews of Germany lose their citizenship rights and their right to marry non-Jews.
March 7, 1936	The German Army begins the reoccupation of the demilitarized Rhineland in violation of the Treaty of Versailles and the Locarno Agreements.
August 1–16, 1936	The Olympic Games are held in Berlin.
September 23, 1936	Sachsenhausen concentration camp is established fifteen miles northeast of Berlin.

July 16, 1937	Buchenwald concentration camp is established.
March 12, 1938	The *Anschluss* [political union between Germany and Austria]. The German army crosses the Austrian border without encountering any resistance.
August 8, 1938	Mauthausen concentration camp is established in Austria.
August 17, 1938	The German government issues a law by which all Jewish women and men are required to add the name "Sarah" and "Israel" to their names. They will be required to carry identity cards with those new added names by January 1, 1939.
September 30, 1938	The Munich "Appeasement" Treaty is signed by Britain, France, Italy, and Germany which yields to Germany the right to annex the Sudetenland, Czechoslovakia. Sudetenland is invaded by German troops and is officially annexed by Germany on October 1, 1938.
September 30, 1938	Jews can no longer practice law or medicine in Germany.
October 5, 1938	Jews must have their passports marked with a bold letter J for *Jude* [Jew].
November 9–10, 1938	During *Reichs-Kristallnacht* [Crystal Night, or The Night of Broken Glass], anti-Jewish pogroms and synagogue burnings take place throughout Germany and Austria. Jewish homes, businesses, and synagogues are destroyed, looted, and burned. About 100 Jews are killed outright, and tens of thousands are deported to concentration camps.
November 15, 1938	The German government in Berlin imposes the *numerus nullus* decree through which all Jewish children are expelled from German schools.
January 24, 1939	The Central Office for Jewish Emigration is opened in Berlin. The SS is given authority over all matters concerning Jewish emigration.
January 30, 1939	In a speech before the *Reichstag* [Parliament], Adolf Hitler states, " . . . If the international Jewish financiers in and outside Europe should succeed in plunging the nations once more into a world war, then the result will not be the Bolshevization of the earth, and thus the victory of Jewry, but the annihilation of the Jewish race in Europe . . ."
March 15, 1939	German armed forces cross the border into Czechoslovakia and occupy Bohemia and Moravia and the capital city of Prague.
May 15, 1939	Ravensbrück concentration camp for women is opened fifty miles north of Berlin.
May 22, 1939	Germany and Italy sign a military alliance known as the "Pact of Steel."
August 23, 1939	Soviet Foreign Minister Vyacheslav Molotov and German Foreign Minister Joachim von Ribbentrop sign the German-Soviet Non-Aggression Pact (a.k.a. the Molotov-Ribbentrop Pact) in Moscow.
September 1, 1939	World War II begins with the German armed forces invasion of Poland.

September 3, 1939	England and France declare war on Germany.
September 10, 1939	Canada declares war on Germany.
October 1939	Adolf Hitler signs the "euthanasia decree" which begins Operation T4, the murder of mentally and physically handicapped individuals in Germany by carbon monoxide gas. An estimated 200,000 people were murdered between 1939 and 1945.
April 9, 1940	German armed forces invade Denmark and Norway.
May 10, 1940	German armed forces invade Belgium, the Netherlands, Luxembourg, and France.
July 10, 1940	The Battle of Britain begins with *Luftwaffe* [German Air Force] attacks on British targets.
September 27, 1940	Germany, Italy, and Japan sign the Tripartite Pact (a.k.a. the Berlin-Rome-Tokyo Axis) in which they agree to collectively declare war on any nation that attacks any one of them.
April 6, 1941	German armed forces invade Greece and Yugoslavia.
June 17, 1941	In Berlin, SS-*Gruppenführer* Reinhard Heydrich briefs *Einsatzgruppen* commanders on the implementation of the plan to exterminate Jews and Gypsies during the imminent invasion of the Soviet Union.
June 22, 1941	Operation Barbarossa begins with Germany's invasion of the Soviet Union.
July 31, 1941	*Reichsmarschall* Hermann Göring sends a memo to SS *Gruppenführer* Reinhard Heydrich to implement the *Endlösung der Judenfrage* [the Final Solution to the Jewish Question].
September 1, 1941	A police decree orders all the Jews of Germany over the age of six to wear a yellow star by September 19.
September 29–30, 1941	In a ravine at Babi Yar outside Kiev, Ukraine, 33,771 Jewish men, women, and children are murdered by members of SS *Einsatzkommando* 4A of *Einsatzgruppe* C.
December 7, 1941	The Japanese attack the U.S. naval base at Pearl Harbor, Hawaii. The United States declares war on Japan on December 8.
December 11, 1941	Germany and Italy declare war on the United States of America.
December 11, 1941	The United States Congress declares war on Germany and Italy.
January 20, 1942	High ranking Nazi officials attend the Wannsee Conference in a suburb of Berlin to formalize the planned annihilation of the estimated eleven million Jews living throughout Europe, known as the "Final Solution of the Jewish Question."
February 2, 1943	Germany suffers a major defeat at the Battle of Stalingrad as the remnants of the 6th Army, under Field Marshall Friedrich von Paulus, surrenders to the Soviet Red Army.
July 24 to August 2, 1943	RAF and USAAF bombers raid the city of Hamburg, igniting massive firestorms. Tens of thousands of people are killed.

July 20, 1944	Col. Claus von Stauffenberg stages a failed attempt to assassinate Adolf Hitler in Rastenburg, East Prussia.
December 16, 1944	The Battle of the Bulge begins when the German 5th and 6th *Panzer* [Tank] Armies launch a major counteroffensive along a forty mile front to break through the Ardennes forests into Luxembourg and Belgium in an attempt to recapture Antwerp.
February 13–15, 1945	RAF and USAAF bombers raid the city of Dresden, igniting massive firestorms. Tens of thousands of people are killed.
April 11, 1945	Buchenwald concentration camp is liberated by the U.S. Army.
April 15, 1945	Bergen-Belsen concentration camp is liberated by the British army.
April 27, 1945	Sachsenhausen concentration camp is liberated by the Soviet Red Army. Three thousand prisoners are found still alive.
April 29, 1945	Dachau concentration camp is liberated by the U.S. Army.
April 30, 1945	Adolf Hitler commits suicide in the *Führerbunker* [Leader's Bunker] in Berlin.
May 1, 1945	Gen. Hans Krebs begins negotiations for a ceasefire with the Soviet Red Army forces surrounding Berlin.
May 2, 1945	The Soviet Red Army occupies Berlin.
May 4, 1945	Oranienburg concentration camp is liberated by the Soviet Red Army.
May 5, 1945	Mauthausen concentration camp in Austria is liberated by the U.S. Army.
May 7, 1945	*Generaloberst* Alfred Jodl and Fleet Admiral Hans Georg von Friedeburg sign the unconditional surrender of Germany at Gen. Eisenhower's Headquarters in Rheims, France. The surrender is ratified by the Soviet Union in Berlin on May 8.
May 8, 1945	VE Day: the war in Europe is over.
July 17 to August 2, 1945	The Potsdam Conference is held. Allied leaders August 2, 1945 Winston Churchill, Harry S. Truman, and Joseph Stalin meet to discuss the future of Europe and Asia in Potsdam, Germany. Winston Churchill is replaced by Clement Atlee after the July 26 British election.
November 20, 1945 to October 1, 1946	The International Military Tribunal of twenty-two major Nazi war criminals is held in Nuremberg.

CZECHOSLOVAKIA

October 1, 1938	German armed forces cross the border into the Sudetenland.
October 6, 1938	Slovakia is given full autonomy and Monsignor Jozef Tiso is made Premier. Anti-Jewish Decrees are put into effect.

March 15, 1939	German armed forces cross the border into Czechoslovakia and occupy Prague.
March 16, 1939	Adolf Hitler proclaims Bohemia and Moravia a Protectorate of the German Reich.
March 23, 1939	German Foreign Minister Joachim von Ribbentrop and Deputy Premier Dr. Vojtech Tuka sign the "Treaty of Protection" whereby Slovakia becomes a German protectorate.
September 3, 1940	Law 210 empowers the Slovak government to "Aryanize" Jewish property.
November 24, 1940	Slovakia joins the Tripartite Pact with Germany, Italy, and Japan.
September 1, 1941	A decree is issued in Prague that requires all Jews to wear the yellow star in Bohemia and Moravia.
September 22, 1941	The Slovak President Monsignor Jozef Tiso orders the Jews of Slovakia to wear the yellow star.
November 24, 1941	The ghetto and concentration camp Theresienstadt is established.
December 1941	Anti-Jewish legislation is passed in Slovakia. Jews are forbidden to congregate, and a curfew is imposed on them.
January 9, 1942	The first transport of Jews leaves Theresienstadt for Riga, Latvia.
March 1942	A concentration camp to imprison Gypsies is opened in Hodonin nad Kunstatem in Southern Moravia.
May 23, 1942	The Slovak government passes a Law permitting the expulsion of the Jews of Slovakia.
July 1942	The Germans remove the civilian population from Theresienstadt. The entire town is then converted into a concentration camp.
September 6–8, 1943	Two transports of 5,007 Jewish men, women, and children leave Theresienstadt for the Auschwitz-Birkenau death camp. There they become known as the "family camp."
July 23, 1944	The International Red Cross visits the Theresienstadt concentration camp. The Germans film the inspection for propaganda purposes.
August 28–29, 1944	German armed forces invade Slovakia.
August 29 to October 27, 1944	The *Slovenská Narodna Rada* [Slovak National Council] leads Slovak National Uprising against the Germans. 2,000 Jewish fighters join the movement.
September 28 to October 28, 1944	18,402 Jews are deported from Theresienstadt to the Auschwitz-Birkenau death camp.
March 16, 1945	The last Jews of Prague are deported to the Theresienstadt concentration camp. In total, 46,067 Jews from Prague were deported to Lodz, Minsk, and Theresienstadt.
April 1, 1945	The Soviet Red Army liberates the Sered transit camp in Slovakia.
April 4, 1945	The Soviet Red Army liberates Bratislava, Slovakia.

May 3, 1945	Theresienstadt is handed over to the Red Cross. 17,247 Jewish inmates remain in the camp.
May 9, 1945	The Soviet Red Army occupies Prague.
May 11, 1945	Theresienstadt and its 32,000 inmates are formally handed over to the Soviet Red Army.
May 15, 1945	Recalcitrant German Army troops in Northern Czechoslovakia and Eastern Germany surrender to the Soviet Red Army.

DENMARK

January 17, 1939	Denmark signs nonaggression pact with Germany.
April 9, 1940	German armed forces invade Denmark and enter and occupy Copenhagen.
September 26, 1940	On King Kristian X's 70th birthday, the citizens of Denmark stage a national demonstration against the Germans. The wearing of a yellow star to identify Jews is never introduced by the Germans in Denmark.
November 1942	SS-*Standartenführer* Werner Best is appointed the *Reichskommissar* [Reich Commissioner] for Denmark.
September 28, 1943	In Copenhagen, the German diplomat Georg Ferdinand Duckwitz warns Danish leaders of the impending roundup of the Jews of Denmark.
October 1, 1943	The Swedish government offers refuge to all Danish Jews.
October 1–2, 1943	The *Gestapo* issues orders to begin the roundup of Danish Jews. This prompts a three-week rescue operation organized by the Danish resistance. Over 6,500 Jews are successfully smuggled in small boats across the Öresund to neutral Sweden. About 500 Jews are arrested and deported to the Theresienstadt concentration camp in Czechoslovakia.
June 30, 1944	Copenhagen stages a general strike.
July 1, 1944	The city of Copenhagen is placed under Martial Law by the Germans. The strike ends July 4.
September 19, 1944	The Germans disband the Danish police in Copenhagen. 1,902 members of the Danish police are then deported to the Buchenwald concentration camp in Germany.
January 2, 1945	In Copenhagen, members of the Danish underground destroy a factory that was manufacturing V2 rocket parts.
April 15, 1945	A Swedish Red Cross convoy arrives in Theresienstadt to transfer 413 Danish Jews to Sweden.
May 4, 1945	In Hecklingen, Germany, at Field Marshal Bernard Montgomery's headquarters, Fleet Admiral Hans Georg von Friedeburg signs the capitulation of all German Army forces in Denmark, the Netherlands, and Northwest Germany.

FRANCE

July 6–15, 1938	The International Conference on German-Jewish refugees in Evian-les-bains is held. It is attended by thirty-two nations. No agreement is reached on how to resolve the plight of the refugees and practically no country is found willing to accept any of them.
September 3, 1939	France declares war on Germany after Germany invades Poland.
May 10, 1940	German armed forces invade Belgium, the Netherlands, Luxembourg, and France.
May 26 to June 4, 1940	The Allies begin the mass evacuation of more than 300,000 troops from the beaches of Dunkirk back to England.
June 3, 1940	The *Luftwaffe* [German Air Force] bombs Paris for the first time.
June 4, 1940	Dunkirk is captured by the German Army and 40,000 remaining Allied soldiers are taken as prisoners of war.
June 10, 1940	Italy declares war on England and France. Italian Army forces invade France.
June 14, 1940	Paris falls as German Army troops enter and occupy the city.
June 16, 1940	Premier Paul Reynaud resigns; Marshal Henri Philippe Omer Pétain becomes Premier and forms a new government. He becomes head of state on 11 July.
June 22, 1940	Gen. Charles Léon Clément Huntziger signs the surrender of France at Compiègne in the same railroad carriage used in the 1918 signing of the armistice that ended World War I.
July 2, 1940	The Vichy government is established in the town of Vichy in Southern France.
October 3, 1940	The Vichy government enacts the first *Statut des Juifs* [Jewish Law] defining who is a Jew and excluding Jews from many public service jobs and other professions and occupations.
October 4, 1940	The government enacts a law that allows the French police to arbitrarily arrest "any foreigner of the Jewish race."
April 26, 1941	The Vichy government passes a decree outlining prohibitions on Jewish employment.
May 14, 1941	The first major *rafle* [roundup, arrests] of Jews takes place in Paris affecting naturalized Austrian, Czech, and Polish Jews.
June 2, 1941	Enactment of the second *Statut des Juifs* which imposes new restrictions on the French Jews.
August 1941	Drancy internment camp is established in the northeast suburb of Paris.
August 20–21, 1941	Over 4,000 Jews are arrested in Paris and interned in the Drancy internment camp.

March 27, 1942	The first transport of 1,112 Jews leaves the Compiègne transit camp for the Auschwitz-Birkenau death camp.
May 29, 1942	The Germans issue a decree requiring all Jews aged six and older in the occupied zone of France to wear the yellow star with the word *Juif* printed on it.
June 22, 1942	A transport of about 1,000 Jewish men, women, and children from the Drancy internment camp to the Auschwitz-Birkenau death camp.
July 16–17, 1942	*La grande rafle* takes place in Paris. During this "Great Roundup" the French police arrest 12,884 Jews. Most of them will be sent to Auschwitz-Birkenau.
November 8, 1942	The Allies invade French North Africa.
November 11, 1942	Vichy authorities sign an armistice with the Allied forces in North Africa. German and Italian Army troops subsequently occupy the southern zone of Vichy.
January 14–24, 1943	A ten day conference is held in Casablanca, Morocco, attended by Prime Minister Churchill, President Roosevelt, and French Generals de Gaulle, Henri Giraud, and Charles Noguès. At the end of the conference, President Roosevelt announces the Allies' demand for the "unconditional surrender" of Germany, Italy, and Japan.
June 6, 1944	D-Day: Allied forces land on the beaches of Normandy.
August 15, 1944	The Allied invasion of southern France begins.
August 17, 1944	The last transport of Jews leaves the Drancy internment camp for the Buchenwald concentration camp.
August 25, 1944	Paris is liberated by troops of the Free French 2nd Armored Division.
August 28, 1944	Marseilles is liberated by French and American troops.
April 14, 1945	In Paris, CROWCASS (Central Registry of War Criminals and Security Suspects) is established by SHAEF (Supreme Headquarters Allied Expeditionary Force).
July 23, to August 15, 1945	The trial of Marshal Philippe Pétain is held in Paris. He is found guilty of "crimes against the internal security of the state" and sentenced to "death with reprieve." This is later commuted to life imprisonment by General Charles de Gaulle.

HUNGARY

May 29, 1938	The first anti-Jewish Law is enacted by Parliament limiting the number of Jews permitted in the professions, business, industry, and government administration to 20 percent.
November 2, 1938	The first "Vienna Award": The Italian and German Arbitration Commission in Vienna, gives Hungary the districts of Southern Czechoslovakia that have a predominant Magyar population.

March 11, 1939	The Hungarian government promulgates the *Munkaszolgálat* Law [Law on National Defense] to establish a Labor Service System. All Jews of military age in Hungary are required to work for the Hungarian Army.
March 15, 1939	Hungarian army troops cross the border into Ruthenia in Southern Slovakia and annex Ruthenia, which includes the city of Munkács.
March 27, 1939	The second anti-Jewish Law is enacted prohibiting Jews from holding positions as judges, lawyers, teachers, or members of Parliament.
August 30, 1940	The second "Vienna Award": Romania is forced to cede Northern Transylvania and Székely Land, an area that comprises about 200,000 Jews.
November 20, 1940	Hungary joins the Tripartite Pact with Germany, Italy, and Japan.
June 27, 1941	Hungary joins the Axis Powers and declares war on the Soviet Union.
December 6, 1941	England declares war on Hungary.
December 12, 1941	Hungary declares war on the United States of America.
July 18, 1942	The United States declares war on Hungary.
December 1942	Prime Minister Miklós Kállay rejects German demands to introduce the yellow star for the Jews of Hungary and to deport them to Poland.
January 1943	The *Va'adat ha-Ezra ve-ha-Hatsala be-Budapest* [Relief and Rescue Committee of Budapest] is established by Fülöp Freudiger, Otto Komoly, and Rezsö Kasztner.
March 18, 1944	President Miklós Horthy is arrested by the Germans.
March 19, 1944	The German army's occupation of Hungary begins. SS-*Obersturmbannführer* Adolf Eichmann arrives in Budapest, orders the establishment of a *Zsidó Tanács* [Jewish Council] on March 20, and starts preparations for the deportation of all Hungarian Jews.
March 20, 1944	German army troops enter Debrecen. A *Zsidó Tanács* and a Jewish police force are established.
March 22, 1944	The Germans promulgate anti-Jewish legislation that orders all Jewish businesses to close. Hundreds of the city's Jews are subsequently rounded up and interned in the Kistarcsa internment camp nine miles Northeast of Budapest.
April 5, 1944	The Germans issue a decree requiring all Hungarian Jews to wear the yellow star.
April 29, 1944	The first transport of 1,800 Jews leaves Budapest for the Auschwitz-Birkenau death camp. Over the next three months, more than 400,000 Hungarian Jews will be deported to Auschwitz-Birkenau.
May 2, 1944	The first transport from the Hungarian provinces to the Auschwitz-Birkenau death camp leaves the country. The deportations are supervised by the Chief of the Hungarian *Czendörseg*, the National Gendarmerie.

July 7, 1944	President Horthy orders the deportations of the Jews halted. Even so, the Germans declare all of Hungary, with the exception of Budapest, *judenrein* [free of Jews].
July 9, 1944	The Swedish diplomat Raoul Wallenberg arrives in Budapest.
September 7, 1944	Hungary declares war on Romania and crosses into Southern Transylvania.
September 23, 1944	The Soviet Red Army crosses into Hungarian territory.
October 15, 1944	A secret provisional ceasefire is signed between Hungary and the Soviet Union. In a radio broadcast, President Miklós Horthy announces that he has signed a separate peace with the Soviet Union that withdraws Hungary from the war.
October 16, 1944	The Arrow Cross, led by Ferenc Szálasi, takes power in coup d'état staged in Budapest.
Late October 1944	Debrecen, Munkács, and Uzhgorod are liberated by the Soviet Red Army.
November 2–6, 1944	76,000 Budapest Jews are taken to the Ujlaki brickyards in Obuda and are then driven out of the city toward Vienna by members of the SS, the Arrow Cross, and the *Csendörség*.
November 13, 1944	The Arrow Cross establishes a ghetto for the city's Jews.
December 1944	Over 10,000 Budapest Jews are forced to the banks of the Danube river, where they are shot by members of the Arrow Cross.
January 17, 1945	The Swedish diplomat Raoul Wallenberg is arrested by the *NKVD* (Soviet Secret Police).
January 18, 1945	The Soviet Red Army enters Pest and liberates the ghetto in the Eastern part of Budapest.
February 13, 1945	Budapest is completely liberated as the German army garrison on the western side of Budapest surrenders to the Soviet Red Army.
March 10, 1945	The Soviet Union restores Transylvania to Romania.

THE NETHERLANDS

May 10, 1940	German armed forces invade Belgium, the Netherlands, Luxembourg, and France.
May 13, 1940	Queen Wilhelmina and the Dutch government decide to flee the country. The Queen establishes a government-in-exile in London.
May 14, 1940	The city of Rotterdam is bombed by the German *Luftwaffe*.
May 15, 1940	Capitulation of the Dutch army. The German army occupies Amsterdam and The Hague.
May 18, 1940	SS-*Obergruppenführer* Arthur Seyss-Inquart is appointed *Reichskommissar* [Reich Commissioner] for the Netherlands.
June 3, 1940	The first anti-Jewish Law is promulgated ordering all Jews to be removed from their government and public service positions.

January 10, 1941	*Reichskommissar* Seyss-Inquart signs a decree ordering the Jews of the Netherlands to report for registration with local branches of the Census Office.
February 22, 1941	Major *razzia* [roundup] of young Jewish men in the centre of Amsterdam.
February 25–26, 1941	An anti-Nazi general strike protesting the arrest and deportation of Jews begins in Amsterdam and quickly spreads to other cities.
March 12, 1941	A decree enabling the "Aryanization" of Jewish property is issued in order to expedite the elimination of the Jews from the economic life of the country.
July 1941	Special identity cards marked with "J" for Jew are issued in The Hague. An order banning Jews from restaurants, movie theaters, swimming pools, and other public places is issued; a nightly curfew from 8:00 p.m. to 7:00 a.m. is also enacted.
November 27, 1941	Decree ordering the establishment of "Jewish quarters" in all of the large towns of the Netherlands is issued.
April 29, 1942	Decree ordering every Jew aged six years or older to wear the yellow star starting on May 3.
July 4, 1942	The Jewish Council is ordered to provide 4,000 Jews for work in Germany.
July 6, 1942	Anne Frank and her mother, father, and sister go into hiding in the "secret annex" at 263 Prinsengracht in Amsterdam.
July 15, 1942	The first transport of Jews leaves Westerbork transit camp for the Auschwitz-Birkenau death camp.
August 22, 1942	The first wave of arrests of the Jews of The Hague. All arrests are made in the Jews' homes according to a detailed list of addresses.
February 21, 1943	A pastoral letter is read that condemns the persecution of the Jews in Protestant and Roman Catholic churches throughout the Netherlands.
March 2, 1943	The first transport of 1,105 Jews leaves camp Westerbork for the Sobibor death camp. Over the next four and a half months more than 34,000 Dutch Jews will be gassed at Sobibor.
March 29, 1943	*Reichsführer*-SS Heinrich Himmler orders the deportation of the Dutch Gypsies to Auschwitz-Birkenau.
September 29, 1943	During a *razzia* on the eve of the Jewish New Year, the last Jews still living in freedom in Amsterdam are arrested and taken to the Westerbork transit camp.
August 4, 1944	Anne Frank, her family, the Van Pels family, and Friedrich Pfeffer are arrested in their hiding place by members of the *Gestapo* and the Dutch police.
September 3, 1944	The last transport of 1,019 Jewish men, women, and children leaves Westerbork for Auschwitz-Birkenau. This transport includes Anne Frank and those in hiding with her.
September 13, 1944	The city of Maastricht is liberated by the U.S. Army.
September 17–25, 1944	British and U.S. Airborne Divisions fail in an attempt to liberate and secure bridges near Arnhem and Nijmegen

	across the rivers Rhine and Waal, and hold them until British ground troops will link up with them.
April 12, 1945	Westerbork transit camp is liberated by the Canadian army.
May 3, 1945	Queen Wilhelmina returns to the Netherlands.
May 5, 1945	The Hague is liberated by Allied forces.
May 7, 1945	Amsterdam is liberated by the Canadian army.
May 8, 1945	Rotterdam is liberated by the Canadian army.
July 1945	Members of the Jewish Brigade arrive in the Netherlands and establish a base of operations to help rebuild the Jewish community.

POLAND

June 6, 1934	The *Endeks* [National Democratic Party] stage anti-Jewish pogroms throughout Poland.
March 17, 1936	Polish Jews, Liberals, and laborers stage a one-day strike and hold mass demonstrations to protest anti-Semitism in Poland.
August 30, 1939	The Polish government announces general mobilization of its troops.
September 1, 1939	German armed forces invade Poland. World War II begins.
September 28, 1939	In Warsaw, the Defense Command of the Polish army surrenders to the German army.
Late September 1939	The Polish *Armia Krajowa* [Home Army] is established.
October 8, 1939	The Germans establish the first ghetto in Piotrków Trybunalski.
October 12, 1939	A German Decree orders the creation of the Generalgouvernement in those areas of Poland not incorporated into the Third Reich. Western Poland is now under German administration, while the eastern part is under Soviet administration in keeping with the Molotov-Ribbentrop Pact of August 23, 1939. Hans Frank becomes the Governor General of the new General Government. Its capital will be Krakow.
November 11–16, 1939	The Germans burn down the synagogues of Lodz.
February 8, 1940	A ghetto is established in Lodz.
April 27, 1940	*Reichsführer*-SS Heinrich Himmler orders the construction of a concentration camp in Auschwitz.
April 30, 1940	The Lodz ghetto is sealed off by the Germans.
May 18, 1940	About 2,800 Gypsies are expelled from Germany to Lublin.
October 12, 1940	The Warsaw ghetto is established.
March 24, 1941	A ghetto is established in Lublin.
April 7, 1941	Two separate ghettos are established in Radom.
June 27, 1941	Bialystok is reoccupied by German Army troops, following the German invasion of the Soviet Union. The next day is "Bloody Friday" when about a thousand Jews are burned alive in a synagogue by the Germans.

July 25–27, 1941	During a pogrom known as *Aktion Petliura*, Ukrainians in Lvov murder two thousand Jews.
August 1, 1941	A ghetto is established in Bialystok.
September 3, 1941	The first trial gassings using *Zyklon B* take place in the Auschwitz death camp.
October 1941	Construction of the Majdanek death camp begins.
October 7, 1941	Construction of the Birkenau death camp begins about two miles from Auschwitz.
November 1, 1941	Construction of the Belzec death camp begins.
November 5–9, 1941	About 5,000 Gypsies from Austria are deported to the Lodz ghetto. They will be killed in gas-vans nearby the Chelmno death camp in December 1941 and January 1942.
December 8, 1941	The first gas-van killings of Jews begin at the Chelmno death camp.
March 1, 1942	Construction of the Sobibor death camp begins.
March 17, 1942	Belzec death camp opens and the first test gassings using carbon monoxide gas take place.
July 22, 1942	Treblinka death camp is put into operation and first gassings take place.
July 22 to September 12, 1942	The mass deportations of Jews from Warsaw to Treblinka are conducted by the Germans. Over 300,000 Jews are murdered in gas chambers.
August 5, 1942	The smaller ghetto in Radom is liquidated.
August 16–18, 1942	The larger ghetto in Radom is liquidated. Most of the 20,000 inhabitants are sent to be killed at Treblinka.
September 5, 1942	20,000 Jews are deported from Lodz to Treblinka.
September 5–12, 1942	*Einkesselung Aktion*: 70,000 Jews are deported from the Warsaw ghetto to be killed at Treblinka.
November 1, 1942	Deportations of Bialystok Jews to Treblinka begin.
December 4, 1942	*Zegota* [the Council for Aid to Jews] is founded in Warsaw by members of the Polish and Jewish underground.
January 18–22, 1943	The first small revolt in the Warsaw ghetto occurs when German units enter.
March 13–14, 1943	The Krakow ghetto is liquidated by the Germans.
April 19 to May 16, 1943	The Warsaw Ghetto Uprising takes place. Large numbers of Jews are killed in the ghetto fighting. The survivors are sent to Treblinka to be gassed. In all, more than 55,000 Jews are killed.
May 30, 1943	SS-*Hauptsturmführer* Josef Mengele arrives at Auschwitz-Birkenau and takes up the position of Camp Doctor.
June 1, 1943	The final liquidation of the Lvov ghetto is conducted by the Germans.
June 11, 1943	*Reichsführer*-SS Heinrich Himmler orders the liquidation of all ghettos in Poland.
August 2, 1943	The inmates of the Treblinka death camp stage an uprising. Armed with a few pistols, rifles, and grenades they overpower and kill several SS men. Though about

	400 of the 700 inmates manage to escape from the camp, most are found and then killed.
October 14, 1943	The Jews working in the labor squad of the Sobibor death camp stage an uprising. Led by Soviet Red Army officer Aleksandr Pechersky and Leon Feldhendler, they overpower and kill eleven SS men. About 400 of the 600 inmates manage to escape from the camp, but about 100 of them are soon recaptured and killed. About 200 inmates are killed during the uprising.
November 3, 1943	Operation *Erntefest* [Harvest Festival]. Tens of thousands of Jews are killed in the Lublin district. It also entails the closure, following the Sobibor uprising, of the three death camps of Operation Reinhard, Belzec, Sobibor, and Treblinka by the end of November.
June 26, 1944	First aerial photographs of Auschwitz-Birkenau are taken by the USAAF.
July 24, 1944	Majdanek death camp is liberated by the Soviet Red Army.
Late July 1944	Lublin, Bialystok and Lvov are liberated by the Soviet Red Army.
August 1 to October 2, 1944	The Polish uprising against the Germans in Warsaw.
August 2, 1944	The Gypsy camp at Auschwitz-Birkenau is liquidated by the Germans. Between 3,000 to 4,000 Gypsy men, women, and children are murdered in the gas chambers.
August 7, 1944	Start of the liquidation of the Lodz ghetto.
October 7, 1944	Crematorium IV is blown up by Jewish members of the *Sonderkommando* at Auschwitz-Birkenau.
November 26, 1944	*Reichsführer*-SS Heinrich Himmler orders the gas chambers and crematoria at Auschwitz-Birkenau destroyed to eliminate all evidence of mass murder.
November 29, 1944	Krakow is liberated by the Soviet Red Army.
January 17, 1945	Warsaw is liberated by the Soviet Red Army.
January 17, 1945	As the Soviet Red Army approaches Chelmno, the SS raze the site of the death camp and then abandon it.
January 18, 1945	The SS evacuate Auschwitz-Birkenau and the death marches begin.
January 27, 1945	The Soviet Red Army liberates Auschwitz-Birkenau.
March 30, 1945	Danzig falls to the Soviet Red Army.
May 10, 1945	The last prisoners of Stutthof are freed as the Soviet Red Army enters the camp.
August 16, 1945	Poland and the Soviet Union sign a border agreement. A new border with Germany and Poland is established.
July 4, 1946	During a pogrom in Kielce, mobs massacre an estimated forty-two Jews. It is the culmination of a year of anti-Semitic incidents all over Poland. Following the pogrom, most surviving Jews of Poland leave for the West.

ROMANIA

May 15, 1937	The Union of Romanian Lawyers votes to bar Jews from its membership.
January 21, 1938	The Jews of Romania lose their citizenship by Royal Decree 169.
February 17, 1938	All Yiddish newspapers are banned by order of the Ministry of the Interior.
June 28, 1940	The Soviet Union annexes and occupies Bessarabia and Northern Bucovina from Romania in accordance with the terms of the German-Soviet nonaggression pact of August 23, 1939.
September 4, 1940	Marshal Ion Antonescu becomes the Prime Minister of Romania and within weeks assumes the title of *Conducator* [leader]. All political parties and movements are banned, except for the Iron Guard.
September 27, 1940	The Romanian government begins to expropriate all Jewish-owned land.
October 12, 1940	German Army troops occupy Bucharest.
March 27, 1941	Romanian anti-Jewish legislation is enacted, which allows the state to expropriate Jewish-owned homes and businesses.
May 15, 1941	Romanian anti-Jewish legislation requires forced labor "for the common good."
June 13, 1941	Soviet deportations of 10,000 Jews from Bessarabia and Bucovina to Siberia commence.
June 29, 1941	"Black Sunday": German troops, the Romanian army, and members of the SSI (Romanian Secret Service) conduct a mass roundup of the Jews in Iasi, Moldavia. Over 1,000 Jews are murdered.
July 6, 1941	Members of *Einsatzgruppen* D and Romanian army troops massacre 3,000 Jews from Bila and Klokuczka in Chernovtsy, Bucovina.
July 24, 1941	Ion Antonescu issues an order to set up camps and ghettos for Romanian Jews.
July 30, 1941	Bucovina's Governor, Alexandru Riosanu, issues a Decree ordering the Jews to wear the yellow star.
August 19, 1941	Ion Antonescu issues a decree to annex Transnistria, the land between the Bug and Dniester rivers, as a new province of Romania. It will become a holding area for Jews deported from Bessarabia and Bucovina, and a penal colony.
September 15, 1941	Ion Antonescu orders the deportation of all the Jews from Bessarabia and Bucovina to Transnistria. About 150,000 Jews are deported, starting in October 1941, by the Germans and Romanians, resulting in over 90,000 deaths.
October 31, 1941	On the banks of the Dniester river, German soldiers and Romanian rural police begin the mass murder of 53,000 Jews deported from Kishinev.

October 13, 1942	The deportations of Jews from Bucharest to Transnistria are halted through the efforts of Dr. Wilhelm Filderman.
September 16, 1943	According to a report submitted by the General Inspectorate of the Romanian Gendarmerie to the Ministry of Internal Affairs, 217,757 Jews had died in Transnistria as of September 1, 1943.
October 1943	The law ordering Jews to wear the yellow star and the restrictions on movement are abolished in Chernovtsy, Bucovina.
December 1943	The first group of 1,500 Jews returns from Transnistria.
March 6, 1944	A group of 1,846 Jewish orphans from Transnistria arrives in Iasi.
March 1944	The Soviet Red Army reaches the border of Romania, recaptures all of Transnistria, and liberates the death camp in Domanevca.
August 31, 1944	The Soviet Red Army liberates Bucharest.
December 19, 1944	All anti-Semitic legislation is abolished in Bucharest.
March 10, 1945	The Soviet Union restores Transylvania to Romania.

GLOSSARY

Aktion: An official Nazi codeword that was widely adopted by the Jews in the ghetto, *Aktion* is German for "action" and refers to any official or organized measured taken against Jews or the Jewish community. The term is very general and covers anything from arrests and violent attacks to confiscation of personal property and deportations to the camps.

amchu: Code word used by Jews to reveal their identity to friends and fellow Jews, with the implied meaning, "Are you one of us?"

Appell: Roll-call. German command that usually refers to the call for camp inmates having to line up in front of their barracks. Often, the inmates were made to line up for roll-call in a designated area occupying a central location at the camp, the *Appellplatz*.

Arbeitslager: A Nazi forced labor camp, such as Mauthausen, Natzweiler-Struthof, and Neuengamme.

Armia Krajowa: The Polish Home Army (AK), an underground military organization that fought to end the occupation of Poland between 1939 and 1945. Although the AK never managed to organize a general revolt, it was responsible for numerous acts of sabotage and resistance, including the Warsaw uprising during the summer of 1944. The Jewish community of Poland had reason to fear members of the AK as much as it did the German military and SS.

Arrow Cross: The Hungarian fascist party created and led by Ferenc Szálasi. The Arrow Cross constituted the main opposition party in the years leading up to Germany's invasion of Hungary in March 1944, and distinguished itself largely by its pro-Nazi foreign policy. For a brief period in the winter of 1944, the Arrow Cross led the Hungarian coalition government and oversaw the deportation of about eighty thousand Jews.

Aussiedlung: An official Nazi codeword that, though it literally translates as "evacuation," usually referred to the forced deportation of Jews to a concentration or extermination camp.

Ausweis: Official identification card that Jews were made to carry at all times.

Blockälteste: The leader of a group of inmates who lived together in the same barracks.

Bricha: Hebrew for "escape." The *Bricha* was an organized and clandestine movement to evacuate large numbers of Jewish Displaced Persons from Europe to Palestine, beginning in July 1945.

Bund: Jewish socialist party established in 1897 to recruit Jews in the popular struggle against the Russian tsarist regime. After the successful Bolshevik revolution in 1917, the Bund all but ceased operations in Russia, growing more active in Romania, France, and especially Poland. During the World War II, the *Bund* developed into a resistance organization and, though its members often held seats on the *Judenräte* of various ghettos, participated in the famed Warsaw ghetto uprising of 1943.

cheder: Literally, "room" or "chamber," a *cheder* is a religious school for Jewish youngsters.

Chetniks: An organization of mostly Serbs who together supported the Kingdom of Yugoslavia. During the war, the Chetniks formed a notable resistance and fought against the Nazis as well as against the *Ustashe*.

chevra kadisha: Group of volunteers affiliated with a Jewish congregation that helps prepare for and perform burial rituals for its community.

Displaced Persons Camp: After VE day, the Allies housed many Jewish survivors who either refused or were unable to return to their homeland in converted Nazi transit and concentration camps. Many Jewish survivors in the British zone, for example, were housed at Bergen-Belsen. They were known as DPs (Displaced Persons). Conditions in the various camps varied, but for the most part life remained extremely difficult as many survivors continued to struggle with overcrowding, poor sanitation, insufficient nourishment, and overt signs of anti-Semitism.

Einsatzgruppen: Special mobile task forces of the Nazi SS, SD (Sicherheitsdienst), and Sipo (Sicherheitspolizei), these elite groups followed in the immediate wake of the advancing German *Wehrmacht* through Poland and Russia. Their orders were to root out indigenous resistance movements. In practice, this meant the mass murder, usually by shooting, of Jews, but also of Gypsies, Communists and other individuals or groups considered undesirable.

Flecktyphus: Spotted typhus fever, an especially deadly and highly contagious disease.

Gestapo: Acronym for *Geheime Staatspolizei*, Secret State police, established in 1933.

gymnasium: European educational institution, a type of high school specially designed to prepare students for study at the university.

Gypsy: Vernacular designation for the Sinti and Roma, a people that are presumed to have emigrated from northwest India to Europe sometime before the end of the thirteenth century. Estimates of the number of Sinti and Roma systematically murdered during the Holocaust range as high as 500,000 though the actual numbers may exceed even that.

Hashomer Hatza'ir: Left-wing Zionist youth group and political party; literally "The Young Guard."

Hatikvah: The Israeli national anthem.

IG Farben: The largest chemical enterprise in the world, I.G. Farben was a conglomerate of eight formerly separate German companies. The company exploited thousands of Jewish prisoners at Auschwitz as slave-laborers.

Irgun: Militant Zionist organization dedicated to the defense of Jewish settlers in Palestine. Originally members of the Haganah, the Yishuv's defense forces in Eretz Yisrael, Irgun's leaders splintered off from mainstream Zionism because of the Haganah's perceived weakness when faced with Arabs and British military pressure. Championing an antisocialist agenda, many members of the Irgun aligned themselves with the radical Revisionist movement and, subsequent to the 1947–1948 war, rejoined the mainstream with the creation of the Israeli Defense Force.

Iron Guard: A Romanian fascist and anti-Semitic movement, established in 1927.

Joint Distribution Committee: American Jewish aid organization that was of major importance in helping resettle the European Jews.

judenfrei / judenrein: Designation meaning that an area has been cleared of all Jews, literally "free of/cleansed of Jews."

Judenrat: A council of Jewish leaders appointed by the Nazis to organize life in the Nazi-formed ghettos and to implement Nazi policies.

kaddish: The Hebrew prayer of mourning. According to Jewish Law, *kaddish* should be recited daily for eleven months following the death of a loved one, and on every anniversary thereafter.

Kanada: A term that refers to the section of Auschwitz-Birkenau designated for sorting and storing the belongings of newly arrived Jewish deportees.

Kapo: The SS appointed prisoner in charge of a work gang. Possibly derived from the Italian word *capo* for chief.

kashrut: Keeping kosher. Adhering to the separation between milk and meat dishes. Jewish dietary laws specify what kinds of meat may be eaten and how it is to be prepared. A ritual butcher (a shochet) must slaughter an animal for it to comply with *kashrut*.

Konzentrazionslager [KL]: German for "Concentration camp." Camps designed for the detention, and sometimes also extermination of Jews, Gypsies, Soviet POW's, and other undesirables. Examples include Buchenwald, Dachau, Bergen-Belsen, and Mauthausen.

Kristallnacht: German for "Night of Broken Glass." A pogrom against Jews in the Reich (Germany and Austria) that lasted three days, November 9–11, 1938. Supposedly a "retaliation" for the assassination of a German diplomat in Paris, Nazis condoned the German looting of the Jewish businesses and homes and the burning of synagogues. Thousands of Jewish men were arrested and sent to concentration camps. Over one hundred Jews were murdered.

Molotov-Ribbentrop Pact: The Nazi-Soviet pact that included a nonaggression agreement between the two nations on the eve of World War II (August 1939). The pact remained in force until Germany invaded Russia under Operation Barbarossa in June of 1941.

NKVD: The Soviet Union's secret police, or the "Peoples Commissariat for Internal Affairs." Formed in 1934, under Stalin.

numerus clausus: Literally "limited number." Official policy that restricts the maximum number of any ethnic or racial group admissible to an academic institution.

Organisation Todt: A large-scale military and armaments construction organization in Nazi Germany, founded by Dr. Fritz Todt (minister for armaments and munitions, 1940–1942). Subordinate to the Nazi army, and divided into task force units (labor battalions), Organisation Todt also employed approximately 20,000 concentration camp prisoners.

Po'alei Zion: Workers' party, whose ideology combined socialism and Zionism; "Workers of Zion."

pogrom: An organized massacre aimed at the destruction of an entire group or community, usually taking place in Russia against Jews.

Schutzpass: German term for a protective pass, such as those provided by Raoul Wallenburg to save the Jews of Budapest.

seder: Ritual reading of the "haggadah" and dinner, the focal point of the Passover celebration.

shabbat: The Jewish day of rest, the sabbath (Saturday).

Sonderkommando: The special squad of Jewish inmates who worked in the crematoria of concentration camps.

SS: *Schutzstaffel* or "protection squad." Elite Nazi organization, headed by Heinrich Himmler, including the party police (blackshirted storm troops), the concentration and death camp guards, and fighting units (Waffen SS).

transit camp: A temporary camp for Jewish deportees, such as Drancy and Pithiviers in France, and Westerbork in Holland. From transit camps, Jews were then deported to concentration and death camps.

Ustasha: A Croatian right-wing fascist organization put in charge of the independent state of Croatia by the Axis powers in 1941. They pursued brutal Nazi collaborationist policies and fought the insurgent and anti-German partisans and *Chetniks*. In 1945, the *Ustashe* were expelled from Croatia, Yugoslavia, and the surrounding areas by the local partisans and the Red Army.

Vernichtungslager [VL]: Death (literally extermination) camp for the systematic murder of Jews, Gypsies, and other undesirables. The six death camps were Auschwitz-Birkenau, Belzec, Chelmno, Maidanek, Sobibor, and Treblinka.

Volksdeutsche: Ethnic Germans living outside the Reich. The adjective is *volksdeutsch*.

Wehrmacht: The armed forces of Germany (1935–1945).

yeshiva: Jewish academy for the study of rabbinical literature and the Talmud.

A variety of sources were used in the compilation of this Glossary.

The Editors

Index

About the Editors

YEHUDI LINDEMAN, a child survivor of the Holocaust, was separated from his family in early 1943. For the next thirty months, and with the help of members of Dutch resistance groups, he moved in and out of more than fifteen different locations in rural Holland.

He is a retired Professor of English at McGill University. He is the founder and past Director of Living Testimonies, an archive for Holocaust Oral History and Documentation at McGill. He is also a co-founder, in the 1990s, of the World Federation of Jewish Child Survivors. He has published on a wide range of subjects, from topics in Renaissance translation to issues surrounding hiding and rescue during the Holocaust.

LUKAS RIEPPEL, a former research assistant at Living Testimonies, received a B.A. from McGill University in Montreal. He is currently working on a Ph.D. in the History of Science at Harvard University. His research focuses on the history and philosophy of biology, with an emphasis on the evolution of animal behavior.

ANITA SLOMINSKA is a former research associate of Living Testimonies, who is working on a Ph.D. in Communication Studies at McGill University. She has worked on issues of historical representation in popular culture. Currently, her research concerns the interplay between modernism, ethno-performance, and national folk art in Canada and the United States.

RENATA SKOTNICKA-ZAJDMAN, a native of Warsaw, lived in the Warsaw ghetto until the start of the ghetto uprising of April 1943. After escaping through the sewers, and obtaining false papers, she was caught by the German police and forced to work in Mannheim, Germany, for the rest of the war as a Polish slave laborer. After living in a DP camp, she came to Canada in 1948.

She has been active in the Montreal Holocaust Memorial Centre and the World Federation of Jewish Child Survivors of the Holocaust where she is the liaison with the Jewish Children of the Holocaust in Poland. She is a member of the Jewish Historical Institute (ZIH) in Warsaw, and is Associate Director of Living Testimonies in Montreal.